The Examined Life

The Examined Life

Advanced Philosophy for Kids

DAVID A. WHITE, PH.D.

PRUFROCK PRESS INC.

Printed in the United States of America.

Library of Congress Cataloging-in-Publication Data

White, David A., 1942–
  The examined life : advanced philosophy for kids / David A. White.
      p. cm.
  Includes bibliographical references and index.
  ISBN 1-59363-008-5 (pbk.)
  1. Philosophy—Study and teaching (Middle school) 2. Gifted children—Education. I. Title.
  B52.W45 2005
  107'.1'2—dc20
                          2005022507

ISBN-13: 978-1-59363-008-9
ISBN-10: 1-59363-008-5

Prufrock Press, Inc.
P.O. Box 8813
Waco, Texas 76714-8813
(800) 998-2208
Fax (800) 240-0333
http://www.prufrock.com

TABLE OF CONTENTS

Part II: Education as Applied Philosophy

Part III: A Philosophical Postlude

Preface

The philosopher Socrates spent his life in Athens, engaging Athenians in discussion of matters that, he believed, were vital for them—and him—to understand as fully as human limits allow. The Athenians eventually grew tired of Socrates in this role, and they carried their deepening ill will to the point of convicting him of capital offenses and, shortly thereafter, presenting him with a cup of hemlock, thereby ensuring the desired fatal results. As one element in the defense Socrates mustered at his trial (immortalized in Plato's *Apology*), he appealed to the principle that the unexamined life is not worth living. This advice is timeless in its wisdom. For if we merely drift atop the uppermost currents of whatever is fashionable in clothes, cars, homes, entertainment, the media—even in whatever currently passes for good thinking in educational circles—without taking the time and energy to reflect on just what we are doing and why we are doing it, then our lives pass as though in a dream, with little solid to provide ballast for support and direction.

The Examined Life offers a series of discussions and reflections inspired by the Socratic view of what people should try to do in order to establish their lives on as firm a foundation as opportunity and ability permit. These materials may contribute, in a small way, to the thoughtful examination Socrates considered so vital to the human condition. The subtitle *Advanced Philosophy for Kids* specifies the area in which such examination will be pursued. It may be assumed that everyone connected with formal education—administrators, teachers, parents, students—has wondered at some point about its purpose, perhaps especially so for those individuals whose purpose is directed toward the education of students identified as gifted. *The Examined Life*, a medley of practice and theory, responds to that wonder through a variety of interactive formats employing philosophy and philosophical approaches in order to achieve this vital pedagogical end, not only for gifted students, but for any student who may benefit from more challenging material. This work is "advanced" in the sense that its approach to philosophy depends, in

Part I, on the use of primary source material and, as such, penetrates more deeply into the doing of philosophy than an earlier work of mine devoted to philosophy and kids.

All the chapters in this book have appeared previously in journals devoted to aesthetic education or gifted education. The positions and proposals described herein, both theoretical and practical, thus represent and distill my efforts in gifted education from 1996 until the present. However, these earlier incarnations have been revised, broadened, and, in some cases, reorganized so that they cohere with one another to form a unified whole.

The Examined Life is offered to educators, parents, and students with the sincere hope that it accomplishes its primary aims: to energize efforts at winning a greater appreciation of who we are and what we are attempting to do in understanding the world around us and, if this goal is attained, to inspire those connected with educating young people to introduce and implement at least some of the ideas and suggestions discussed in this book.

Acknowledgements

As noted in the Preface, sections of this work have already been published: Chapters 1–10, 12, and 14–16 originally appeared in *Gifted Child Today*:

"The Oldest Cave Art: An Essay on Giftedness and Excellence" originally appeared in 1996, *Gifted Child Today*, *19*(3), pp. 28–31, 46–47 [with Maureen Breen]. Copyright ©1996 by Prufrock Press Inc. Reprinted with permission.

"Edutainment: Gifted Education and the Perils of Misusing Multiple Intelligences" originally appeared in 1998, *Gifted Child Today*, *21*(2), pp. 12–14, 16 [with Maureen Breen]. Copyright ©1998 by Prufrock Press Inc. Reprinted with permission.

"Gifted Education: The Event—and Advent—of Theory" originally appeared in 1999, *Gifted Child Today*, *22*(6), pp. 60–64. Copyright ©1999 by Prufrock Press Inc. Reprinted with permission.

"Gifted Students and the Adventure of Philosophy" originally appeared in 1999, *Gifted Child Today*, *22*(1), pp. 40–45, 49. Copyright ©1999 by Prufrock Press Inc. Reprinted with permission.

"Philosophy and Gifted Students: Where Has the Time Gone . . .?" originally appeared in 1999, *Gifted Child Today*, *22*(3), pp. 23–29. Copyright ©1999 by Prufrock Press Inc. Reprinted with permission.

"'Do We Really Know What We Think We Know?': Philosophy and Gifted Students" originally appeared in 1999, *Gifted Child Today*, *22*(5), pp. 44–51. Copyright ©1999 by Prufrock Press Inc. Reprinted with permission.

"Gifted Students, Philosophy—and the Existence of God" originally appeared in 2000, *Gifted Child Today*, *23*(2), pp. 22–28. Copyright ©2000 by Prufrock Press Inc. Reprinted with permission.

"Gifted Students and Philosophy: The Sound of a Tree Falling in the Forest . . ." originally appeared in 2000, *Gifted Child Today*, *23*(4), pp. 28–33, 53. Copyright ©2000 by Prufrock Press Inc. Reprinted with permission.

"Philosophy and Gifted Students: 'I Don't Want to Do What the Class Wants to Do!'" originally appeared in 2000, *Gifted Child Today 23*(6), pp. 42–48. Copyright ©2000 by Prufrock Press Inc. Reprinted with permission.

"Freedom and Responsibility: Existentialism, Gifted Students, and Philosophy" originally appeared in 2001, *Gifted Child Today, 24*(2), pp. 48–53, 65. Copyright ©2001 by Prufrock Press Inc. Reprinted with permission.

"Gifted Students and Philosophy: On Social Justice in a Violent World" originally appeared in 2001, *Gifted Child Today, 24*(4), pp. 48–53. Copyright ©2001 by Prufrock Press Inc. Reprinted with permission.

"Gifted Students and Philosophy: Feminism and Social Justice" originally appeared in 2002, *Gifted Child Today, 25*(1), pp. 40–45, 64. Copyright ©2002 by Prufrock Press Inc. Reprinted with permission.

"Gifted Students and Philosophy: Technology—Servant or Destroyer" originally appeared in 2002, *Gifted Child Today, 25*(2), pp. 22–27, 64. Copyright ©2002 by Prufrock Press Inc. Reprinted with permission.

"'The Bohemian Life': Opera and Gifted Education" originally appeared in 2002, *Gifted Child Today, 25*(3), pp. 34–39, 64 [with Cynthia Sprague]. Copyright ©2002 by Prufrock Press Inc. Reprinted with permission.

"Critical Thinking and Artistic Creation" originally appeared in 2001, *Journal of Aesthetic Education, 35*(2), pp. 77–85 [with Robin Robinson]. Copyright ©2001 by University of Illinois Press. Reprinted with permission.

"The Philosophy of French Funetics: An Essay in Applied Gifted Intelligence" originally appeared in 1996, *Roeper Review, 19,* pp. 44–50 [with Maureen Breen]. Copyright ©1996 by The Roeper Institute. Reprinted with permission.

"Philosophy and Theory in the Study of Gifted Children" originally appeared in 2003, *Roeper Review, 26,* pp. 16–19. Copyright © 2001 by The Roeper Institute. Reprinted with permission.

I would like to thank the editors of these journals for permission to reproduce this material in *The Examined Life*. A special note of thanks to Susan Johnsen, who was the editorial stimulus behind the production of a series of articles for *Gifted Child Today* devoted to presenting primary source philosophy to gifted young people. Thanks as well to Joel McIntosh and Jennifer Robins of Prufrock Press for their support in continuing to make philosophy available to younger audiences.

I also want to acknowledge Robin Robinson for providing the foundations in teaching methods for young actors analyzed in Chapter 11, Cynthia Sprague for her diligence in developing the program in middle school opera production discussed in Chapter 14, and Maureen Breen—French teacher extraordinaire—for her remarkable creativity in producing Funetics, a unique method for learning foreign language (Chapter 13) and for collaborating in producing the argument represented in Chapter 16. It is both my privilege and pleasure to recognize here the work and inspiration of these caring and creative teachers.

And to Sheila Schlaggar—the primary cause (as Aristotle would say) of my initial ventures into philosophy with gifted students—this book stands as a tribute to and record of her passionate concern that only the highest levels of thinking are appropriate for those young people endowed with the ability and diligence to appreciate it.

GENERAL INTRODUCTION

Who am I and what am I doing here?

—"Are you a philosopher or do you just teach philosophy?"—

The question froze me; it was as if I had been sheathed in ice. The speaker was a 7th grader, a young lady who had not been very active in our class discussions of primary source readings in philosophy—that is, until now, and to my considerable chagrin. In one obvious sense, the question was off the point. We had been analyzing some important philosophical issue—we were *not* indulging in autobiographical confessions or talk-show fashion from the visiting teacher. But, how could I indulge in a sophistical dipsy-do around such a splendid question? I was doubly moved by its perceptiveness—first, how did she so neatly detect the crucial difference between (a) parading standard philosophical positions in front of students and (b) actually doing philosophy? Furthermore, I had been wondering about the answer to this very question in rare moments of awkwardly intense self-scrutiny for—oh—some 35 years. Was I indeed a philosopher or only a teacher of philosophy?

This anecdote should alert the reader that we are about to venture into areas of practical education that, it seems, have not been particularly well charted among the often rugged terrains of educational theory; as a result, the positive statements presented in this book should be approached as tentative, if reasoned, speculation, rather than as firmly established pedagogical dogma. But first, let me try to answer the young lady's question (just in case the reader might also be wondering). The following is an amplified version of what I told her in class.

I once wrote an article for a philosophical journal in aesthetics on what it means to describe classical music as "profound." Now, I believe—although I cannot be altogether certain—that in this small work I attained a level of philosophical interest. For that moment then, a painfully brief moment, I was a philosopher. But, the vast majority of my time—through the written word (7 books, some 50 articles) and more than 30 years of classroom discussion—has been occupied by telling various audiences what I think other philosophers mean by what they have said. In that respect, I have been and continue to be much more a student of philosophy than a philosopher.

An additional autobiographical note: Since 1991, I have been teaching programs in primary source philosophy to students in grades 6–8 in various gifted programs of the Chicago Public School system. And since 1993, I have also taught philosophy to gifted students at Northwestern University's Center for Talent Development. During those years, I have sought wisdom in the company of literally thousands of younger students. As I review this busy period, I observe that I have learned about aspects of philosophy hidden to me while I was teaching the subject at the university level (which I have been doing since 1967). And I have learned a great deal about young students—how they think, feel, and interact with one another, as well as with people who appear before them representing an often eccentric, yet intriguing discipline.

A word, then, about the background required for understanding what follows in this book. That word is—*none*. All of us are philosophers to some extent; it is just that some individuals have concentrated more than others on thoughtfully developing these common concerns. Thus, no special knowledge or skill in philosophy is presupposed here. Indeed, the reader should be aware that the attempt to become clear in one's own mind as to exactly why a given philosophical position has run afoul of the truth is itself an extremely healthy and worthwhile exercise. As noted in the Preface, the Socrates who graces Plato's dialogues spent much time attempting to show Athenians that they did not know what they thought they knew—it may be supposed, then, that, despite Socrates' personal destiny, at least some of these individuals were better off as a result of his efforts. For now, I hope that, when readers find themselves in disagreement with what is said, their interior response will strengthen their beliefs and clarify their understanding of the pedagogical principles and practical attitudes they embody and direct toward their students.

The Genesis and Scope of This Book

This work is in three parts. Part I, "Kids and Philosophy," includes 10 readings in primary source philosophy, each with discussion, commentary, and analysis for educators, parents, or students who want to think about important questions in the company of noted philosophers who share this concern. Part II, "Education as Applied Philosophy," offers four discussions enhancing students' abilities in critical thinking, drawing, language acquisition, and music. Finally, Part III, "A Philosophical Postlude," presents three perspectives dominated by theoretical concerns on philosophy and education, with special emphasis on educating gifted students. As an aside, the titles of the chapters in Parts II and III mention gifted students and gifted education, but the discussions in all these chapters have, whenever possible, been contoured to fit any student with the ability to confront interesting—and challenging—material.

As noted in the Preface, my own adventures with philosophy and young students began in 1991 and are ongoing. The chapters in Part I represent more than 10 years of reading and discussing primary sources in philosophy with students in grades 6–8 and, on occasion, students younger and older than this age group. The comments concerning each of the primary source readings represent encapsulations of, in most instances, hundreds of classroom experiences. During the course of my classes with younger students, I have been extremely fortunate to have collaborated with and observed many conscientious and creative teachers. Three of these individuals have contributed curriculum ideas for the discussions in Part II (all are appropriately recognized in the Acknowledgments). For these chapters, field testing was undertaken and supervised by the teachers who originated the ideas and projects for classroom use. Thus, chapters 11–14 present classroom exercises in a format including introductory material, descriptions and analysis of the projects, and a review of their implications for more traditional areas of the curriculum.

Suggestions for Using This Book

This book is designed for use in a variety of ways: philosophical, practical, theoretical.

Philosophical

Educators and parents who wish to explore ideas through lively and profound discussions are invited to investigate Part I. This part contains 10 chapters, each with a primary source reading devoted to a single question or issue in philosophy (topics and corresponding authors are listed in the Table of Contents). This part begins with an introduction that includes more detailed suggestions for presenting the readings. In fact, for those without a background in philosophy, this introduction is recommended as a prelude to examining any of the three parts of *The Examined Life*. (A hint: Any young person who wants to go "where the philosophical action is" may proceed straight to Part I without concern for Parts II and III.)

Practical

For educators interested in a direct application of philosophy to the classroom, the chapters in Part II will be of immediate interest. The applications in this part include activities pertinent to critical thinking (Chapter 11), drawing and visual design (Chapter 12), language acquisition (Chapter 13), and music (Chapter 14). All four chapters in Part II contain activities that not only can be readily introduced into the classroom, but also provide a substantive, challenging, and enjoyable contribution to students' growth in these areas.

Theoretical

Part III appears at the conclusion of the book because it contains the most consistently theoretical discussions, illustrating the level of reflection underlying the scope of the book as a unified venture in educational theory and practice. Chapter 15 analyzes the place of theory in the history and practice of gifted education. Chapter 16 pinpoints a concept that enjoys wide popularity in contemporary educational theory—multiple intelligence—and critically evaluates this concept in light of considerations pertinent to curricula for gifted students. Finally, Chapter 17 presents ideas articulated by some Stoic philosophers who flourished in ancient Rome juxtaposed with a treatment of justice by a contemporary philosopher, John Rawls, illustrating the relevance of such sustained reflection on current understanding of vital questions in gifted education.

Educators with a special interest in the presence and implications of theory may, of course, review Part III of *The Examined Life* first to familiarize themselves with the approach taken toward curricular matters throughout the book. Those who employ the practical discussions and activities in Parts I and II may, however, find themselves drawn to the more theoretical underpinnings for these adventures. If so, they may then be attracted to Part III even if initially their concerns seemed more practical than theoretical. In the end, the order in which the various components of this book are traversed is not significant as long as the user appreciates the extent to which a philosophical dimension permeates the vistas opened by the work as a whole.

It is also worth mentioning that the present book—in particular Part I—may be used as a sequel to my *Philosophy for Kids* (Prufrock Press, 2001). That work has introduced many young people, gifted or not (and, if anecdotal evidence is reliable, not a few curious adults as well), to the wonders of philosophy by posing 40 questions arranged under the headings Value, Knowledge, Reality, and Critical Thinking. These questions are then answered with a brief account based on the position of an important figure in philosophy. However, everything said in that book is filtered through my own sensibilities; as a result, the challenge—and excitement—of working through a given philosophical position as stated in the philosopher's own words is an experience that *Philosophy for Kids* does not provide. Part I of *The Examined Life* contains exactly that kind of adventure, thereby advancing—and deepening—the approach taken in the earlier book and giving anyone who has seen or had experience with *Philosophy for Kids* the opportunity to continue to develop his or her skills with an insight into the concerns that have animated the philosophical enterprise for almost 3,000 years. (In fact, six of the chapters in Part I of *The Examined Life* contain the readings that inspired corresponding questions in *Philosophy for Kids*.)

Philosophy for Kids and *The Examined Life* thus form a natural pair, a set of works defined by a shared concern for the relevance and importance of philosophy. It should also be emphasized, however, that *The Examined Life* in no way presupposes any familiarity with its predecessor and is perfectly capable of standing by itself as a contribution to philosophy and its place in the education of young students. As a result, the work in hand is "advanced," as its subtitle states, only in the sense that the contents of Part I allow young people—indeed, any interested reader—to approach and interact with philosophy as it has been written by great philosophers.

PART I

Kids and Philosophy

INTRODUCTION

Young Students and the Adventure of Philosophy

"I wonder . . ." According to the ancient Greeks, philosophy—the love of wisdom—begins in wonder. It is frequently observed in this regard that young students are exceptionally curious, wondering about many things. Once this natural sense of wonder has been introduced to the issues philosophers find fascinating and vital, young people may well be in a position to expand that wonder into the kind of interest—perhaps even the kind of love—that drives the impetus to know about things in a philosophical sense. One wonders then . . . would kids like philosophy? Indeed, would they not only like it, but also be *good* at it? Based on my own personal experience, the answer to both questions is a resounding "Yes!"

This introductory discussion describes some of the general features of philosophy that are especially pertinent to gifted education and offers strategies to the interested educator (and parent) for incorporating philosophy into more traditional curricula for the gifted, as well as for any group of students intrigued by the fundamental resonance of interacting with philosophical issues.

Questions arise immediately: What is the value of studying philosophy? Which philosophers should be read? And *how* should they be read?

Reasons to Study Philosophy

Philosophy is valuable for a number of reasons. Young students know about mathematics, science, language arts, social studies, foreign languages, and other traditional academic disciplines. But, although they have doubtless heard the word *philosophy*, it is unlikely that they have had an opportunity to read, study, and discuss examples of a philosopher's work in anything like a formal setting. Such study will make the student aware of this important way in which human beings have attempted to understand themselves and their place in the general scheme of things. For these students, philosophy can then become another element in the set of educational instruments with which they construct their own personal approach to dealing with the opportunities and problems of life. The following areas are especially fertile territory for realizing the relevance of philosophy:

A. Critical Thinking

The intellectual processes involved in understanding philosophical concepts and positions enhance the student's ability to think critically. To study philosophy properly requires skill in formulating ideas, recognizing conclusions of arguments, and assessing the strength of the reasoning that leads to those conclusions. Furthermore, a degree of adeptness in any or all of these areas is readily carried over from the analysis of philosophical issues proper to different, but related forms of thoughtful literary expression. Although history, novels, and poetry are not read in the same way as philosophy, the intellectual patterns and habits that are formed when grasping and analyzing philosophical issues will assist the student in many other forms of reading and writing. (Note that Chapter 11 develops an especially imaginative approach to critical thinking.)

B. Cultural Differences

Philosophers from all cultures have made contributions to the stock of human wisdom. It is a commonplace that our world is shrinking in the sense that advances in technology have virtually nullified spatial and temporal distances. The long-range effects of such technologies are unknown; however, it remains true that the world as a whole still contains many diverse cultural attitudes and practices, some of which are viewed with distrust or dismay. The more experience young people have in confronting differ-ent beliefs and attitudes while they are still young, the more likely they are to be receptive to understanding and accept such differences and not react to them in irrational, hurtful, and destructive ways.

C. Practical Applications

Philosophy affects life in that it affords us the opportunity not only to learn in an abstract way what great minds have offered us, but also to apply what we have learned to the practical matter of living. In one obvious sense, philosophy is theoretical in that it is written in books and developed, as a rule, according to strict logical procedures. But, theory is itself part of life, and the theoretical dimension is only the threshold to the reality of philosophy when its conclusions are put into practice during the helter-skelter business of life as it is actually lived. In this regard then, philosophy is not just an isolated body of knowledge devoted to expounding wispy esoterica; rather, it is a reservoir containing sustenance of considerable value for those who allow its teachings to be understood and then to be acted upon—with courage when necessary—as the problems and decisions that define our lives are being resolved.

The first practical advantage is that the study of philosophy instills in the student a greater tolerance for views that differ from his or her own, especially on matters of fundamental importance. Students of philosophy are continually confronting beliefs and conclusions that run in direct opposition to their own personal convictions. The concerned and caring individual will attempt to understand the other viewpoint, discuss that viewpoint if possible, and, if nothing better can be secured, agree to disagree and attempt to resolve the issue at another time.

The second advantage is more personal and perhaps, in the final analysis, even more valuable. To reflect about the issues of philosophy is ultimately to reflect about oneself—what do I think about this question, about that problem, about those concepts? Thus the young student becomes more self-aware about matters that are vitally important to everyone. This enhanced degree of self-knowledge can only contribute to the student's ability to grow and mature, not only in academic settings, but also in every department of life.

Elements of Philosophy

The nature of philosophy is itself a philosophical question, since philosophers—unlike, say, mathematicians or natural scientists—have disputed among themselves, sometimes with great vigor and heat, as to the purposes and methods of their discipline. Despite this sporadic history of foundational disagreement, it may be affirmed that if philosophy is understood to encompass a series of significant figures from the Greeks to the present, the following list of elements may safely be said to characterize its basic structure:

A. Concepts

Philosophers describe and analyze ideas or concepts that are basic to human experience—happiness, virtue, knowledge, time, matter, causality, goodness, freedom, purpose, beauty. Indeed, the list of viable philosophical topics is coextensive with the concerns of the human condition.

B. Distinctions

Since these concepts are so general, it is essential to draw distinctions in their elaboration in order to make our understanding of these concepts more accessible and more accurate.

C. Definitions

The goal of the philosopher is, as a rule, to establish a definition of a concept: a clearly described and comprehensive set of conditions that will fully explain that concept by covering all relevant circumstances. Needless to say, if the concepts under analysis are general and also the subject of dispute—which is nearly always the case—it will be difficult to secure a definition that will command consensus.

D. Reasoning

The standard method for producing definitions is reasoning, which for present purposes may be described as the movement in thought from certain basic beliefs or facts (premises) to certain other claims (conclusions) that follow from these premises according to the rules of logic. It is true that not all philosophers proceed in this formally regulated way (e.g., Confucius, Francis Bacon, Nietzsche), but it is also true that so many philosophers do use this approach that it is not inappropriate to offer it as one of the basic elements of the discipline.

Primary Source Philosophy

Which philosophers should be read? Here again there will be differences of opinion among professional students of the discipline. For me, it is safe to say that, even if one is thoroughly convinced of the extreme view that the history of philosophy has systematically distorted our understanding of and our place in reality, it remains essential to know something about that history in order to be in a position to recognize these errors. Thus, there are philosophers who simply must be read, starting with Plato and Aristotle and including a number of

seminal figures throughout the history of thought until we come to the 20th century—at which juncture the student has a veritable smorgasbord of philosophical fare from which to select.

How then should the thought of these philosophers be approached? My own work with gifted students has been based exclusively on primary sources, although usually in excerpted form. The main advantage of primary sources is that the student has the opportunity to meet philosophers firsthand as they actually thought and wrote, rather than as filtered through a contemporary interpreter who has attempted to paraphrase, condense, and perhaps "simplify" that thought for those who may not be well-versed in the sometimes intricate byways of philosophy. In the example of Aristotle to be discussed first, the passages included are only excerpts—a format that should be employed with certain precautions in mind. Thus, anyone working through these passages should reserve final judgment as to his or her impressions of Aristotle (or, of course, any philosopher) until the entire work has been examined with care. It is fair to add, however, that the treatment of these passages, even though excerpted, will respect the discipline of philosophy as it has been practiced by the primary exemplars of that discipline (e.g., Aristotle and all other philosophers featured in Part I).

The Readings— Principles of Selection and Organization

1. The 10 readings in Part I are all primary source selections. These readings have been chosen because they satisfy the following requirements:

a. All are classical issues and questions drawn from the history of philosophy, Plato to the present.

b. The topics are of concern in various ways to students from grades 4 through high school.

c. The readings, although brief, represent a unified, comprehensive philosophical position. Students who work through a complete reading will experience in a forceful way the challenge and satisfaction of confronting a philosophical text and mastering the main purpose of that text.

d. Each reading appears on a single page (for ease of reproduction and use in a classroom setting). The passages constituting each reading are quoted verbatim, with the exception of occasional ellipses and brief interpolations, indicated by brackets, for the sake of clarity and to establish transitions.

2. Each reading consists of a series of numbered passages. It is important to realize that these numbers are not those of the philosopher and are not in the original source. The numbers divide the text to facilitate discussion. Each numbered text corresponds to a discussion of that text with the same number; this discussion appears in the commentary section immediately following the reading.

3. The numbered sections in the commentary accomplish various ends, depending on the purpose of the reading, as well as the specific function of each passage. The commentary may (a) define unusual or technical terms; (b) explain theoretical positions, if necessary; (c) suggest questions to pose in order to initiate discussion of key points made in a given passage; or (d) note anticipated responses as based on my experience presenting these readings to diverse younger audiences.

4. The sequence of readings is arranged in approximate historical order, although punctuated with several exceptions. First, the reading on Aristotle precedes that on Plato (which reverses the actual historical order, since Aristotle was Plato's student)—the reason: the topic, friendship, is one of the most important to young people and serves as an especially penetrating introduction to philosophical thinking. The second historical anomaly is that the reading on determining the nature of time by Augustine comes second (rather than third, after Plato and Aristotle) because the content of this topic is suitably abstract as an introduction to more of this kind of thinking to come later. Finally, the reading that concludes the set in Part I—by Martin

Heidegger (who died in 1976) on technology—occurs at the end since it may be argued that this topic, with its potentially apocalyptic overtones, supercedes in importance all the topics that precede it.

5. A teacher or presenter is, of course, free to select a given reading for a particular purpose, regardless of where that reading occurs in the sequence. In addition, the current sequence can also be reorganized to suit a teacher's curricular interests and opportunities. It may be observed, however, that if the sequence is followed according to the order deployed in the book, then the student will gain some sense for the historical flow that is so crucial to philosophy in its almost 3,000-year existence.

6. The analysis of the topics offered by the 10 readings can be integrated with humanities, social studies, or language arts courses that include components on critical thinking. And, in general, philosophy can be integrated with virtually all standard disciplines—science, mathematics, literature, social studies, and art. Specific suggestions for such curricular integration are, when relevant, included toward the conclusion of the commentary sections for the readings.

7. Most of the 10 readings in Part I include links for accessing the complete texts for these readings. Some translations of the complete texts differ from those appearing in the readings, but the differences are minor and readily recognized. Anyone interested in pursuing topics outlined in these readings is invited to explore the entire work. For example, the first reading, on friendship from Aristotle's *Nicomachean Ethics*, includes a link to the online text of this classic work. A prospective philosopher entering a thoughtful analysis of friendship and watching Aristotle develop that con-

cept in context quickly discovers that friendship is connected to a number of equally important concepts. To pursue these connections is challenging, rewarding, and enjoyable.

Some Ideas on Presenting or Teaching Philosophy

The following points present a few general guidelines for presenting philosophy to younger students:

1. As noted in the general introduction, no specialized background in philosophy is required in order to present the readings in a classroom setting or at home. Since the readings are self-contained, unified, and comprehensive, it is recommended, however, that the presenter—teacher, parent, student, onlooker with an interest in philosophy—review each reading and then note the connections established in the commentary to each passage.

2. The principal function of the presenter/ teacher is to explain and to defend the philosophical position represented in the passages read. Since the excerpts are brief, it is recommended that there be a minimum of explanatory lecturing and a maximum of Socratic dialogue. This is where the fun starts, especially with students endowed with special abilities or interests; it is also where the teacher must blend humility, alertness, and judiciousness.

3. Two basic principles for interpreting a philosophical text are (a) What is the philosopher trying to say (i.e., Can the point of the position be paraphrased in ter-

minology that will allow students to return to the texts with enhanced understanding?) and (b) is this position true and can it be known to be true?

Answering the first question shows that the philosopher's position has been understood to the best of one's ability; answering the second question—clearly the more difficult of the two—shows the extent to which the philosopher's thoughts have affected one's own beliefs. Of course, the teacher need not have secured final and definitive answers to both questions for each and every passage to be discussed with the students. As noted above, however, it is advisable to spend some time beforehand reflecting on the passages individually and on the position as a unified whole.

4. The teacher should be receptive to functioning as a member of a democratic discussion (i.e., as both leader and peer). This divergent function implies (a) that a response from the teacher may and probably will be criticized by the students; (b) that the students, especially gifted students, may be entirely capable of pursuing the point on their own, with only occasional guidance from the teacher; and (c) that the admission of ignorance on a given point or inference is perfectly justified and should not be looked on as reflecting a lack of intelligence or preparation on the part of the teacher, but rather as an index of the difficulty of the problem. Socrates, as he is depicted in Plato's dialogues, often says, in so many words, "I don't know the answer to that . . . let us think about it." The teacher is only being Socratic in emulating this humility while confronting the issue under scrutiny.

When such guidance is at hand, the classroom can then become an arena of inquiry, with everyone involved clearly recognizing that it is the issue that is important, rather than the display of personalities who may tend to dominate discussion. It is well to keep in mind that *everyone* is a student when philosophy is the subject being studied. Some students just happen to be older (and, perhaps, a little more experienced in philosophical practice) than others. In philosophy, we are often confused, we are often wrong, our "absolutely final" positions are often refuted. These are facts of life about philosophy understood—following its Greek etymology—as the love of wisdom. They are facts that in large measure contribute to the difficulty of the discipline, but they also season and accentuate its intrigue and allure.

5. Every student opinion counts, but those opinions advanced with some form of justification are more reliable, at least philosophically, than those that are merely asserted. Asking a student "Why do you say that?" is a common occurrence when discussing philosophical issues. Thus, the pedagogical problem amid the swirl of classroom discussion is to balance the twin goals of allowing everyone to have his or her say and exploring a given response if it appears fruitful—this while hands are energetically waving, their owners awaiting recognition to speak.

6. When young students state or justify an opinion, their assertions or reasons may initially appear to be "off," that is, the student seems to be thinking in areas that differ widely from those developed by the primary source and, perhaps, within the teacher's own mind. On occasion, students do stray from the point. But, it is important to note that frequently what appears at first to be "off" may in fact be a route of development unforeseen by the teacher—and

well worth investigating in its own right. This kind of unexpected development is common among gifted students, testifying to both their energy and insight. I have been through this experience countless times, and the range of creativity of students in this regard continues to amaze me year after year.

When such routes of divergence occur, the teacher must decide—on the spot—whether to pursue the new line of thought or note its importance to the class, but then redirect the discussion to the point previously under scrutiny. It is important not to give the contributing student the impression that his or her response was "wrong"; rather, this response may well have been entirely justified, but in philosophy it is axiomatic that not everything can be done at once—that is, issues must be introduced and analyzed one at a time. It may happen, of course, that a particular response opens a line of discussion that the teacher judges to be worth pursuing even if that discussion threatens to move onto paths other than those the teacher had intended to follow. Such "unplanned" relevance is not unusual in philosophical discussions, is always exciting when it happens, and will require the teacher to exercise discretion (and a measure of restraint leavened by wisdom) in terms of changing the direction of a discussion in mid-session. Finally, regardless of how often discussions of a given topic have occurred, surprising—and revealing—comments and questions will doubtless be raised. In sum, be ready for anything. Gifted and inquisitive children are quite wonderful, especially when they seek wisdom in the wake of a crew of famous philosophers.

7. Although the primary intended audiences for these readings are younger students, it

should be noted that all the readings can be used as topics for self-study and the growth of our own personal understanding of important issues. In Plato's dialogue *Theaetetus*, Socrates describes thinking as "the dialogue of the soul with itself," a wonderful way of characterizing how a thoughtful person can stretch his or her limits by debating a point internally with the self as the only audience and with no place to hide as far as being honest about where he or she stands on a given question.

In the *Phaedrus*, Plato tells us that "all things noble are as difficult as they are rare." Philosophy is a noble enterprise, one of the finest achievements of the human intellect. Although philosophy is difficult, it returns to its students at least as much as, if not more than, they put into it. My experience with philosophy and younger students is that, on the whole, they relish being introduced to these works and revel in the thoughtful regions they have entered as a result. It is an experience that I hope to share with any teacher who has the spirit of adventure and discovery to begin exploring the possibilities of philosophy.

CHAPTER 1

"Who Are My Friends?"

A Friendly Philosophical Prelude

Young people value their friendships highly. But, it is one thing to value a friendship, another to understand clearly what friendship is and why it is valued. Friendship is one of the most common concepts found in the everyday experience of young students. This experience, in tandem with conversation based on that experience, already contains the seeds of fruitful philosophical analysis. For example, the teacher can initiate discussion by asking the class to define the difference between a friend and a "good" friend. It is extremely unlikely that whatever answer is provided will not be challenged by another student. Once debate on this question is joined, the students will be hooked—after all, the question is personal, timely, and engaging. Discussion of related issues may be engendered by asking, "Why do some friendships end?" And then the question "How long does it take to make a friend?" can be introduced. Any or all of these questions, used informally as a sort of philosophical "warm-up," will provide a well-prepared corps of young philosophers ready to confront Aristotle's classical—and, for some students of ethics, problematic—treatment of friendship.

Aristotle on Friendship

The following selections are excerpted from the eighth book of the *Nicomachean Ethics* by Aristotle (384–322 B.C.). In this work, Aristotle devotes two books, about 50 pages, to the concept of friendship, a fact suggesting that friendship was highly significant to the Greeks and that Aristotle was well aware of the importance of understanding that concept. The passages listed here constitute a

1. No one would choose to live without friends, even if he had all other goods.

2. When people are friends, they have no need of justice, but when they are just, they need friendship in addition.

3. We conclude, therefore, that to be friends, men must have good will for one another, must each wish for the good of the other on the basis of one of three motives [i.e., the good, the pleasant, or the useful], and must each be aware of one another's good will.

4. The three motives differ from one another in kind, and so do the corresponding types of affection and friendship.

5. Now, when the motive of the affection is usefulness, the partners do not feel affection for one another as such, but in terms of the good accruing to each from the other. The same is also true of those whose friendship is based on pleasure; we love witty people not for what they are, but for the pleasure they give us. . . . Accordingly, with the disappearance of the motive for being friends, the friendship, too, is dissolved, since the friendship owed its existence to these motives.

6. The perfect form of friendship is that between good people who are alike in excellence or virtue. For these friends wish alike for one another's good because they are good people, and they are good as such. . . . Hence their friendship lasts as long as they are good, and that means it will last for a long time, since goodness or virtue is a thing that lasts.

—From Book 8 of the *Nicomachean Ethics* by Aristotle

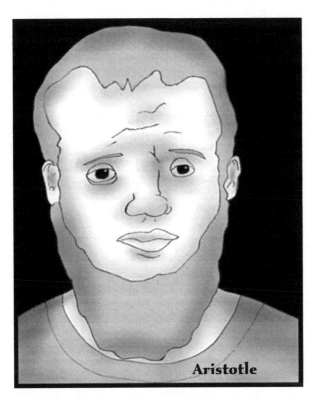

Aristotle

central portion of the core of his teaching on this vital concept. (It may be observed that the translations are not politically correct; thus the teacher, or anyone for that matter, should feel free to alter the detail of the translations as deemed proper.)

Suggestions for Presentation

The following comments are not intended to provide anything like a blueprint or "lesson plan" for teaching Aristotle's theory of friendship. Rather, as noted in the Introduction, they are sketched here only to give a teacher the general "feel" for what it is like to present this position to younger students.

Passage 1

Aristotle asserts this claim without offering a reason. He does so because for him its truth is self-evident. If the class is asked whether they would be happy if they had all the money, power, and fame they wanted—but were completely and utterly alone—almost everyone says he or she would not want to lead this sort of life, thus supporting the self-evident character of Aristotle's claim. However, occasionally someone will say, "Well, if you have all the money you want, then you can buy friends." As a rule, another student will quickly critique this objection—"But, if you buy them, then they are not really friends!" This brief exchange is excellent philosophizing all around—the first student is attempting to evaluate critically Aristotle's claim, the second student is negating the force of the criticism. If this kind of response occurs early on, the class is naturally tuned in to philosophy.

Passage 2

This passage also does not receive supporting reasons, again because Aristotle believes its truth is obvious. The students might be asked what reason Aristotle would give if he were challenged about the first part of this claim (i.e., why friends have no need of justice). Typically, the students readily produce the answer: just because they are friends! Students can see that friendship entails justice by the very nature of friendship—even though at this point in the argument friendship (as well as justice) remains undefined. The second half of the claim is more subtle; one way to approach it is to ask the students what the atmosphere in the classroom would feel like if each student acted justly to every other student, but that was the extent of the way they interacted with each other while they were in the room. Although this question requires a little thought, the relevant kind of answer usually comes quickly—my favorite response is "cold"; the room would feel impersonal and even boring if justice were the only interactive order of the day. The point is not that justice is a derivative virtue—far from it, of course. But, Aristotle wants to insist that we need friends in order to feel that we are leading a properly human life. In a word, although it is good to be just to each other, it is better for us to be both just and to have friends.

Passage 3

This is Aristotle's definition of friendship, one of a number of epochal moments in Greek ethics. Note that the definition has three parts; all three parts must be fulfilled before friendship has been established.

a. The notion of "good will" is not directly analyzed. My advice is not to try to analyze it until, or unless, discussion warrants it. The students almost always think they know what bearing good will means; after discussion of particular examples of friendship, they frequently learn that the concept is not entirely clear, at least not in terms of the passages given here.

b. Aristotle has earlier established the three motives for friendship by simple inspection; it is a fundamental distinction of crucial importance for his position. The motive of usefulness nearly always occasions cries of disagreement: "How can you be a friend if you're just using somebody!" Aristotle's answer is that (a) you have freely entered into this relationship, (b) you are getting something from it (as is the other party), and (c) you both know that usefulness is controlling the relationship. Clearly if A is using B and B doesn't know it, then friendship would not be present—the reason: A is not bearing good will toward B in using B without B's awareness. In this case, B has, in effect, been reduced to a tool, albeit a living one, for A's advantage.

Younger students frequently refuse to accept that friendships can be based on usefulness. They insist that friends must "like" each other and they do not see how people who are using each other, even if they fulfill

all three of Aristotle's conditions, can legitimately be called friends. One response is to note that friends who "like" each other are friends based on the motive of pleasure, which for Aristotle is a perfectly legitimate type of friendship. But, prepare for some serious philosophical wrangling in defense of the type of friendship based on usefulness!

c. The awareness of the other party's good will is essential to friendship; in other words, bearing good will must be reciprocal and *known* to be so by each party. Thus, one could bear good will to another person by giving charity to that person, but in this case the recipient and giver would not be friends since the bearing of good will went only in one direction.

Passage 4

This inference is one of the most valuable points in Aristotle's discussion. Young people, in fact human beings generally, do not tend to think of friendships in terms of types, except perhaps "friends" vs. "good friends." But, Aristotle, after noting these types, proceeds to draw some very pertinent inferences about them in the following passage.

Passage 5

This discussion explains why some friendships end. Thus in the case of friendships based on usefulness or pleasure, we do not really like the person as such; rather, we like a certain feature of his or her personality. Without that feature, the friendship has lost its motivation and, inevitably, is dissolved. A provocative question at this point is to ask the students what percentage of their friendships are based on either pleasure or usefulness. The answers vary, but usually cluster between the 80 to 100% range. The implication is that they will tend to change friends fairly often, especially as their interests and needs develop over time.

What then about friendships based on the third type, the good?

Passage 6

A friendship based on the good is not the same as a "good friend." For Aristotle, friendships based on the good exist only between people who exhibit virtue. Thus, they will be the highest kind of friend because they are attracted to each other by reason of something—virtue—that will guarantee their individual success as human beings. Aristotle's assumption at this point (he argues it elsewhere in the *Nicomachean Ethics*) is that, if one is virtuous, one would want to remain that way since it would be clear to the virtuous person that leading a virtuous life is better than leading one that is riddled with vice. Thus, it follows that this kind of friendship will be the most long-lived—and, of course, it also follows that it will be the least frequently found and enjoyed, since the number of truly virtuous people in the world is not high.

A footnote: Students will often want to know what it means to be "virtuous." When this question occurs, I reply that this is another topic, one on which Aristotle spends much time and energy in the *Nicomachean Ethics*. Recall that, in philosophy, we deal with only one topic at a time; also, if students are left wondering what it means to be virtuous, that is something good for them to wonder about.

Some Questions to Anticipate

As one should expect, younger students, especially if gifted, produce relevant and incisive questions and objections. Here are just a few that occur fairly often:

a. Can one be a friend for more than one motive (e.g., pleasure and usefulness)? [Yes. Aristotle's argument appears to allow this inference.]

b. What is the difference between a friend and an acquaintance? [I generally sidestep this one by saying that it will be hard enough to define a friend and to defend that definition; if we also have to define and defend the concept of acquaintance, we will be in the room for a long time! However, the question is a good one. It usually arises because students commonly produce perceptive counterexamples to Aristotle's theory (and to philosophical positions generally), that is, cases that apparently fulfill the conditions of the definition, but do not seem, in the case at hand, to be meaningfully called instances of a friend. Examples: a polite exchange between a customer and a salesclerk; helping an older person across the street, saying "Hello," but little else, to someone (a classmate, perhaps) on a regular basis.]

c. Can we make a friend, in Aristotle's sense of friendship, in half an hour? [This one is difficult to answer, at least on the strength of the passages given above. I leave it to the reader's philosophical acumen and ingenuity to provide an appropriate response in the Aristotelian spirit.]

A Brief Philosophical Coda

Teaching philosophy to young students is a challenge that offers considerable measures of satisfaction but, it should be added, potential frustration, as well. To provide these students the opportunity to read and discuss philosophy is to pitch the challenge of learning at an academic level higher than many educational challenges normally occupy. However, it should be noted that there is no guarantee in approaching this challenge that the outcome will always be successful—just as there is no guarantee that anyone beginning a work by one of the great philosophers will discover that this adventure in reading and thinking has comfortably achieved anything like a satisfactory conclusion.

To do philosophy is to risk a potentially drastic alteration in one's beliefs; to teach philosophy to young students is to compound that risk exponentially. But, there is every likelihood that just the attempt to be philosophical in this way will be respected by both students and teacher. Furthermore, if the attempt is successful, then the teacher can be duly proud of having introduced philosophy to human beings at an age when they may well remember—and value—the experience for the rest of their lives. Plato's Socrates said that the unexamined life is not worth living—a principle that, as explained in the Preface, inspired the title *The Examined Life*. If this principle is true, the sooner students begin such examination, the better for them and for all concerned.

Reference:

Aristotle. (1941). *The basic works of Aristotle.* New York: Random House.

Web address for online text:
http://www.constitution.org/ari/ethic_00.htm

CHAPTER 2

"Where Has the Time Gone?"

"What's the time?" The answer to this question is straightforward, assuming one has access to a watch or clock. "What is time?" This question, although similar in form to the first, is quite different. Answering this question has cost philosophers considerable energy and effort.

Ethics and Metaphysics

The Introduction to Part I sketched the nature of philosophy in general terms and outlined its relevance for younger students. Chapter 1 followed with an examination of Aristotle's approach to the concept of friendship using passages drawn from Aristotle's own words in the *Nicomachean Ethics*. This concept, friendship, stands as one of many pivotal ideas in the domain of philosophy designated as ethics. The word *ethics* comes from the Greek *ethos*, custom or habit, and its use in a philosophical context evokes how we habitually lead our lives. So, when we study ethics, we learn about living and, presumably, living well—since it would not take much study or, indeed, all that much effort in order to live badly.

Ethics is probably the area of philosophy that people tend to equate with the discipline of philosophy itself. Such questions as "What is the meaning of life?" or "Why are we here?" represent questions popularly associated with the scope and function of philosophy. These questions are perfectly legitimate (although very broadly stated), and they initiate reflection on concepts and issues that have always attracted philosophers concerned with ethics. But, such questions, although obviously of great importance, comprise only one of the major areas in philosophy. Another area of equal and perhaps even greater significance is metaphysics.

The word *metaphysics* is also Greek and it means literally "after the physics." An early Greek editor of Aristotle's writings placed a work analyzing the basic princi-

21

1. What, then, is time? There can be no quick and easy answer, for it is no simple matter even to understand what it is, let alone find words to explain it.

2. I know well enough what it is, provided that nobody asks me; but if I am asked what it is and try to explain, I am baffled.

3. All the same I can confidently say that I know that if nothing passed, there would be no past time; if nothing were going to happen, there would be no future time; and if nothing were, there would be no present time.

4. Of these three divisions of time, then, how can two, the past and the future, be, when the past no longer is and the future is not yet.

5. [Thus] it is not strictly correct to say that there are three times, past, present, and future. It might be correct to say that there are three times, a present of past things, a present of present things, and a present of future things. Some such different times do exist in the mind, but nowhere else that I can see. The present of past things is the memory; the present of present things is direct perception; and the present of future things is expectation.

6. It seems to me, then, that time is merely an extension, though of what it is an extension I do not know. I begin to wonder whether it is an extension of the mind itself.

7. It is in my own mind, then, that I measure time. I must not allow my mind to insist that time is something objective. . . . I say that I measure time in my mind. For everything which happens leaves an impression on it, and this impression remains after the thing itself has ceased to be. It is the impression that I measure, since it is still present, not the thing itself, which makes the impression as it passes and then moves into the past. When I measure time it is this impression that I measure.

8. It can only be that the mind . . . performs three functions, those of expectation, attention, and memory. The future, which it expects, passes through the present, to which it attends, into the past, which it remembers. No one would deny that the future does not yet exist or that the past no longer exists. Yet in the mind there is both expectation of the future and remembrance of the past.

—From Book XI of the *Confessions* by Augustine

ples of reality—the work now known as the *Metaphysics*—chronologically "after" Aristotle's treatise on physics. A less pointedly historical and more inclusive characterization would bring out the fact that metaphysics describes the nature of reality using extremely general and abstract concepts. Metaphysics is considered the most abstruse and difficult area in philosophy. It is also, for the author, the most intriguing—after all, what is more real than reality? Furthermore, if we know and can describe what reality truly is, then we control at least part of what we need to know in order to lead a decent and meaningful life. But, describing reality is a tricky business. We are all real and we all live in reality. It's just that, when we interrupt our busy lives in order to think about and articulate what "reality" really is, we become confused in our own minds and often contentious with others who may share this concern, but who disagree with our particular version of the real.

The Importance of Metaphysics

It was claimed above that metaphysics is arguably more important than ethics. Let me sketch an example illustrating this claim. If I believe in God, especially a Christian God, then I may also believe that God has a plan for me insofar as I have a place in God's universe. If I follow the divine plan, then I will be happy in this life (or at least as happy as this life allows), and I am also likely to believe that I will be completely happy forever in the next life. This notion of happiness is an ethical belief. As a result, how I lead my life will be governed by what I believe God wants me to do. Furthermore, the answers to any ethical questions that might arise in my life depend on understanding the intimate connection between my notion of ethics and my belief in a loving and beneficent God.

St. Augustine

In a word, then, all my ethical beliefs ultimately rest on the existence of God. But, what if God does not exist? If there is no God, then these beliefs lose their foundation and I would seemingly find myself adrift in a world lacking obvious or clear moral guidance. Once I reflect on this set of ethical beliefs and also on their foundation, then I realize that I must be certain of the *existence* of the being who serves to ground these beliefs. But, from a strict philosophical standpoint, the question of the existence of God belongs to metaphysics since it is a question dealing with one component in the nature of reality. Is God real or a figment of our collective imagination? And, if God does exist, can anything be said about characteristics of such a being (e.g., God's knowledge, power, goodness, love)?

These questions are and remain one of the primary concerns of philosophers when they pursue metaphysics to its ultimate foundation (it may be noted here that Chapter 4 offers one of the most famous attempts in the history of philosophy to prove God's existence rationally). But, for present purposes, the point is that the ethical position sketched above is in a sense derivative, since it depends on the existence of a particular being for its attractiveness and compelling force in guiding our conduct. Or, more generally, one's ethics depends ultimately on one's metaphysics.

These matters are weighty and complex, but they are not our present concern. What is our concern is that we are now in a better position to realize that metaphysical questions are important, indeed essential, to the philosophical enterprise. And one of these questions revolves around the subject of the initial paragraph above: What is time?

Augustine on the Nature of Time

The following selections are taken from half a dozen pages in the 11th book of the *Confessions* by St. Augustine (354–430 A.D.). When Augustine was young, he was in no way a saint, and in the beginning of this work, he "confesses" a variety of misdeeds he inflicted upon the world. But, Augustine converted to Christianity and became one of the most important figures in the early church in both philosophy and theology.

Although the following discussion of time is unreservedly philosophical, the way Augustine finds himself involved in this question is of interest. As a believer in God and also in divine creation, Augustine poses the question whether time existed *before* God created the universe. Investigation reveals that intriguing and important questions arise either way this matter is resolved. But, before attending to these questions, Augustine reasons out the nature of time as such, apart from any possible theological relevance, as a prerequisite for such inquiry. The eight selections given on the opposite page represent the core of his thinking on this fundamental concept.

Passage 1

As a philosophical warm-up, ask your audience—or, of course, yourself—for a definition of time. The standard reply is in terms of measurement (i.e., various references to clocks or calendars). But, is the length of a class period what time is? Is time simply what human beings measure it to be?

Augustine says that time is neither easy to understand in a purely conceptual way, nor is it easy to find words to articulate what we believe is in our minds when we are thinking about time. Later, when we examine Augustine's position critically, the wisdom of this opening remark will become evident.

Passage 2

Time is around us all the time (so to speak), but we take its precise nature for granted. We tend to restrict our thinking about time to practical matters, such as keeping appointments and deadlines, or to vague ruminations, as in "Where has the time gone?" Augustine says that he is baffled by a direct question as to the nature of time. But, he will nonetheless offer an explanation of this nature as best he can.

Passage 3

This passage is in three parts. The first part asserts that, if nothing "passed" (or happened), then there would be no past. Students find this point relatively straightforward if they are asked to imagine a yesterday where absolutely nothing happened or moved at all.

The second part, about the future, may be secured by asking the students to imagine what would happen to time if the entire universe were to come to a sudden stop at this very instant. By reversing the direction of the point made about the past, this question facilitates recognition of the fact that future time would cease to exist if nothing were going to happen anywhere in the universe.

The third part, concerning the present, is the most elusive to convey. First, I ask the students to provide a synonym for *were*, emphasizing that the synonym cannot be another form of the verb *to be*. A little digging may be required, but soon someone comes up with *existed* or perhaps *happened*. *Existed* is preferable, I think, because it is more abstract and it indicates an awareness that appropriate language can be procured at this level of generality.

Passage 4

This passage sets the scene for Augustine's approach to time, and it does so with subtle drama. Here is one way to establish the point and have fun in the process. For purposes of illustrating the relevant distinctions, draw a horizontal line on the blackboard and trisect it, labeling the three sections "past," "present," "future." Then ask, "Where is yesterday?" (Asking "*When* is yesterday?" is misleading, since the answer offered tends to be "yesterday," which, given the stark simplicity of the question, is hardly wrong. "Where is yesterday?" or, perhaps, "What happened to yesterday?" invites the students to think of yesterday from a different perspective.) Answer: "It's gone." Question: "Will it ever return?" Answer: "No." Comment: "Yesterday is gone and it's gone forever—it will never return."

Establishing that yesterday, and the past in general, has ceased to exist is relatively straightforward. Showing the parallel point for the future is, however, another matter.

"Where is tomorrow?" "In the future." Now the slightly sneaky question: "Will tomorrow ever come?" At first, a resounding chorus: "Yes!" Question (posed with subtly raised eyebrows): "Oh . . . ? Does it?" Chorus (now somewhat hesitant): "Yes . . ." At this juncture, it pays to wait a bit—although the interval varies, someone will usually say (with a mixture of sudden discovery and resultant pride): "No, it doesn't! Because when tomorrow comes, then it's today." This takes a little time (!) to sink in, but when the point is absorbed, there is general murmuring, "Yeah, that's right . . ." Question: "So, when tomorrow comes, what is it?" Answer: "Today." Question: "So, does tomorrow ever come?" Answer: "No!" Does the future exist then? Well . . . no, or at least only, as Augustine states it, as a "not yet." The reaction at this point is wonderful to behold—brows are furrowed, heads are scratched, more quizzical muttering . . . the students are aware that something metaphysically strange, almost magical, is happening right in front of their probing minds.

Footnote: Occasionally, someone adept at abstract thinking will extend the point just made about the past and the future to include the present. Thus, our youthful metaphysician will say something along the following lines: If you try to put your finger on the present (as it were), it keeps slipping away. As soon as you say "now," then the now is gone; it vanishes. So, in a sense, the present doesn't exist either!

Passage 5

Distinguishing time into past, present, and future is fundamental to our basic experience of reality. But, for Augustine, these divisions are misleading. In fact, he wants effectively to collapse the three phases of time into one—the present. Each phase is then associated with a certain kind of psychological function: the past with memory, the future with expectation, the present with direct perception.

a. *Past*: Ask the students the following question, with the warning that, although the question is simple, they will get the answer wrong unless they *think* before they respond: "When do we have a memory?" Fairly often, someone will blurt, "In the past!" This answer is incorrect. We have the actual experience of a memory in the *present*—what memories are *of*, their particular content, evokes the past. In fact, for Augustine that is exactly what the past is (i.e., our experience of memory).

b. *Present:* Hold up a piece of chalk or a marker. Ask, "When are you seeing this chalk?" "Now," the students chorus. "How do you know you are seeing it now?" This question is slightly odd, and there may be some hesitation. But, fairly soon, someone will say, "Because we are seeing it." Ask, "So, when do you know you are in the present?" The answer: "Whenever we are seeing [or hearing, etc.] something." Augustine's point is made.

c. *Future:* Ask, "Will there be a 6:00 this evening?" The answer nearly always is: "We don't know." Strictly speaking, this is true, since the universe might pop out of existence at the end of the school day. But, such a cataclysmic event is unlikely. Nevertheless, even if the universe were to cease to exist at the end of the school day, it would still be true to say now that we expect there to be a 6:00 this evening. Why? Because yesterday there was a 6:00 p.m., the day before yesterday, etc. So, the future exists in our mind in the sense that we *expect* things to continue to exist—even if, in fact, this expectation turns out to be unwarranted.

In sum, there is a present of past things—memory; a present of present things—perception; and a present of future things—expectation.

Passage 6

Note Augustine's caution in this passage. He wonders whether time is not objective in the sense that it exists on its own, outside of our experience. He also wonders whether the mind grounds the existence of time.

Passage 7

At this point, Augustine has become convinced that time is not "objective." Rather, when we measure time, we measure a mental *impression.* Two examples: Ask someone what he or she had for dinner last night. The eating of last night's dinner is gone, but the impression of that perhaps undramatic event remains; hence, when we remember, we recall that impression. Strictly speaking, we cannot remember what has never left an impression on our mind. A slightly more complex example is to ask why we are certain there will be a 6:00 this evening. Answer: because there was a 6:00 p.m. yesterday evening; in fact, every previous day had a 6:00 p.m. Sometimes, we were aware of this particular moment, sometimes not. But, on those occasions when we were so aware, this moment left an impression and this is the impression measured when we say, "I expect there to be a 6:00 p.m. today."

The conclusion: Whenever we measure time, we are measuring impressions that exist in the mind and *only* in the mind.

Passage 8

The first sentence might be read as if Augustine has limited the mind to only three functions. But, he means that, although the mind has many functions, only three of them are sufficient for adequately analyzing the nature of time.

One way to convey the middle section of the passage is to have the students think of time as a stream that flows entirely in the mind—the future lies in front of us through expectation, edging into the present, which is experienced right now whenever we perceive anything, slipping into the past, which we evoke through memory. This process runs continually throughout our conscious life.

The conclusion of the passage restates the pivotal point, that the three classic dimensions of time—past, present, future—exist in the mind through impressions determined by three of the mind's primary functions.

Augustine's Theory Assessed

Augustine's position has now been developed. I remind the students that one of the ways philosophers assess their conclusions is to test them by seeing whether, or to what extent, they apply in different sets of circumstances. We will now assess Augustine's position in this way. Draw a circle on the board. Tell the students that every existing thing—the entire universe—is in this circle. Then say that this universe is a duplicate, a clone, of our universe—with one exception. In this parallel universe, there are no minds! When I first did this reading, I described the parallel universe as identical to ours, but without *human beings*. This was a tactical mistake because the evaluative investigation is intended to determine whether time exists in this parallel universe, and gifted students quickly indicated that, if *animals* have minds, then a universe without humans would still be a universe with minds (i.e., the minds of animals). What typically happened then was an argument—more or less spirited depending on how many students were animal-lovers—concerning whether or not animals have minds. This is an important question by itself, but strictly speaking it is not germane to the metaphysical point under analysis. To avoid being ambushed by this issue, I realized that the parallel universe should be described as without minds. To reinforce the thrust of the example, write "no minds" inside the circle representing the parallel universe. Then ask the key question: "What does Augustine's position imply about this universe?" The answer is usu-

ally instantaneous: "There's no time in it!" As soon as this consequence is stated, consternation breaks loose, its expression not always kind and gentle. "That's stupid!" "That's crazy!" "Huhhhh . . .?" "How can that be?"

This example dramatically makes the point that, although time certainly exists for Augustine, it exists *only* in the mind. It follows then that, if there are no minds, then there is no time. The students are nearly always convinced that this conclusion is impossible. If so, then it is important to bring out the logical implication that Augustine's overall position becomes questionable, if not false.

Curricular Integration

At this juncture, philosophical considerations can be conveniently blended with other curricular concerns.

A. Language Arts: "Begging the Question" and the "Burden of Proof" in Critical Thinking

Students are generally quite eager to confront Augustine's theory once its unorthodox consequence has been indicated. Their responses can take many forms, but two frequent attempts present opportunities for instruction in a pair of procedures with important applications in logic and critical thinking.

1. Some of the most passionate students will proclaim, "Augustine's just wrong! Time exists whether or not human beings are around!" This is an honest response, but it does not pass the bar of minimal rationality. In fact, it illustrates the logical fallacy known as *begging the question*. A question is begged if the conclusion to be established is assumed in the statement of the position at issue. In this case, the question whether or

not time exists in the mind is the point under dispute. Someone cannot state "Time exists outside the mind" and expect this conclusion to be accepted merely by the fact of its being so baldly stated. It should be pointed out to the students that they cannot simply deny Augustine's conclusion and expect that this denial will be embraced by anyone interested in determining the nature of time. Additional reasoning must be provided by the individual asserting this denial.

2. After explaining the logical concept of begging the question—a basic rule guiding correct argumentation—I then defend Augustine's position against all comers with, I confess, a certain measure of quasi-malicious glee. Let it be noted, however, that I conscientiously warn the students beforehand that it is difficult to refute Augustine's position. However, I also indicate that the burden is on them to refute what Augustine has argued, and at this point the second procedure relevant to critical thinking may be introduced.

Rarely does anyone object to Augustine's position while it is being developed; students typically become agitated only when it is pointed out that this position entails that time exists entirely within human minds. Now, Augustine may be wrong here. But, the *burden of proof* is on the student to show that the theory is false and perhaps, for those duly inspired, to produce a more persuasive account. The burden of proof rests on the student because Augustine has developed his position using standard tools of philosophy: principles, distinctions, reasons, and logic. Once the position has been established, it must be accorded minimal respect. This respect is ensured by the concept of burden of proof since this procedure indicates which side in a dispute must do the arguing.

My experience has been that few students knew the meaning of "burden of proof" prior to its being explained. This logical concept is important in keeping order during any kind of dispute or discussion, and, of course, it is a prerequisite for formal debate. Showing its relevance in a discussion on the nature of time will impress the students with the fact that such inquiry is not entirely free-wheeling, at least not if one intends to make substantive headway on a difficult—yet fascinating—issue in metaphysics.

It should not occasion surprise to learn that any student actively involved in this discussion is hardly daunted by having to follow basic logical considerations pertaining to rational argument. In general, such students love to attack philosophical positions, especially those carrying such seemingly skewed consequences. As a rule, however, the typical counter-examples offered to refute Augustine assume the truth of that position in the very attempt to refute it.

For instance, a common student response is appealing to dinosaurs as the paradigm extinct animal and then arguing as follows: Dinosaurs existed before human beings existed. But, dinosaurs are now extinct. Therefore, there must have been time while the dinosaurs existed since human beings did not exist when dinosaurs did. As a result, since time can exist without human minds, Augustine's theory is false.

This argument, although ingenious, does not refute Augustine. He would admit the existence of dinosaurs, but deny that their existence occurred in time. Reason: No human observers were present while dinosaurs were on the earth. Human beings know now that dinosaurs existed only because of the fossil record. But—and here is the crucial point—we contribute the temporal framework within which the dinosaurs existed when we experience and describe the fossil record. Strictly speaking, Augustine's position allows for dinosaurs, fully existent and fully in motion, but denies that such existence and motion occurred in time, since time by virtue of his argument requires human observation to contribute the dimensions proper to the engendering of time.

In general, Augustine's position concentrates attention on psychological aspects of our awareness of time—memory, perception, and expectation. The consequences of his theory also compel a sharp distinction between *motion* and *time* as the measure of motion. One metaphysical lesson to be learned from reflecting on Augustine and time is that understanding the concept of motion seems to require that we must distinguish between things moving and the time in which those things move. Admittedly, however, these are difficult lessons to learn, especially amidst the argumentative thrust and parry ringing throughout a classroom of young people actively philosophizing about time!

Student reaction toward the end of a session on this topic ranges from sullen frustrated silence to fiery metaphysical discontent—almost all are convinced that Augustine's position is incorrect, but they find it difficult to show why or to present another theory that will avoid the bizarre consequence of a universe replete with motion, but bereft of time. One way to deal with this gamut of unsatisfied response is to recall the first passage in Augustine's treatment: "it is no simple matter even to understand what [time] is, let alone find words to explain it." For Augustine, time can be explained as an interplay of various mental functions. But, if this account seems unconvincing, then we as philosophers have additional work to do to provide a more satisfactory explanation. Time is indeed hard to understand . . .

To be honestly perplexed about an issue as fundamental as the nature of time is, as a rule, a healthy intellectual condition, regardless of how youthful the students may be. If, however, a teacher would like to provide a measure of relief to the students' philosophical bewilderment, then the following two avenues of thought may be explored. It should be emphasized at the outset, however, that these avenues include potential potholes, not to mention a number of sudden—and hidden—twists and turns.

First, here is a question that offers a direction for critical inquiry: If, as Augustine says, time exists in the mind, then . . . whose mind is it in? This question may lead to others of a related sort. For example, are psychological functions such as memory and perception reliable as far as temporal accuracy is concerned?

It appears that Augustine's position can be assessed, first, by assuming that its conclusion is true—that time exists only in the mind—but, second, by eliciting problems, perhaps even contradictions, when the supposed truth of this conclusion is confronted with facts about the psychological functions that circumscribe time. One obvious example, a fact real to all of us, is the stark difference between the experience of an exciting class in contrast to the suffocating feeling of incarceration in a class that is deadly dull.

B. Science: Time and the Big Bang

A different approach to determining the nature of time, one that will be receptive to students with an interest in science, is to present a version of the Big Bang theory concerning the origin of the universe and then to investigate, as carefully and rigorously as possible, what that theory says or implies about time. Students captured by this topic will typically be able to provide imaginative models that depict the Big Bang and also focus on time and the relation between time and matter in motion. Discussion of these models will clarify the students' understanding not only of the Big Bang as such, but also how this important and widely discussed topic in cosmology pertains to our grasp of the nature of time in a theoretical context far removed from Augustine's. For Augustine, time is basically anthropomorphic; for proponents of the Big Bang, time is already in some sense "out there" in the makings and structure of the cosmos. Which position should we as philosophers accept?

Postlude

The title of this chapter is "Where Has the Time Gone?", and I would venture that this question will arise in the minds of more than a few teachers who try these readings with their students. At the end of the class, these teachers will wonder at how quickly the time sped by, and I predict they will also marvel at the ability of their students to produce pointed and perceptive metaphysical comments and questions on this venerable issue. Of course, at another level of significance, the question in the title also describes our collective state of knowledge concerning the subject of this inquiry: Just where *has* the nature of time gone now that we have started to think about it? Augustine's

theory remains a candidate for careful and sustained philosophical reflection. But . . . it cannot be true . . . Or can it?

We must continue to reflect on the matter. Yet, as this reflection continues, it should be evident now that metaphysics as a branch of philosophy is not the cold and dry plaything of desiccated intellectuals. It is as real and vibrant as the wonder animating children and driving them to investigate so many things in their world—including, perhaps, the very nature of time itself.

Reference:

Augustine (St.). (1961). *Confessions*. London: Penguin.

Web address for online text:
http://www.stoa.org/hippo

CHAPTER 3

"Do We Really Know What We Think We Know?"

"It's the right thing to do!"

"That's your <u>opinion</u>. But, how do I <u>know</u> that it's right?"

This or a similar exchange has occurred many times in the past and doubtless will reoccur many times in the future. The speakers are two adults, or two adolescents, or—the language suitably modified—parent (or teacher) and child (or student). The dispute concerns whether or not a given decision or course of action is right, either in a moral or practical context. The theoretical resolution of these common disputes is rooted in an area of philosophy as old as the ancient Greeks. As a practical matter, of course, the resolution may be a stark appeal to authority—"Just do it! It's right because I say so!" If, however, the rightness of the action or decision is to be based on something other than mere authority—in a word, on knowledge—then the question becomes one of establishing that rightness and explaining it on the basis of principles and concepts that should be acceptable to all thoughtful parties involved. The area in philosophy concerned with analyzing the nature of knowledge is called *epistemology.*

Epistemology is a Greek word, meaning literally "the study (or the science) of knowledge." This study concerns how we know whatever we know and the degree to which we know it. Its principal focus is directed at the processes and objects involved in instilling what we call knowledge into the human animal. Thus, the processes that come into play in knowing that God exists, that 3 + 2 = 5, and that some apples are red will presumably differ because deity, numbers, and fruit represent different kinds of reality. For the knower, the processes central to epistemology include sensation, perception, intuition, and thinking, each of which is a complex phenomenon in its own right with its own set of concepts and engendering its own philosophical issues.

It should be noted that modern psychology, especially in its experimental modes, has essentially taken over analysis of the empirical aspects of these processes. To that extent, psychology has supplanted (perhaps "supplemented" is preferable) traditional philosophical approaches to the study of knowledge. However, the interpretation of the data produced by empirical psychological investigation remains of concern to those contemporary philosophers whose interests lie in explaining what goes on whenever we think that we know something. Indeed, the fundamental questions of epistemology remain timeless, and some version of these questions animates all disciplines devoted to studying this feature of human activity.

Chapter 1 dealt with friendship in Aristotle; Chapter 2 analyzed Augustine's treatment of time. Friendship and time are classic concepts in the areas of ethics and metaphysics, respectively. Epistemology is generally considered to be the final member of philosophy's basic triumvirate of subdisciplines. After all, any claim in ethics or metaphysics—"friendship is . . .", "time is . . ."—can be prefaced "How do you know that friendship is . . .?" or "How do you know that time is . . .?" Whenever we assert something to be true, whether that something is philosophical or otherwise, we are implicitly depending on an embedded understanding of what it means to know that something is the case. Upon close scrutiny, however, it becomes evident that the division of philosophy into ethics, metaphysics, and epistemology is a rubric based more on convenience, since it appears that an inquiry originating in any one of these three areas inevitably leads to questions and problems that encroach on and eventually enter the domains of the other two. Nonetheless, for our purposes, we will follow this division since it allows us to examine a fundamental distinction in epistemology discussed

Plato

in a passage drawn from the *Crito*, one of the most dramatically moving dialogues of Plato (427–347 B.C.).

Background

The *Crito* is one of Plato's early dialogues, and is short (about 12 pages in the standard English translations). Here is the situation: The year is 399 B.C. After a life spent thinking and questioning, the 70-year-old Socrates resides in prison, awaiting execution after an Athenian court has convicted him of two capital offenses related to his philosophical investigations. Crito, about the same age as Socrates, has been his lifelong friend; unlike Socrates, however, Crito is wealthy and knows others who are wealthy. Crito visits Socrates and proposes that money is available to take care of (i.e., to bribe) the relevant authorities; Crito then offers Socrates a series of reasons that he hopes Socrates will accept to justify this proposal. But, although his life hangs in the balance, Socrates responds to this timely offer as he has always done in circumstances requiring a moral decision: If rational argument convinces him that leaving Athens under these circumstances is the right thing to do, then he will do it. If, on the other hand, argument shows that acting on this proposal is not right, then Socrates will reject it and accept the legally decreed punishment of death. Here, as elsewhere, Socrates' actions follow from his reasoned thoughts.

One of the reasons Crito wants to convince Socrates to escape concerns what the Athenians will think of Crito and Socrates' other friends if they do not make the most strenuous effort—including the expenditure of funds to appropriate parties—to ensure that Socrates' life is preserved. Since Crito believes that public opinion is very important, not only in the urgent matter at hand, but also in general, Socrates must critically examine this belief in order to evaluate its relevance. The section of the dialogue analyzed below appears at this juncture in the *Crito*. Its primary point is to show that failing to recognize the difference between knowledge and opinion will be harmful to both body and spirit.

Procedural Suggestions

The following (47a–48b in the Greek text of the *Crito*) is one continuous passage divided into 8 sections in order to clarify the reasoning in the exchanges between Socrates and Crito. This arrangement also allows comment on the typical responses to this reasoning provided by young students. The text is verbatim except for two brief ellipses.

1. Have different students read the parts of Socrates and Crito, a pair of students for each of the eight segments. Even the most sophisticated gifted students enjoy "performing" this episode drawn from a remarkable philosophical drama.

2. As the students discuss the exchanges, it will become evident that both Socrates and Crito make a number of assumptions. These assumptions are not considered during the explicit reasoning exhibited in this passage. However, it is certainly open to the teacher to pursue these assumptions if student interest suggests that such inquiry will prove engaging and informative.

3. In the discussion of Augustine on time in Chapter 2, suggestions for integrating elements in this discussion were made in two curricular areas: critical thinking and science. These suggestions concerned the relevance of Augustine's position to the Big Bang theory of the origin of the universe and to several areas in logic important for critical thinking. The present passage from the *Crito* is marked by a spaciousness of argument that makes such curricular integration not readily available. However, the very generality of the Socratic conversation makes this passage suitable for "spin-off" discussions that could be pursued in relation to other subjects or as supplemental topics of general concern to students. These discussions will be noted where applicable in the commentaries appended to each of the eight passages.

Passage 1

The easy flow of conversation in a Platonic dialogue masks the fact that Plato's Socrates almost always makes his point in compressed and precise language, avoiding mere chit-chat. This initial passage is an excellent test of the students' ability to read closely and carefully.

It is helpful to divide Socrates' observation into two parts: (a) not valuing all the opinions of people, but some and not others; (b) not valuing the opinions of all people, but those of some and not others. The "some and not others" locution occurs twice, but it refers to differ-

1. **Socrates:** Consider, do you not think it a sound statement that one must not value all the opinions of people but some and not others, nor the opinions of all people but those of some and not of others? What do you say? Is this not well said?
   Crito: It is.

2. **Socrates:** One should value the good opinions, and not the bad ones?
   Crito: Yes.
   Socrates: The good opinions are those of wise people, the bad opinions those of foolish ones.
   Crito: Of course.

3. **Socrates:** Come then, what of statements such as this: Should a person professionally engaged in physical training pay attention to the praise and blame and opinion of anyone, or to those of one person only, namely a doctor or trainer?
   Crito: To those of one only.

4. **Socrates:** The person in training should therefore fear the blame and welcome the praise of that one individual, and not those of the many?
   Crito: Obviously.
   Socrates: This person must then act and exercise, eat and drink in the way the one, the trainer and the one who knows, thinks right, not all the others?
   Crito: That is so.
   Socrates: Very well. And if this person disobeys the one, disregards the opinions and praises while valuing those of the many who have no knowledge, will he or she not suffer harm?
   Crito: Of course.
   Socrates: What is that harm, where does it tend, and what part of the person who disobeys does it affect?
   Crito: Obviously the harm is to his body, which it ruins.

5. **Socrates:** Well said. So with other matters . . . and certainly with actions just and unjust, shameful and beautiful, good and bad, about which we are now deliberating, should we follow the opinion of the many and fear it, or that of the one—if there is one who has knowledge of these things and before whom we feel fear and shame more than before all the others.

If we do not follow the directions of this person, we shall harm and corrupt that part of ourselves that is improved by just actions and destroyed by unjust actions. Or is there nothing in this?

Crito: I think there certainly is, Socrates.

6. **Socrates:** Come now, if we ruin that which is improved by health and corrupted by disease by not following the opinions of those who know, is life worth living for us when that is ruined? And that is the body, is it not?

Crito: Yes.

Socrates: And is life worth living with a body that is corrupted and in bad condition?

Crito: In no way.

7. **Socrates:** And is life worth living for us with that part of us corrupted that unjust action harms and just action benefits? Or do we think that part of us, whatever it is, that is concerned with justice and injustice, is inferior to the body?

Crito: Not at all.

Socrates: It is more valuable?

Crito: Much more.

8. **Socrates:** We should not then think so much of what the majority will say about us, but what that person will say who understands justice and injustice, the one, that is, and the truth itself. So that . . . you were wrong to believe that we should care for the opinion of the many about what is just, beautiful, good, and their opposites.

—From the *Crito* by Plato

ent things. Passage (a) contrasts opinions; passage (b) contrasts people. Thus (a) says that some of our opinions are valuable while others are not; (b) says that some people are worth listening to for their opinions but some people are *never* worth listening to about anything.

It is usually not difficult to have the students recognize the point of (a). The teacher might ask when we should listen to someone's opinion, and the answer typically given is "When they know what they are talking about." If people do not know what they are talking about, then we might listen to their opinion (e.g., for the sake of politeness), but we do not believe what they have to say nor, if we had a choice, would we typically act upon that opinion.

Recognizing the point of (b) is, however, another matter, especially in a democracy when people can have an opinion on a given issue—and then cast a vote based on that opinion—and know little or nothing about that issue. It has been my experience that students usually do not hesitate to identify some people as so thoughtless that their opinions are virtually useless, regardless of the subject. These students agree with Socrates. On the other hand, it is not uncommon to find other students arguing against Socrates by claiming that everyone knows a little about something, thus whenever a person expresses an opinion on that something, whatever it may be, this opinion should be valued.

Spin-off #1: Are gifted students "better" than nongifted students?

The distinction Socrates introduces here could readily be adapted to a discussion of the attitude gifted students should display toward the "nongifted"—in short, the "elitism" question couched in a particular context among the students themselves.

Assume that some students never have any worthwhile opinions. Are gifted students "better" than these students? The egalitarian answer is no, they are just different. Whenever this issue has emerged in discussion, it is evident to me that gifted students tend to be uneasy about this point; thus, denying that gifted students are any better or worse than other students is an almost universal refrain coming from the gifted students themselves. But, if this is true, then what follows for the attitude gifted students should display toward nongifted students? It may be inferred that gifted students should act in precisely the same way toward nongifted students as they do toward other gifted students, even if the nongifted students have little or nothing to say about anything that interests or concerns gifted students.

A related question: Should gifted students receive more funding for their school programs because they can learn more and do more with what they learn than their nongifted peers? If so, doesn't this make gifted students an elite group even if the word *elite* is not used to describe them? One way to approach answering this question rests on the value assigned to formal education in terms of long-range results. If it is true that gifted students do learn more and faster, then it could be argued that, because their knowledge is greater, they will accomplish more for the society in which they live than if equivalent funding is given to nongifted students who lack the capacity to move from the level of opinion to the higher level of knowledge. I offer this observation not as an answer, but as an inference that could be drawn from the flow of the dialogue, an inference that could—and should—be discussed and dissected to unearth hidden assumptions and to produce additional possibilities. The issue is a vexed one. In context, the point of this paragraph is only that one aspect of this kind of problem in social and educational policy could be based on the distinction between opinion and knowledge and overall outcomes in society as derived from that distinction. It is evident, I think, that students not designated as "gifted" would be just as interested in this question (if not more so!) than their gifted counterparts.

Passage 2

In this exchange, Socrates connects the goodness of opinions with wisdom, the badness of opinions with foolishness. Ask the students for an example of a foolish opinion. It would, at present, be a foolish opinion to say that the earth is flat, although this was an opinion that for centuries held sway among many people. And, given what we now know, it would also be a foolish opinion to maintain that smoking is harmless to the smoker. Although views on particular instances of wisdom and foolishness will differ, most students will accept, usually without demur, the distinction between those who are wise and those who are foolish. But, the connection Socrates wants to establish between wise opinions and goodness in contrast with foolish opinions and badness raises interesting difficulties.

Spin-off #2: Are foolish opinions "bad" opinions?

Consider smoking. Most students admit that it is foolish to hold the opinion that smoking is harmless. However, they then often deny that the person holding this opinion is "bad" since such a conclusion is "judgmental." These students will claim that an individual has the "right" to hold a foolish opinion if he or she wants to, and although this opinion is considered "bad," this right makes it inappropriate to label this person as "bad." Thus, if the opinion is a value judgment (e.g., "smoking is harmful to your health" or "cheating is always wrong") then if values are subjective and private, people can hold whatever opinion they wish and no one can claim to know what values should be held by society.

On the surface, there seems to be a vast difference between the opinions "the earth is flat" and "smoking is okay." The first opinion can be refuted as unfactual whereas the second depends on the individual's own sense of what is right and wrong. The fact-value distinction seems to be thoroughly ingrained in the modern mind. Facts are public and subject to verification; values are private and are produced by individual interests. But, for Socrates, this distinction is too simple; in fact, the stark dichotomy between fact and value and their respective characteristics is unwarranted and incorrect. Of special note in this context is the point that what we refer to as values can be known just as facts can be known (a type of knowledge Socrates pursues in other dialogues).

For a rousing discussion, ask the students whether they can identify a value that is *not* private and, if they can, to give reasons why it is not private. The point of this discussion is to invite students to think about the difference between opinion and knowledge in the context of values. Although some students can appreciate Plato's "absolutist" position on objective values, my experience has been that the majority will side with accepting an essential link between values and opinions. In other words, values are not susceptible to being known, but at best merely express personal opinion, which may or may not be shared by society at large. Once this link is accepted, it is difficult to agree with Socrates in asserting that a person who holds a foolish opinion holds a "bad" one and is, for that reason, also "bad." Even if it is a foolish opinion, if the person holding that opinion feels that it is good, then it is good—for that person. But, it might be asked, is acting on such an opinion truly good for the person just because the person may feel that it is good at the time?

Passage 3

To reinforce Socrates' point, ask the students why someone involved in physical training should heed the praise and blame of only one person if that person is a doctor or trainer. As a rule, the answer comes quickly: because

that person knows. It is also advisable to ask why "the praise and blame and opinion of anyone" should be ignored. There are two answers, one fairly obvious, the other more subtle and not as frequently produced. The first answer is that "anyone" might not know anything about physical training, although that person might be of the opinion that he or she knows. Stating that one knew something that one in fact did not know would illustrate Socrates' conception of a "foolish" opinion (as indicated in Passage 2 above).

The second answer is that, if this individual listened to more than one person at the same time, then the opinions stated might (and doubtless would) contradict one another. In this case, if all the opinions given are deemed of equal value, then how would one decide which opinion to use as a guiding principle of action? If the opinions as a set are indeed contradictory, then attempting to act on them becomes impossible. As Aristotle pointed out long ago, we cannot do A and not-A (e.g., load up on carbohydrates and not load up on carbohydrates) at one and the same time and in the same respect. In such cases, logical contradiction rests on straightforward physical impossibility.

Passage 4

Here the factor of knowledge is made explicit. The person in training must act in all ways according to the directions of the individual with knowledge: the doctor or trainer. Socrates also infers that advice from the many will be harmful, either because it is based solely on opinion or because it will be contradictory (or both). Note that Crito draws the conclusion that the harm will be to the body, which it "ruins," a conclusion that Socrates endorses.

Students will often comment that this conclusion is overstated as it stands, since one could follow foolish advice and harm the body only slightly, rather than ruin it. Crito is apparently considering a "worst case scenario," where the opinions are such that they will cause the most dire consequences to the body if acted upon. If the students press this objection, Crito's main point can still be saved—for if the harm to our body is only slight, rather than severe, we would surely prefer not to undergo even that minimal degree of harm, especially if we suffered it because we listened to people who were uttering ungrounded opinions, rather than knowledge.

Passage 5

This complex and rich passage offers considerable room for development and discussion.

a. Note the pattern of opposition present in the sequence: just/unjust, shameful/beautiful, good/bad. The end points of each type of opposition are left undefined. Ask the students whether some actions are just and other actions unjust. As in the case of wisdom and foolishness above (Passage 2), although they might disagree about a particular example, students will not deny that *some* kind of difference exists between what is just and what is unjust.

   Now ask the students who is the "someone" who has knowledge of "these things" (i.e., justice, beauty, and goodness). One factor that pertains to answering this question concerns when in the students' curricular history this discussion of the *Crito* is offered. If classes devoted to other philosophical issues have already occurred, then the students will readily identify the "someone" in question as "a philosopher." If, however, the Plato passage is the initial text discussed, then some prodding might be required in order to get the students in a position to recognize that the individual who studies these kinds of abstract realities is the philosopher.

b. Ask the students what is "that part of ourselves" that is improved by just actions and

destroyed by unjust ones. Engaged students are usually quick to determine that, if there is a "part" of us that is not the body, this part must be the mind or, to use the Greek term, the soul. However, someone will doubtless challenge this conclusion by asking "What evidence is there that we have a soul?" To circumvent disputes arising from the fact that "soul" is frequently used in a religious context, the teacher can suggest that soul be understood as mind or perhaps as "the human spirit" or something equivalently ethereal. But, regardless of whether it is soul or mind or spirit, for Socrates we are harmed by doing unjust actions; in addition, we are harmed merely by holding an opinion that is bad or unjust, regardless of whether or not we ever choose to act on that opinion.

Spin-off #3 (from Passage 6): Is euthanasia ever justified?

It seems that Socrates and Crito would answer this question in the affirmative: If our body is ruined and corrupted by disease, then, as Socrates says and Crito agrees, life is not "worth living."

Ask the students whether human life should be preserved at all costs. Socrates does not analyze the question in any detail at this juncture, although his point in the blanket affirmation that life is not worth living with a corrupt body suggests that we need a functioning body in order to live a properly human life. I have heard gifted students assert that, even if the body has been thoroughly ruined, life is still worth living as long as the mind continues to function. Their position is that, if you can think, then you can and should continue to live. The virtually immobilized physicist Stephen Hawking is a particularly dramatic—and remarkably productive—example of this conclusion. But, here again the question is vexed, and reflection on it will introduce considerations pertaining to the quality of life and also to social policy, since maintenance of individuals when they continue to exist in such conditions can sometimes be at public expense.

Passage 7

Crito asserts that the soul is more valuable than the body, but he does not explain why he believes this to be true. Ask the students to give reasons to justify the claim that the soul is more valuable than the body. One frequent answer is that the soul is immortal, whereas the body perishes. At this point, one might ask, "How do we know that the soul is immortal?" and, as a parallel question, "Can we know that the soul is immortal for reasons other than religious belief?" Finally, it is also worth asking, "Even if the soul is immortal, why does that make it more valuable than the body?" As an aside, if the soul is indeed immortal as some students will maintain, then it appears difficult to affirm consistently that the soul can be ruined, as Socrates seems to claim in Passage 5 above. One way to resolve this logical tension is to indicate that a ruined soul is not destroyed; rather, a ruined soul is one that cannot function properly in its role as giving direction to and controlling the body. On Socrates' principles, then, the more bad and foolish opinions we hold and things we do, the less the soul is able to provide order and stability to the person as a unity of body and soul. But, even such a disrupted and disoriented soul will continue to exist.

Issues pertaining to the soul are fascinating to pursue, but they are also fraught with pedagogical peril since, depending on the degree of religious belief held by the students, the discussions can become occasions for emotional appeals to religious works, passionate assertions of divine revelation, and, on occasion, even some Elmer Gantry-type sermonizing. It is important to emphasize to the students that this discussion has nothing to do with religion,

given the immediate context of the inquiry. For Socrates and Crito, as Greeks, the soul is an essential part of being human and, although they, again as Greeks, did believe in an afterlife, the existence of the soul after death is not directly relevant to their present concerns. Thus, are we harmed by doing evil even if we are not religious? Socrates' answer is yes, since evil harms the soul and the soul is an integral element in the human person, whether or not that person happens to be religious. For Socrates, we do evil things because we are not thinking clearly, not because we are caught in the clutches of Satan.

Passage 8

The conclusion of the argument shows that what the majority says about values such as justice and goodness should be ignored. There is, however, a qualification of sorts. We should ignore the majority in these cases and listen to someone who knows about justice, beauty, and the good—in other words, to a philosopher who can help us learn about the true natures of these realities. It is obvious, of course, that philosophers imbued with this kind of intellectual desire and achievement are rarely met with in ordinary life. However, we can all be philosophers, or at least think and act philosophically, if we take the time to reflect on our choices and justify them in terms of our best long-range interests in conjunction with the interests of those with whom we share our lives. Here is an example pertinent to all students, gifted and otherwise.

If the majority of one's classmates says, or implies by actions, that cheating is okay, does this make it acceptable? There are two related, but distinct issues here: (a) Is cheating ever morally acceptable? (b) Does the fact that a number of people say that cheating is acceptable make it so? Thus, one could perhaps maintain that some circumstances justify cheating, but deny that cheating is acceptable if the only

reason put forth on its behalf is that many people say that cheating is acceptable. Most students readily recognize that (b) is an instance of what logic textbooks call the fallacy of common belief (i.e., that a conclusion is not established as true merely because a number of people believe that it is true). However, to interject a personal impression, it has been continually unnerving to see the number of gifted students who assert that cheating is acceptable "if you really need a grade in a course" or "if your parents will give you grief should you get a bad grade."

Although the *Crito* does not address the moral ramifications of (a), the dialogue does offer a criticism of (b). This criticism is that many people holding an opinion do not transform that opinion into knowledge. Students are, of course, extremely susceptible to peer pressure. Therefore, the more aware they are of reasons against relying on the opinions of peers, the greater the possibility that such students will not emulate behavior simply because they are implicitly—and thoughtlessly—of the opinion that, since "everyone does it," it is morally acceptable.

Socrates' position is that acting on a bad opinion harms the person performing this action, quite apart from consequences such as a cheater getting caught by the teacher. For Socrates, cheating is no less harmful to the student even if the student gets away with it. The harm is to the soul, and if the argument in the *Crito* is correct, then a student who cheats does more harm to the self because of damaging the soul than if that student had overindulged in food or exercise and thereby harmed the body. From Socrates' perspective, there is no "private" realm of value—even if I am the only person who knows I did something wrong, I have still harmed myself by that action.

Concluding Thought

This brief excerpt from the *Crito* suggests some practical reasons for believing that a distinction between knowledge and opinion is important. However, in the course of the discussion, many related questions have emerged and been left unresolved, for example, is there indeed a soul? And, if we do grant the difference between opinion and knowledge, just how is knowledge to be defined? Plato's Socrates takes up these questions in dialogues written after the *Crito* (e.g., the *Phaedo* and the *Republic*). For present purposes, the *Crito* will have accomplished its aim if the above passage has alerted us to the possibility that the distinction between knowledge and opinion is a topic worthy of continued reflection. Furthermore, inviting younger students to reflect on this difference and on the meaning of knowledge in general will make them more aware of the need to be receptive to all levels and types of experience. This awareness will contribute toward preparing them to maximize their knowledge in as many subjects as possible and to solidify their knowledge in areas of special interest to them.

The first three chapters in Part I have been devoted to ethics, metaphysics, and epistemology—the basic triumvirate of disciplines constituting the philosophical enterprise. Aristotle, Augustine, and Plato were the philosophers illustrating this series. The primary sources highlighting each of these chapters constituted only small samples from the seminal works from which they were chosen. Despite their brevity, however, my hope is that readers have recognized how much the ancient thinkers still have to offer to us in the present. Of course, the search for wisdom did not come to an end in antiquity. As long as there are thoughtful human beings, there will always be at least a few philosophers trying to be heard. And, by way of preview, subsequent chapters will explore other examples of philosophical concepts in the areas of ethics, metaphysics and epistemology, but with examples drawn from philosophers working in later historical periods.

Following this sequence of sources from the ancient world of philosophy into the modern era will accomplish at least two ends: First, it will contribute to the reader's awareness of the immense richness offered by the panoply of philosophers available for our consideration, an awareness that can then be transferred to students by developing the primary source texts contained in each chapter. Second, traversing the ideas of this series of thinkers in its entirety will enhance students' overall awareness of history and how the values of contemporary culture are the product of a reservoir of prior thought drawn from a variety of the world's cultures. To strive to achieve these goals is a noble enterprise, well worth the effort expended even if, in the end and as one might realistically expect, the pursuit falls short of complete success in instilling a comprehensive awareness of all the philosophical figures covered. Be that as it may, the process of inquiry accompanying this pursuit can only help students (and, of course, the teachers who accompany them) become more reflective and sensitive human beings. In such awareness are planted seeds of wisdom that, properly developed, will contribute to a more sensitive and fulfilling life for all concerned.

Reference:

Plato. (1981). *Five dialogues* (G. M. A. Grube, Trans.). Indianapolis, IN: Hackett.

Web address for online text:
http://www.constitution.org/pla/crito.htm

CHAPTER 4

Younger Students and the Existence of God

Does God exist? Most individuals at one time or another have posed this question either silently to themselves or aloud to others. Kids are no exception to this common quest. In this chapter, we discuss one of the most well-known and respected philosophical pathways to God.

The first three philosophers encountered in Part I have been Aristotle, Plato, and St. Augustine, all thinkers from the ancient world. We now move into the medieval era in philosophy, a thousand-year period roughly dating from the fall of the Roman Empire to the dawn of the Renaissance. There was considerable philosophical activity during this millennium, so much so that it is a decided misnomer to refer to this as the "dark ages," at least from the standpoint of philosophical productivity. Much light was shed on a number of important issues, not the least of which was the question of God's existence and nature. It should be noted that virtually all the significant philosophers working during this period were religious—to mention only two especially prominent figures, the Arabic thinker Avicenna (980–1037), a follower of Islam, and the Jewish philosopher Moses Maimonides (1135–1204). Although doctrinal differences existed among these and a number of other supremely gifted individuals, their beliefs spoke to their reason, and much worthwhile philosophical thought was the result.

Thomas Aquinas (1225–1274) is universally recognized as one of the greatest medieval philosophers and theologians. In the massive *Summa Theologica*, Aquinas discusses a wide variety of problems and questions pertaining to Catholicism, using a blend of philosophical and theological concepts, distinctions, and argumentative strategies. Early in the *Summa*, as a prelude to sustained inquiry on a singularly important subject—the nature of God—Aquinas produces five "ways" toward rationally proving that God exists. Each way takes a different theoretical path to this destination, and one of these ways will occupy us here.

The following discussion is based on the fifth way, a demonstration traditionally known as the "Argument From Design." This argument is short—five sentences in the standard English translation of the *Summa Theologica*—and although the reasoning is accessible, its expression is extremely compressed, so much so that the argument is best handled sentence by sentence.

Introduction

Ask the students, "How many of you believe in God?" Almost all hands will go up. Then ask, simply, "Why?" Answers tend to fall into patterns: (a) Some students' religion includes God as part of their belief system; thus, if they accept that religion, then they accept the existence of God. (b) Some students' parents have instilled in them a belief in God. (c) Some students have concluded to the existence of a supreme being on their own and for a variety of reasons: (i) life would make no sense without God; (ii) an explanation is necessary for why they as human beings exist at all; (iii) to keep things in the universe in harmony and under control.

The students can now be challenged with the following claim: According to the philosopher Thomas Aquinas, the existence of God can be *proven rationally*, that is, just by thinking and reasoning. Keen interest is aroused by this bold assertion. However, before starting Aquinas' argument, I have found it useful to make two prefatory observations.

First, alert the students to the fact that they will be participating in a philosophical exercise and that its purpose is in no way to undermine or even to challenge anyone's religious beliefs. For some students, God is a sensitive topic, and discussion of this concept is inflected with various emotional responses that should be respected. Also emphasize that the students' religious beliefs—or lack thereof—are their own business and will not be touched by the ensuing discussion. Second, Aquinas' fifth way is a reasoned account, therefore it is prudent to

reacquaint students with the nature of reasoning, especially from the standpoint of formal structure. For present purposes, reasoning may be defined as the progressive movement from a set of premises to a conclusion. Here is a straightforward, and extremely pedestrian, example of reasoning:

All dogs are mammals.
All mammals are users of oxygen.
Therefore, all dogs are users of oxygen.

Here the mind has moved to a new (if prosaic) bit of information by combining two propositions and then drawing a conclusion from this juxtaposition. It will soon become evident that the reasoning in the Argument From Design is complex, both in terms of the content of the argument and as far as strict logic is concerned. However, it is essential for the students to be aware from the outset that Aquinas is not just venturing an opinion; rather, he is moving from certain facts about the natural world through valid principles of logic to the conclusion that only if God exists could those facts be adequately explained.

Finally, some of the concepts driving the argument of the fifth way are relatively abstract, so students will have to concentrate and be alert in order to comprehend and contribute meaningfully to discussion of this intriguing and important issue.

The Argument From Design: Proof and Discussion

The fifth way comprises five sentences. In this section, each of these sentences is quoted verbatim from the standard English translation of the *Summa Theologica*. Then, as in all the chapters in Part I, each passage is followed by an

1. The fifth way is taken from the governance of the world.

2. We see that things which lack knowledge, such as natural bodies, act for an end, and this is evident from their acting always, or nearly always, in the same way, so as to obtain the best result.

3. Hence it is plain that they achieve their end, not fortuitously, but designedly.

4. Now whatever lacks knowledge cannot move towards an end, unless it be directed by some being endowed with knowledge and intelligence; as the arrow is directed by the archer.

5. Therefore some intelligent being exists by whom all natural things are directed to their end; and this being we call God.

—From the *Summa Theologica*, Part. 1, Question 1, Article 1, by Thomas Aquinas

explanation and also by an account of typical student reactions to the reasoning at that juncture.

Passage 1

The word *governance* resembles *government*, and the intended sense in context is similar. Ask the students what, in general, a government does. Whereas a government helps organize and order the affairs of human beings, *governance* is restricted by Aquinas to a region of reality that has nothing whatsoever to do with human beings. It is important to emphasize this point at the outset even though its import will not become clear until later in the argument.

Passage 2

This is a complex passage and it requires a fair amount of discussion. Aquinas now indicates what region of the natural world he will consider in this argument: "things which lack knowledge, such as natural bodies." But, prior to illustrating and discussing this premise, it is advisable to explain how Aquinas is using "end."

The concept of "end" is used in a special sense that Aquinas borrowed from Aristotle. (Aquinas often refers to Aristotle as "the philosopher," as if the great Greek were uniquely seminal in this regard.) "End" means the realization of a natural process; thus, the end of an acorn is to become an oak. Although certain conditions must be fulfilled (e.g., sufficient soil, moisture, sunlight), once those conditions have been satisfied, then an acorn will necessarily become an oak. In general, then, the "end" of a natural body that lacks knowledge is to become what is in its nature to become and also to realize fully that nature. The end of a robin's egg is to become a robin, and the end of a robin, once grown, is to live and act as long as a robin naturally exists.

It is now possible to identify the regions of nature that concern Aquinas. He is referring to natural bodies that function as they do without any kind of knowledge, as the acorn becoming the oak (and, of course, all plants of this sort) and the activities of certain animals, such as birds migrating for the sake of self-preservation. The latter example frequently engenders debate over whether or not birds "know" what they are

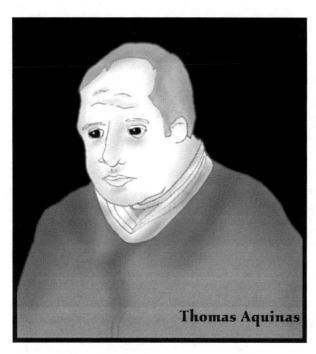

Thomas Aquinas

doing. The disputed concept is, of course, knowledge, and although it is fascinating to argue about the extent to which animals know what they are doing, such discussion will quickly assume a life of its own, rapidly moving away from the specific issue at hand. Thus, even if animals do in fact possess knowledge, hosts of other natural bodies clearly lack knowledge of any sort, and this is the sector of nature that concerns Aquinas.

Assume that birds act on instinct, rather than knowledge. Why do birds migrate? They do so in order to survive, which is the "best result" of which Aquinas speaks. Note that Aquinas is careful to qualify his conclusion: He says that natural bodies that lack knowledge always act in the same way—or "nearly always." This qualification is important. Aquinas knows that nature is characterized by uniformity— natural bodies repeat the same processes over and over and over again. But, he also knows that there are occasional exceptions.

Passage 3

This step is short, but intricate, in terms of both language and logic. First, several termino-

logical points. (a) Make certain that the referent of "they" is clear. Those students who have been reading closely will readily recognize that "they" refers back to "things which lack knowledge, such as natural bodies." (b) The adverbs—for-tuitously and designedly—are occasionally unfamiliar. If it appears that students are some-what troubled by them, suggest that they plug in synonyms—"by chance" for *fortuitously*, "on purpose" for *designedly*.

After these meanings have been clarified, ask what the word *hence* means at the start of this sentence. Answers are swift—*therefore* or *so*. Then ask, "What is *hence* a sign of as far as logic and reasoning are concerned?" Answers come, although typically not quite as fast—*hence* is the sign of a conclusion. Thus, Aquinas is estab-lishing a conclusion with this sentence.

It is worth indicating at this juncture that the fifth way contains, in effect, two arguments. The first argument has just been completed. Ask the students, "What reason has Aquinas given in the discussion that allows him to draw the logical conclusion that natural bodies achieve their end not fortuitously, but designedly?"

This is not an easy question to answer; stu-dents must follow the argument closely and also connect the information given in step 2 with the conclusion stated in step 3 by seeing what would happen if step 2 were *not* true. The answer usually can be elicited with the follow-ing hint: If natural bodies that lack knowledge acted strictly by chance, what would we expect to see in nature? At this point, students can dis-cern the relevant point: If natural bodies acted by chance, then we would expect to see enor-mous if not bizarre variations in nature (e.g., the seasons following each other haphazardly and in no special order, things growing every which way and forming all manner of odd and unusual shapes, etc.). Nature would become an Alice-in-Wonderlandish nightmare fantasy of constant change and disorder.

But, such chaos is not our experience of nature. Natural bodies that lack knowledge always—or nearly always—do exactly the same thing, over and over and over again. For Aquinas, such repetition cannot be the result of chance; it cannot be due to random movements of material bodies. Therefore, since only two alternatives are given, chance and design, and since natural bodies cannot exhibit the order they do by chance, then—"hence," as Aquinas indicates—natural bodies must have been *designed* to reach their end.

Passage 4

Can one oak tree tell another oak tree how to grow? No, because oak trees do not have the capacity for discourse. Aquinas generalizes this point so that it applies to all natural bodies that lack knowledge. If natural bodies move toward an end, they cannot do so by themselves. Aquinas then infers that they must have been *directed* to move toward an end by something other than themselves. Furthermore, this something cannot be of the same kind (i.e., it cannot be another natural body without knowledge since, as the oak example has just shown, such beings lack the required capacity for discourse and giving direction). Therefore, Aquinas reasons, the only possibility is that the being who has directed natural bodies must be endowed with knowledge and intelligence in order to be capable of providing such direction. Just as the arrow will go only where it has been directed to go by the archer, so also beings that lack knowledge will move toward their end only insofar as the being endowed with knowledge and intelligence has directed them to do so.

Passage 5

This proposition is the conclusion of Thomas Aquinas' fifth way to the existence of God. Aquinas reasons that there must be "some intelligent being" who exists to perform the direction we discern in nature. Once it is noted that the "all" encompasses not only every natural thing on earth, but every natural thing throughout the universe, then it becomes evident that the "intelligent being" must be omniscient and omnipotent, all-knowing and all-powerful, in order to provide direction for such cosmic complexity. Only one being exhibits such properties. This is the being "we call God". And, since it is evident from simple observation that natural bodies lacking knowledge do indeed act for an end, then such a being must exist in order to provide this direction. Final conclusion: God exists. Furthermore, God *must* exist, otherwise nature would have collapsed into randomness and chaotic disorder eons ago, which we know from long-standing experience has not been the case.

Thomas Aquinas has proved—rationally and without any appeal to anything in Scripture—that there must be a supreme being, God, who has provided natural bodies that lack knowledge with direction.

Student Response

In my experience, students seldom absorb Aquinas' conclusion without responding, usually in a critical vein. However, on those rare occasions when the conclusion, once stated, does not instigate inspired reaction, I have reminded the students that it is part of the philosopher's task to evaluate an argument critically. Anyone with a serious interest in philosophy should not merely sit back, sponge-like, and rest content with a sequence of reasoning without casting a critical eye on that reasoning—especially in this instance, since the reasoning in question purports to demonstrate the existence of God, a conclusion that, if soundly established, will surely affect all human beings in some sense. Once this reminder is in place, then one, some, or all of the following points have been made. The range of these responses (excluding the first one discussed below) is testimony to the ability of young students to think critically and perceptively on one of the deepest of all philosophical issues. ●

"God Exists" is Just an Opinion!

This cry is not heard that often, but frequently enough to mention. Students who say this have not fully appreciated that Aquinas is not asserting "God exists" just because he feels, from religious motives or something similar, that it represents an opinion that must be true. The claim that God exists is a *reasoned* proposition; that is, Aquinas has concluded to the existence of God based on the interlocking effect of prior assertions and premises employed as reasons in a logically structured argument. The appropriate form of criticism is therefore not a simple blanket rejection of Aquinas' conclusion as "just an opinion"; rather, the student must reexamine the reasoning and find a flaw in the movement of thought from the beginning of the argument through each succeeding step and then to the conclusion. If the demonstration is faulty, the problem lies somewhere along the path of Aquinas' reasoning, not simply in the conclusion—God exists—based on that reasoning.

Who Created God?

Discussion of the conclusion of Aquinas' argument tends to follow certain patterns. One of the most common is the following response: "Well, if God created nature, then who created God?" This question is typically posed in a vigorous, forthright manner, suggesting that its point is not only crucial to the argument, but also fatal to the supposed truth of its conclusion.

The question is serious and subtle: serious because it has connected the point of the argument, the causal function of deity, to a being—God—who appears to be itself part of the cosmic network of cause-and-effect relation-

ships. In other words, the question presupposes a fairly high order of sustained abstract thought. It is also subtle because underlying the question is an implied logical strategy, the nature of which, it is safe to assume, even gifted students are not fully aware.

Here is one way to respond. Take the question as posed and ask, "If God had a creator, what kind of being would be capable of creating God?" The question is readily answered: "Another God." Let's call this creator "God_1." Sometimes, the next move requires a bit of prodding, but generally students will see it on their own. "Well, who created God_1?" The answer: "God_2." (Writing the names of these deities on the board is helpful, each joined to the next by an arrow.) The causal round dance is now in full swing, and there is no need to continue the performance once the students see what is being generated. The question that should be raised is: "When will this series end?" Usually a vocal, unified, and loud response: "Never!" This answer is correct. And, at this juncture, it is essential to explain the notion of a *vicious regress*, of which this ever-proliferating series of deities is an example. This kind of explanation is a *regress* because it keeps moving back and back and back; it is a *vicious* regress because the explanation never gets anywhere. As a rule, an explanation that collapses into a vicious regress is rejected since, as we have just seen, it never really explains anything because it ends up chasing and devouring its own tail.

This result leaves the students perplexed. What's the answer to the question that instigated this frustrating train of thought?

The way to handle this question is straightforward: We must reject the question! After all, "Who created God?" assumes that God had a creator. At this point, one can ask the students for some of the attributes or properties commonly attributed to God. More often than not, a student will note that "God is eternal." If this is true, what follows? If God is eternal, then it follows that God had no creator because God had no origin. God always was, is, and will be. So, the answer to the original question is *no one* created God because God is not the sort of being that can be created.

The question that instigated this line of thought is perceptive, but, as noted above, it is slightly off the point. To speak of God's eternity is to describe an aspect of the nature of God. The five ways are intended only to show the existence of God. In fact, Aquinas devotes a large section of the *Summa Theologica* to discussing the nature of God, one aspect of which concerns whether or not God had an origin. So, students who pose this question are certainly thinking along Thomistic lines of inquiry, although not quite on the particular point at issue.

Couldn't There Be More Than One God?

Aquinas' conclusion refers to "a being" that we call God, as if it were obvious and necessary that there is only *one* God. Students who are aware of the pantheon of Greek gods and goddesses (or indeed any culture marked by polytheism) will, on occasion, ask whether there could be more than one God. This is also a good question; but, again, it is aimed at the nature of divinity—whether there could be a plurality of gods—rather than at the issue of the existence of God.

Here is one way to respond: Is God omnipotent (i.e., all-powerful)? Yes, is the typical reply. Could there then be *two* omnipotent Gods? Once this question sinks in, there is usually considerable excitement. No, someone says, there could not be two Gods who are both omnipotent because one of them—either one—would have a property that the other did not and therefore the other god would not be omnipotent and, as a result, not be God. The feeling of exuberance when a student reasons to and expresses this conclusion is palpable; it is as if recognizing and thinking through this impli-

cation provides a legitimate intellectual thrill—and so it should! This point is exquisitely abstract, a fine instance of metaphysical reflection and is, in fact, the argument Aquinas gives when he discusses later in the *Summa* how there could be only one supreme being.

What About Evolution?

This question is often posed. Students argue that God is not necessary as the source of natural order in the universe; all that is required is a belief in evolution. Two points should be made by way of introduction: First, it is usually prudent to note that, although evolution is widely held, it is still a theory and therefore can be considered questionable depending on an individual's religious beliefs. Thus, a debate on the cogency of evolution at this juncture would lead the discussion astray. Second, it should be mentioned that evolution is a 19th-century theory in its origin and thus one that Aquinas, living in the 13th century, could not have known. The question then becomes whether the fifth way can accommodate the theory of evolution and remain rationally viable.

The answer is yes, and in my experience students frequently discover the answer by themselves without much prodding. Couldn't God have created species to evolve very slowly over vast reaches of time? Of course! Therefore, simply pointing to evolution will not refute Aquinas' fifth way. The only modification the argument requires in the face of evolution is to say that the order exhibited by natural bodies that lack knowledge is slowly changing over time. It may be noted, however, that this conclusion is incompatible with the account of creation in Genesis if it is assumed from this account that God created all species to exist in a completely fixed and determinate way. However, this incompatibility arises from the intersection of religion and philosophy and need not be addressed here—or in class!

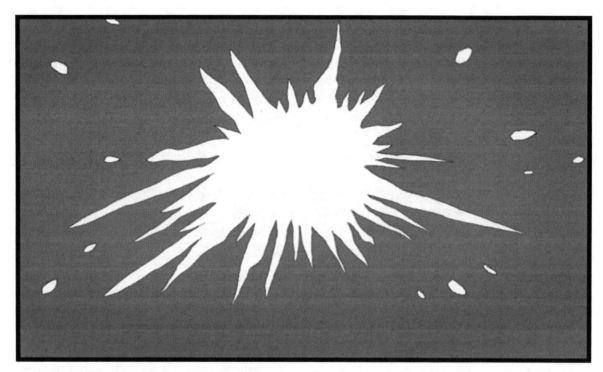

What About the Big Bang Theory?

This question is also common, although slightly less so than queries derived from evolution. Many students in the 6th–8th grades are conversant with this theory, at least in general outline. Their argument: If the universe began with a big bang, then why is God necessary in order to introduce order? Here again, and even more so than for evolution, it may be noted that this theory is the product of 20th-century science and, as such, represents a position Aquinas could not have known. But, the relevant question is can the fifth way accommodate the Big Bang Theory? Yes, and as a rule, students are again quick to recognize the response Aquinas would probably give. After all, where did the big bang come from? Isn't it possible that God created the "stuff" of the big bang and then allowed it to take its inevitable developmental—or evolutionary!—course through the vast reaches of time and space? Yes, this possibility is also quite real. In fact, Aquinas would argue that it is essential that God created the stuff of the big bang since, for Aquinas, some-

thing cannot come from nothing. It may be noted in this regard that contemporary physicists who appeal to the Big Bang Theory to account for the origin of the universe are not, from a philosophical standpoint, asking the crucial question—for even if this theory is correct, where did the big bang come from?

What if Matter is Eternal?

This question is, admittedly, rare. But, it has indeed been asked, and the fact that it has been asked at all is remarkable and indicates abstract thinking of the highest caliber. Aquinas' position rests on the general principle in metaphysics, already mentioned above, that something cannot come from nothing; or, as it is more tersely put, "from nothing, nothing comes." Even if this principle is accepted, however, there remains the possibility that something—matter—could have always existed. If, therefore, matter is eternal, then it would not necessarily require a deity to impose order on it. Furthermore, what we call "the order of nature" could refer only to the current forms in which matter has contoured itself. For as the limitless reaches of time slowly edge forward, these forms could alter significantly, but do so based on causes that lie deep in the heart of matter itself—and not on the designing impulse of a deity. Contemporary cosmologists would probably embrace this position since, if true, it would eliminate the need to explain where the stuff of the big bang originated. The answer: It did not have an origin. Matter always existed.

Curricular Integration

Aquinas' fifth way is a classic example of a carefully reasoned and extremely compressed demonstration in philosophy. However, once the argument has been scrutinized with commensurate care, as illustrated by the above discussions, its subject matter quickly radiates from a metaphysical core—is there a really existing God?—to epistemology—how do we know what we claim we know about God? These allied issues then inevitably engender much broader debate in the domains of religion, science, and critical thinking. And it is this radiation effect that can be readily and incisively applied to standard areas in the curriculum.

A. Language Arts

Just the effort to recognize the vocabulary and then follow the close reasoning in this argument provides an excellent exercise in critical thinking. How conclusions in reasoned argument "follow from" premises is aptly illustrated by the progression of thought in the fifth way. The abstractness of the concepts also guarantees that even a rudimentary discussion of their import will enhance the students' abilities in the area of conceptual analysis. Students who can understand and reason with and about the concepts in Aquinas' fifth way are well on their way toward being able to understand and reason about virtually any concepts of similar generality.

B. Humanities

Different cultures approach God in various ways, and discussion of the characteristics of God as they emerge from critical analysis of the reasoning in Aquinas' argument will elicit an appreciation of these differences. A greater comprehension of differences pertaining to our understanding of the existence and nature of God will foster an increased understanding of differences in worship and religious practice found among different cultures and nationalities. Thus, could God be something less than perfect, something less than omnipotent, something less than omniscient? Could there be a plurality of deities, as the ancient Greeks thought (and as some contemporary cultures still believe)? Indeed, is a God necessary at all in order to explain natural phenomena?

C. Science

Inquiry into the concepts of animal intelligence, the order found in nature, and the structure of matter are legitimate "spin-offs" from the ramifications of Aquinas' philosophical demonstration in the fifth way.

1. How should the line be drawn between the way plants react to their surroundings and the more complex ways animals react? Is it essential to define knowledge in order to establish this distinction? Do animals know what they are doing? How can we tell for sure one way or the other?
2. Is it conceivable that matter could assume all the myriad forms that it does in nature from purely physical and mechanical causes—without a guiding and intelligent force?
3. Can we determine whether or not matter is eternal by scientific (or philosophical)

means, or is this a question that must be left undecided? If we believe that matter is not eternal, are we compelled to accept the existence of God in order to explain how matter begins to exist?

These questions are obviously challenging, but students will be invigorated by the attempt to investigate them. It is not essential that clear-cut and fully persuasive answers be produced in the classroom; rather, the excitement of inquiry and the extension of knowledge through debate and discussion will provide tangible and worthwhile results. Aquinas' fifth way may not have conclusively proven that God exists, but the content of its premises and the sequence of its reasoning provide a fascinating entry into a constellation of concepts well suited for the adventurous minds of younger students to explore.

Reference:

Aquinas, T. (1945). *The basic writings of Saint Thomas Aquinas* (A. C. Pegis, Ed.). New York: Random House.

Web address for online text: http://www.ccel.org/a/aquinas/summa/home.html

CHAPTER 5

The Sound of a Tree Falling in the Forest

Groans might greet anyone posing the question, "If a tree falls in the forest with no one around, does it make a sound?" This venerable poser is, however, laden with philosophical intrigue. In fact, the issues that this question raises typically tantalize gifted students (indeed, anyone with a serious interest in philosophy) for two reasons: First, the question, although immediately relevant to certain basic forms of personal experience, is difficult to answer satisfactorily, doubtless because, second, the question revolves around issues that go straight to the core of a particularly fundamental region of philosophical reflection.

Earlier chapters have included Plato's concern for establishing theoretical grounds to show how we have knowledge and St. Augustine's thoughtful and penetrating inquiry into the nature of time. These two classic questions illustrate the areas of philosophy known as epistemology and metaphysics, respectively. As we have seen, epistemology addresses questions and problems pertaining to knowledge and how human beings obtain it; metaphysics discusses the nature of reality (e.g., time) in general and abstract terms. When philosophy is pursued as an ordered discipline, these areas are typically kept separate in order to keep the analysis of their problems within manageable bounds. However, the question of whether or not an unperceived tree falling in the forest makes a sound effectively intersects these two areas, especially if that question is approached from the standpoint of the Irish philosopher George ("Bishop") Berkeley (1685–1753). Berkeley's account undercuts this distinction by showing how questions pertaining to knowledge play directly into questions pertaining to reality. Here, then, metaphysics implies epistemology and vice versa.

With Berkeley (pronounced "BARK-lee," as in Charles Barkley, former NBA great) we are squarely within the modern period of philosophy. "Modern" philosophy is usually dated to begin with the work of René Descartes (1596–1650). Descartes' quest to establish the same certainty in philosophy that he saw—and contributed to himself—in the sciences and mathematics inaugurated an extended period of intense philosophical reflection on human knowledge. Descartes' answer to the basic question of knowledge, that certainty derives from the self and how we experience and understand our ideas, was deemed inadequate by many of his philosophical successors, primarily John Locke (1632–1704), who as an empiricist insisted that the materials of knowledge originated from outside the mind and were processed and made meaningful by the mind.

George Berkeley, usually referred to as Bishop Berkeley (he was a prelate in the Anglican church), continued to think about knowledge along these lines. In a work entitled *Three Dialogues Between Hylas and Philonous*, Berkeley extended Locke's empiricism in an unusual and distinctive direction. Few philosophers after Plato wrote dialogues since they did not want to be seen as trying to compete with Plato in expressing difficult ideas in a literary form of which the great Greek master was the exemplar. Berkeley is an exception, however, and in this work he presents a series of short dialogues between two fictional characters with etymologically significant names: "Hylas" is from the Greek for "matter" while "Philonous," also Greek, means "lover of mind or spirit." Thus, the dialogues record a conversation between, in essence, matter (Hylas) and spirit (Philonous). The three excerpts cited below present key representative statements of Berkeley's overall position.

George Berkeley

Preliminary Discussion

Pose the question: "If a tree falls in the forest with no one around, does it make a sound?" As noted above, this question may seem banal, but my experience has been that students nonetheless find it fascinating, with discussion of the question quickly becoming energetic and, at times, somewhat heated. Have the students dis-

cuss their answers and allow discussion to continue for a few minutes, inviting students to critique the reasons given by those arguing for each side of the issue. Then, conclude this discussion by wondering out loud whether there might be a third answer to this question, an answer other than yes or no. (There is such an answer, as we shall see.)

Now, modify the original question by posing the following variation: "Does a tree in the forest continue to exist if no one is around to see it?" The typical response is immediate and forceful—"Of course the tree continues to exist!" Young students believe they discern a clear distinction between (a) the existence of the tree when no one is around and (b) the sound a tree might—or might not—make if it falls when no one is around. The existence of the tree is more fundamental than a sound the tree might make. Therefore, existence is less dependent upon a human observer than sound. In fact, students nearly always assert that the

1. **Hylas:** ... I tell you once for all, that by sensible things I mean those only which are perceived by sense; and that in truth the senses perceive nothing which they do not perceive immediately; for they make no inferences ...

   Philonous: This point is then agreed between us—that sensible things are those only which are immediately perceived by sense.

2. **Philonous:** The tree or house therefore which you think of is conceived by you?

   Hylas: How should it be otherwise?

   Philonous: And what is conceived is surely in the mind?

   Hylas: Without question, that which is conceived is in the mind.

   Philonous: How then came you to say, you conceived a house or tree existing independent and out of all minds whatsoever?

   Hylas: That was I own an oversight; but stay, let me consider what led into it—it is a pleasant mistake enough. As I was thinking of a tree in a solitary place, where no one was present to see it, methought that was to conceive a tree as existing unperceived and unthought of, not considering that I myself conceived it all the while. But now I plainly see that all I can do is to frame ideas in my own mind. I may indeed conceive in my own thoughts the idea of a tree, or a house, or a mountain, but that is all. And this is far from proving that I can conceive them existing out of the minds of all spirits.

3. **Philonous:** But how can that which is sensible be like that which is insensible? Can a real thing, in itself invisible, be like a color; or a real thing, which is not audible, be like a sound? In a word, can anything be like a sensation or idea, but another sensation or idea?

   Hylas: I must own, I think not.

   Philonous: Is it possible there should be any doubt on the point? Do you not perfectly know your own ideas?

   Hylas: I know them perfectly; since what I do not perceive or know can be no part of my idea.

   Philonous: Consider, therefore, and examine them, and then tell me if there be anything in them which can exist without the mind: or if you can conceive anything like them existing without the mind.

   Hylas: Upon inquiry, I find it is impossible for me to conceive or understand how anything but an idea can be like an idea. And it is most evident that no idea can exist without the mind.

   Philonous: You are therefore, by your principles, forced to deny the reality of sensible things; since you made it to consist in an absolute existence exterior to the mind. That is to say, you are a downright skeptic. So I have gained my point, which was to show your principles led to Skepticism.

   Hylas: For the present I am, if not entirely convinced, at least silenced.

—From *Three Dialogues Between Hylas and Philonous* by George ("Bishop") Berkeley existence of something does not in any sense require an observer in order to guarantee that thing's existence.

But, Berkeley asks, how do we know that this claim about the unperceived existence of the tree is true? Why can we be certain that a tree in a forest continues to exist if no one is there to perceive it as existing?

The excerpts from Berkeley's *Three Dialogues* present a reasoned account that answers this question. (Suggestion: Have the students "perform" these excerpts, with a different Hylas and Philonous taking their parts for each of the three passages.)

Passage 1

The key concept in this passage is the meaning Hylas gives to "sensible things." In nonphilosophical contexts, the word *sensible* is often used to refer to human conduct, as when a teacher intones to a student, "Please act in a sensible manner." Here Hylas brings out the root meaning of the term: what is "perceived by sense." Hylas also adds the important characteristic that the senses function immediately, or, as he puts it, the senses "make no inferences."

This last point may be demonstrated. Hold up a piece of chalk (or marker, etc.). Ask, "What color is this?" The students will chorus an answer (e.g., white). Then ask, "Can you tell what this object feels like just from seeing its color?" Occasionally someone will blurt out "Hard!," but this response is unthinking. Someone who sees a piece of chalk and who has also held a piece of chalk can *remember* what the chalk feels like, but he or she cannot *see* what the chalk feels like. If we hold a piece of chalk, we *feel* its hardness, but if we just *see* a piece of chalk, there is no way, just from the sense of sight alone, to infer that this white object is hard. From what is seen, we cannot infer touch; from touch, we cannot infer what is seen. Thus, the senses "make no inferences."

This definition of "sensible" establishes the

meaning of a concept that will become important later in the discussion. In general, this brief interchange brings out the distinction between what we *perceive* and what we *know*: We perceive that the object is white, but we know that this object is (a) a particular piece of chalk, which is (b) hard and (c) capable of being used as a tool for writing based on what perception has taught us and also what our minds have added to perceptual data through memory and reasoning. In analyzing the nature of knowledge, it is essential to keep processes such as perception and knowledge separate from one another as much as possible in order to clarify the structure of each of these components and to be aware of questions and problems that might arise as a result of such clarification.

Passage 2

Ask the students, "Do you believe that things exist outside the mind?" "Of course," they will say. Then, ask them this, a more challenging variation on the same question: "When you think of things existing outside of the mind, do these things exist *apart from* the act of thinking about them?" The answer, after a bit of reflection, will be yes, since it is in effect the same question. Now, take a particular thing—say, a tree existing in a solitary place. Does the existence of this tree depend on our thinking about that tree existing in a solitary place? The students will say, no, it does not. But, Philonous wants to know how one can claim that the tree is existing alone and unperceived if this tree is being thought of as existing unperceived and alone. For surely the thinker remains in the company of that tree insofar as the thinker is in the act of thinking about it. Therefore, the tree is *not* alone and unperceived; it is, in fact, being thought of by someone as alone and unperceived. How then does the individual thinking this thought know for certain that this tree will continue to exist if one does not think about it at all?

Passage 3

(This passage leads to the primary philosophical conclusion—and also answers the lead question about the tree falling in the forest.) Ask the students—or yourself: "Who won this exchange?" Those who have been paying attention to the rhythm of thought will say, "Philonous!" Hylas does not exactly cede the point at issue, but he does admit that he cannot think of anything to say in response to Philonous' reasoning. What, then, has the reasoning demonstrated? Consider the following summary of the passage:

A. Philonous asks us to consider a real thing, such as a tree. Is this tree "audible," that is, does it produce a sound? Not as such, that is, not as a tree. But, sound is, by itself and necessarily, audible. Therefore, if sound when sensed is something perceived, then how can something inaudible (e.g., a tree) even be like such a sensation? Philonous insists that no basis of comparison will allow us to connect the perception of sound with something that, by itself, is without sound.

B. We know the ideas we have based on whatever we perceive. If I do not perceive something, then what I do not perceive cannot be part of my idea of that something. Therefore, only an idea can be like another idea, in the same way that only something perceived can be like something else perceived. The question then becomes whether, for example, an idea of a tree existing in our mind can be like the "real" tree existing "outside" our mind.

C. Hylas had said that reality was "sensible things," things that existed absolutely outside of the mind, just as we might say that the tree exists absolutely apart from, or outside of, the mind of an observer (or

observers) seeing the tree. The relevance of the definition of "sensible" in Passage 1 now emerges. Sensible things are things immediately perceived by the senses. When what is perceived by the senses strikes the mind, the sensory experience produces an idea. But, ideas derived in this way exist only in the mind. Furthermore, Passage 2 has shown that ideas resemble only other ideas—not what the ideas are ideas of. Therefore, the question becomes: How do we make the transition from the idea of a tree that exists in our mind to the actual tree existing outside our mind?

Philonous' reasoning (based on Hylas' own stated principles) demonstrates that we cannot make such a move and be confident of any success. For if all that exists is only what is sensible, then we can never be completely certain that what is perceived through the senses really and in fact exists out there, "outside" our senses. We are reduced to a condition of skepticism about the existence of the sensible world. All we know, and apparently all we are capable of knowing, are our own ideas. According to Philonous, it is therefore impossible for us to assert with certainty that things outside our ideas actually do correspond to these ideas. We cannot get outside of the ideas we have in our minds in order to assert that material things exist apart from these ideas.

The general meaning of skepticism may have to be explained. One standard dictionary definition of skepticism is "the doctrine that the truth of all knowledge must always be in question." It should be emphasized that the skepticism of which Hylas is accused concerns not just a state of suspended belief about knowledge concerning particular things, but about the very existence of all sensible things—everything perceivable by the senses, which is everything we see, touch, taste, and so forth.

Here is another way to approach the conclusion established at the end of the three excerpts. To say "Something (e.g., a tree) is real" seems to assume the truth of the claim that "I know that this tree is real." For if something were real, but we could not know this something, then by what right do we assert that this something is real in the first place? This philosophical priority is reflected in ordinary situations whenever someone says, "How do you know?" in response to a claim. A question about the justification of knowledge usually refers to a claim that appears dubious or, perhaps, controversial. But, in theory, "How do you know?" could preface every claim anyone has ever made! If I say "There's a tree outside," I must be willing to answer the question "How do you know?" As a rule, people in civilized society would not pose such a seemingly uncivil question about routine perceptual observations—assuming, of course, that the senses of the parties involved are all functioning properly—because it is "obvious" that the claim refers to something that truly exists. But, such existence is "obvious" only because everyone involved in the discussion *sees* a particular sensible object—or, as Berkeley might put it, we *think we see* a particular object.

Berkeley's position may be summarized as follows: "To be is to be perceived," the Latin version of this principle—*esse est percipi*—being almost as well known in philosophical circles as Descartes' *cogito ergo sum* (I think, therefore I am). This position is sometimes referred to as *absolute idealism*, since it requires that a mind must exist and function as a mind thinking about things before anything else can be said to exist. In a sense, then, the mind "holds" all existing things within it insofar as human beings perceive and think about these things. Without such perception and thought, the existence of "external" objects becomes uncertain.

Once this conclusion has been established, ask the students the original question—"If a tree falls in the forest and no one is around, does it make a sound?"—and have them state the answer that can be inferred from Berkeley's principles. The answer is . . . "We don't know!" Whether or not the falling tree will make a sound without an observer present to hear that sound cannot be determined. Thus, the venerable tree-in-the-forest-question admits of more than a "yes" or "no" answer; the third possible answer is that of the skeptic: "We do not know." In general, then, Berkeley's reasoning has shown the close intimacy between metaphysics and epistemology: What we believe to be reality depends directly on what we are actively perceiving when in the presence of this reality.

This conclusion is important, fascinating, and well worth serious and sustained philosophical reflection. But, aside from the definite possibility of inciting some intriguing and doubtless volatile classroom discussion about perception and existence, both of which are decidedly abstract philosophical concerns, does Berkeley's thinking carry with it any practical pedagogical relevance?

Curricular Integration

Previous chapters have offered specific suggestions for integrating aspects of the philosophical positions discussed into a more standard school curriculum. Since, however, the intimate connection between perception and the existence of things is developed with considerable generality in Berkeley's thought, the most fitting curricular application is not so much to any particular subject, but rather to an attitude that can affect the way students approach many subjects, as well as, in a larger sense, certain important areas in life outside the classroom. This attitude is the *skepticism* that often characterizes students, gifted and nongifted alike.

A. The Specter of Skepticism

Skepticism appears in a variety of educational contexts. For present purposes, consider skepticism in the attempt to gain knowledge of a poem. Why are the results of an experiment in science not subject to the kind of skepticism that affects—or, perhaps, infects—the interpretation of a poem (or, of course, any literary work), where discussion so quickly and so often reduces to "That's your opinion!" or even "Well, no one can say what the poem really means . . ."? Ask the students in a language arts class: Can we know the meaning of a poem in the same way that we can know the meaning of an experiment in science? Or, more generally stated, how is objectivity possible when doing a scientific experiment in contrast to the apparently unavoidable subjectivity that prevails when interpreting a poem? In fact, where does the supposed "objectivity" of science come from in the first place?

It is relevant here to observe that the clear distinction between the "objective" reality of scientific study and the "subjective" values of literary criticism cannot be maintained within Berkeley's thought. For Berkeley, whatever is "objective" is no less governed by the need to be perceived by the mind to guarantee its existence than is whatever may be only "subjective." What elements in scientific investigation allow

us to conclude that the results of such thoughtful activity have indeed put us in touch with its subject matter—the "objective" physical world?

Scientific experiments depend on observation and can be repeated by other individuals to verify observable results; as a result of these and related considerations, we believe that science places those who practice it directly within a public and commonly shared world. Reading and interpreting a poem is, by contrast, a private activity, and since such interpretation produces results that exist entirely in the realm of "meanings," whatever results are produced do not enjoy the status of the perceptible and public shared reality that encompasses the activities and practices of the scientist. But, consider the following line of thought: A poem is real, just as the material "stuff" that becomes subject to the scrutiny of science is real. If, therefore, a poem is taken to exist as an artifact, something made from a human source, then there seems to be no reason why students of a poem could not discuss the structure of this rhythmical bit of reality with a care and rigor that fits its subject matter and with expectations of producing concrete results that can be defended or amended, as the twists and turns of discussion and analysis so indicate.

B. A Berkeleyian Antidote to Skepticism

The point of these observations is not to transform studying literature into a clone of scientific research—that would be neither possible nor desirable. Rather, it is to become aware of what would have to be done to reshape attitudes toward the study of literature (and other nonscientific subjects) so that students will not automatically be tempted to dismiss such study as so much personal and subjectivist patter. It is a singular virtue of reflecting on Berkeley's thought that it invites students to question how they as individual human beings experience the world—and this includes, of course, the world of literature—in order to be in a position to discuss that experience meaningfully with others. For Berkeley, any form of inquiry presupposes the observer and whatever the observer contributes to that inquiry. Berkeley shows the need to pay attention to what is perceived and to describe it as accurately as possible so that other observers, hearing this description, can verify its sense through their own perceptual experience.

The frequency with which skepticism is met in younger students can therefore be diminished, or at least rendered less virulent in its effects on the educational enterprise, if students learn to get "outside" themselves as much as possible—to move the individual mind from its own inherent concerns and preconceptions to the object of study, whether this object be a poem in language arts or an experiment in science. One way to achieve this transition is to maximize the amount and depth of discussion of whatever students are experiencing—and, of course, perceiving—thereby taking advantage of the fact that much of our experience of the world is shared with others. The more we are aware of what we feel and think in relation to what others feel and think, the less insular and isolated we will become in studying what exists "out there" in the world.

C. Skepticism and Values

The skepticism affecting the study of certain subjects in a school curriculum also permeates one of the most important areas in life, both within and outside of school. Ask students whether cheating on an essay or exam is morally wrong. An answer that occurs all too frequently runs along these lines: Cheating is wrong for you if you feel, or believe, that it is wrong; if, however, cheating is a useful expedient to rectify lack of preparation for an assignment or test, then who's to say that cheating is wrong in these circumstances? And, if cheating is an

acceptable option in school, why shouldn't it also be viable later in life, in nonacademic situations?

Another route to the same destination: Ask a class of students "Is honesty a good thing?" Most, perhaps all, will say yes. But, then ask *why* being honest is a good thing. Reasons and justifications will come quickly and be wide-ranging; however, what nearly always happens is that the reasons soon appear to conflict with one another and are also not developed sufficiently to answer objections based on concrete circumstances. The result is a creeping skepticism that begins to infiltrate the group perception of the value of honesty.

Facts are public and verifiable, values are private and variable depending on the person. The reality of values is defined by the limits of an individual's feelings and perceptions about his or her world; in fact, values simply are what that individual feels is an appropriate attitude or behavior in a given set of circumstances. This belief is very common among young people (as it is, of course, among adults). But, how reliable is this belief?

As noted above in the context of skepticism and education, it is essential to determine the boundaries of the "I," that is, what I sense and perceive and think—the sum total of my own individual experience—and then place these boundaries in juxtaposition with what others sense and perceive and think. Our perceptual activity is in some important respect a social activity, that is, what we see and experience as individuals has something essential to do with what we as members of a group have been conditioned to see and experience. What we then label "reality" insofar as it emerges from this common source of experience is determined at least as much by our collective perceiving of what is "out there" as by whatever this reality may be "in itself" or "as such."

This conclusion about the close connection between the way we experience the world and the existence of the world as such has an essential bearing on the conclusions we wish to draw about our personal beliefs and values. Skepticism concerning moral values—happiness, goodness, justice, honesty, and other forms of virtue—derives from the unexamined belief that we cannot move beyond our own individual conceptions, or perceptions, of the patterns and consequences of human behavior. Berkeley's thought invites us to reconsider this encrusted distinction that so permeates the fabric of contemporary life. From Berkeley's perspective, values and facts are suffused with personal experience; it follows that either facts are no less personal than values or values may be considered to have as much solidity as facts—assuming that they are approached and described in a way that displays their existence in a world beyond that of an individual observer of human behavior. Thus, if I say "Cheating is wrong," I must be willing to support that claim with reasons based, in some respect, on features of the world as the world actually exists. Thus, a persuasive justification of honesty will not be based merely on the fact that the speaker of this claim *feels* that honesty is something good or morally praiseworthy, but rather on *perceived* aspects of a common world going beyond the fact that the speaker, as a single human being, approves of honesty.

The currently popular attempt to institute character education in schools is certainly laudable. But, with Berkeley's position in view, this attempt should be supplemented by inviting (and, perhaps, compelling) young people—whether gifted or nongifted—to examine the experiences they have had of the world, whether enjoyable, unpleasant, or indeterminately "blah," and to integrate this complex cycle as

fully as possible with the closely similar experiences of other human beings. When such integration has been successful, then the understanding of values and the essential role they play in the development of character may be established on something more substantial than individual inclination. Thus, honesty, as one virtue among many, could then be established as a feature of the world defined by structures that incorporate a public sphere of considerations, rather than simply asserted as a value on the strength of the individual attitudes of people who "feel" that honesty is morally praiseworthy.

In retrospect, then, the apparent whimsicality of wondering whether or not unattended falling trees make sounds in forests takes on a very different and far more serious tone. For when, with Berkeley's assistance, we think through a philosophical answer to this chestnut, we appreciate more fully and urgently the central character of our individual experience of the world and the need to integrate that experience with all that encompasses "reality" and "value" as perceived and thought by those with whom we share that world.

Reference:

Berkeley, G. (1995). *Three dialogues between Hylas and Philonous: Classics of Western philosophy* (6th ed.). Indianapolis, IN: Hackett.

Web address for online text:
http://www.bartleby.com/37/2

CHAPTER 6

"I Don't Want to Do What the Class Wants to Do!"

The philosopher Aristotle was not given to witty one-liners, but in the *Politics* he says that a person who lives alone is "either a beast or a god." Much later in the history of Western thought, Thomas Hobbes (in *Leviathan*) describes the life of human beings when it is driven solely by desire and occurs outside of society as "solitary, poor, nasty, brutish and short." For both these important thinkers, it is evident that human beings are social by nature; they need association with one another not only to secure basic techniques and strategies for survival, but also to provide more subtle and elevated forms of humanity in order to find fulfillment as individuals.

In the modern era, formal education typically occurs in a classroom, with the inhabitants of such a class comprising a small society, the composition of which changes over time. As these children grow into adults, they will eventually take their place in "society" writ large. How, then, are human beings to understand their place as individuals existing within a common social order?

Philosophers since the Greeks have studied the nature and structure of society for purposes of establishing, in thought if not in deed, the form of government that best serves the interests of its members. Previous chapters have offered examples of philosophizing in *ethics* (Aristotle), *epistemology* (Plato and Berkeley) and *metaphysics* (Augustine and Aquinas). In this chapter, we venture into *political philosophy*, often subsumed as a branch of ethics. The philosopher to be discussed is Swiss-born and French-writing Jean-Jacques Rousseau (1712–1778). The work to be excerpted is his *Social Contract* (1762). Emphasizing the date when this work was published is important for reasons that will become clear later in the discussion.

The following eight passages are excerpts from the *Social Contract*, followed, as usual, by comments clarifying the pivotal concepts in this important and influential work and sketching typical responses to Rousseau as they have occurred in classrooms for students intrigued by the prospect of reflecting on their place in society.

1. The problem is to find a form of association which will defend and protect with the whole common force the person and goods of each associate, and in which each, while uniting himself with all, may still obey himself alone, and remain as free as before.

2. **[Definition of the social compact]**: Each of us puts his person and all his power in common under the supreme direction of the general will, and, in our corporate capacity, we receive each member as an indivisible part of the whole.

3. In fact, each individual, as a man, may have a particular will contrary or dissimilar to the general will which he has as a citizen.

4. In order then that the social compact may not be an empty formula, it tacitly includes the undertaking, which alone can give force to the rest, that whoever refuses to obey the general will shall be compelled to do so by the whole body. This means nothing less than that he will be forced to be free; for this is the condition which, by giving each citizen to his country, secures him against all personal dependence.

5. What a man loses by the social contract is his natural liberty and an unlimited right to everything he tries to get and succeeds in getting; what he gains is civil liberty and the proprietorship of all he possesses. . . . we must clearly distinguish natural liberty, which is bounded only by the strength of the individual, from civil liberty, which is limited by the general will . . .

6. However the acquisition be made, the right which each individual has to his own estate is always subordinate to the right which the community has over all: without this, there would be neither stability in the social tie, nor real force in . . . Sovereignty.

7. . . . instead of destroying natural inequality, the fundamental compact substitutes, for such physical inequality as nature may have set up between men, an equality that is moral and legitimate, and that men, who may be unequal in strength or intelligence, become every one equal by convention and legal right.

8. . . . the social compact sets up among the citizens an equality of such a kind, that they all bind themselves to observe the same conditions and should therefore all enjoy the same rights.

—From *Social Contract* by Jean-Jacques Rousseau

Passage 1

Rousseau states his purpose in authoring the *Social Contract*, and although this initial passage is generally clear, it is stated paradoxically, doubtless by intent. If students are asked to note what in it appears to be unusual or displaced, they readily spot the problem: How can a person be a member of an association—membership implicitly entailing rules, which in turn entail some kind of restriction—and still "remain as free" as they were before becoming a member of this association? It seems obvious that obeying rules signals a curtailment of freedom—all students are keenly aware of this consequence. How, then, can individual human beings become members of an association that will protect them and all their property and at the same time allow the same degree of freedom they possess prior to their acceptance of this association?

Passage 2

This passage defines the social compact, the fundamental element in Rousseau's vision of a well-ordered society. Three parts of this definition require comment: (a) "the general will" to which all members entrust themselves and their individual abilities; (b) the qualification "an indivisible part of the whole"; and (c) what it means to exercise "corporate capacity."

For Rousseau, (a) "the general will" is a real force or power that differs from the sum total of individual wills. As such, the general will is always aimed at the common good for all members of the society who agree to form a social compact. How the general will functions within a society will become more evident as the discussion continues.

(b) The concept of being "indivisible" is familiar from the Pledge of Allegiance, and once reminded of this context, students quickly determine that indivisible means incapable of

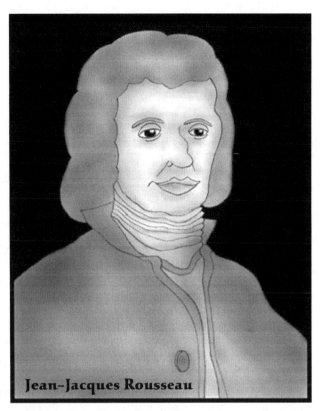

Jean-Jacques Rousseau

being broken up into parts. A relevant example: If a new student joins the class during the year, then the class will (or, perhaps, should) welcome and accept that new student as a new and "indivisible" part of the class. In other words, no individual who has become a member of the class can be ostracized or shunned, for this negative response would sunder the indivisible character of the class as a whole.

When the students embrace the new member, they act (c) in their "corporate capacity," that is, not as unique individuals with their own concerns, but as members of a group defined by a common interest. Thus, for Rousseau, human beings exist in at least two senses simultaneously: as individuals and as members of a group or society. In this respect, then, a society defined by the presence of the social compact is understood as a whole greater than the sum of its parts.

However, difficulties arise from this joint mode of existence, and Rousseau faces them directly in the following passages.

Passage 3

This assertion states the obvious objection to the definition of the social compact. What if I, as an individual, want to do something other than what is sanctioned by the general will? This conflict occurs often in the derivative kind of social compact that characterizes a classroom. If the class has agreed to go on a field trip and I would prefer to go elsewhere (or, perhaps, not go anywhere at all), what, if anything, can I do? And, if my own particular will as an expression of my individual interests runs counter to the will of the class and this communal or general will has its way, have I not thereby lost the freedom that Rousseau has promised will be mine once I embrace the social compact? What incentive do I have for sacrificing my seemingly unlimited individual freedom for the sake of those decisions that reflect and accept the will of the group?

Passage 4

The word *tacitly* plays a crucial role in this passage, thus the meaning of this word must be explained. One way is to contrast a classroom rule that is explicit, clearly stated by the teacher either verbally or in writing, with its opposite, a classroom rule that is implied, or tacit. It is an essential element of Rousseau's thought that the social compact is present and alive (i.e., tacit) even if it has not been explicitly brought into the language of rule or law.

It is apparent that the note of paradox is struck again in the phrase "forced to be free," and students quickly remark on its presence. The paradoxical air of this idea can, however, be reduced or even dissolved if the context of discussion is shifted from the miniaturized social compact exemplified in a classroom to the social compact understood as a fundamental structure in society and as the foundation underlying specific forms of government.

The following philosophical mini-drama helps show how we tacitly embrace the social compact and are thereby forced to be free: Ask the students what they can do if they discover that they do not like the government and laws of a certain state (e.g., Illinois). "Move to Wisconsin!" is the cry. Then, ask what they can do if they discover that they don't like the laws of Wisconsin. "Move to X [substitute a preferred state]!" Allow the sequence to broaden geographically until the students recognize that the point is to determine where a person would go if he or she did not like any laws whatsoever. "Go to a desert island!" is a frequent cry.

At this juncture, ask the students, "Are you free on this island?" "Yes!" is the almost universal shout. The students are voicing—without a great deal of thought—the popular notion that freedom means being able to do whatever you like to do. On our hypothetical desert island, there are no laws, no rules, no teachers, no parents, nothing to interfere with the continuous fulfillment of one's most heartfelt desires—a perfectly idyllic existence! But, wait . . . There is also no society on this island, not to mention the complete absence of all the necessities and luxuries that society provides to those who have adopted, whether explicitly or tacitly, the social compact. Ask the students, "How will you be spending your time on this island?" There is usually a brief pause as young minds focus and reflect: "Doing whatever you like!" blurts a devout hedonist, but others will recognize the utter ominousness of the situation: "Hunting for food!," "Looking for shelter and clothing!," and related expressions of reality-based needs. I then ask (with, admittedly, a slight air of perverse pleasure), "What is your life like on this deserted island?" Almost invariably someone will say, in a voice inflected with a grudging acceptance of dire inevitability, "It will be just like the life of an animal . . ." The final Rousseauian query: "Would you really want to lead that sort of life?"

According to Rousseau, this would be a form of natural bondage of the highest order. If a human being must spend virtually every waking hour seeking food and shelter, this human being is not free. So, the relevant opposite to the social compact is not unfettered freedom— it is the state of nature that, as Hobbes' tart trope rings in our ears, is not a pleasant place to be (unless, of course, one is indeed an animal!). Rousseau's point is that, once we realize the immeasurable benefits we receive from the social compact, then anyone who would claim to want to live outside the bounds of the social compact will be "forced to be free" by those already enjoying the type of existence guaranteed by the social compact. There was much in the European civilization of his day that Rousseau thought excessive and unnatural, and

therefore ultimately harmful to humans with respect to their inborn goodness of character. However, the many benefits—both tangible and immaterial—that the social compact has engendered and fostered for human beings are essential to realizing our humanity, especially since the nature of that humanity is a social enterprise and must be acknowledged as such.

If all the members of a social compact recognize that they are truly free only insofar as they collectively band together and bind themselves under common observances and laws, then each and every member of the social compact has been "forced to be free," but in a way that truly liberates the humanity of each individual as such and in relation to pursuits and interests sought in common with peers in the society. In sum, "freedom" is not equivalent to absolute license or complete lack of external restraint. Freedom in Rousseau's social compact means having the ability to realize who one is as a human being, both individually and as a member of a society comprised of other individuals who are seeking the same self-actualization.

Passage 5

The key step here is the distinction between natural and civil liberty. To illustrate the force of the distinction, I wander around the classroom looking for something of value to appropriate—a special pen, a wristwatch, a calculator. I then pick up the object, asking what, according to the passage just presented, will limit my acquisition of this and any other object I desire to possess. The students typically review the passage, then answer "strength," that is, strength in a straightforward physical sense, and only my strength. Thus, if I am stronger than you, then I will take whatever I want from you. This is natural liberty. Your only recourse in wishing to preserve your property is to try to fight me. And I will win because, simply, I am bigger (and a lot meaner!). Ask: Who, then, will control this society? The answer: The biggest, strongest dude! Then, ask how much property this dude will be able to control. The answer, and someone usually sees this consequence, is not very much! Why? Because the dude, although a potent individual, has only himself as a source of power; thus, the dude is unable to enlist the support of others since doing so will drain his natural liberty. The most powerful person according to natural liberty will indeed be better off than anyone else in the neighborhood, but not by all that much.

Under civil liberty, the unrestrained boundlessness of natural liberty has been renounced. But, says Rousseau, what has been gained is something much more pervasively powerful and better for all concerned: civil liberty. In the case at hand, if a big bully pilfers one's property, then when civil liberty is in place, one can appeal to the authorities and to the law. Civil liberty rests on the social compact; thus, all the forces amassed and controlled by that common bond are (at least theoretically) at the service of the person whose property has been taken. It is true that, under natural liberty, we have the "right" to whatever we can acquire by power and guile. But, this right, once applied in a social setting, is severely limited by the unavoidable limits inherent in being an individual human being. For Rousseau, the contrast between the two senses of right is clear, and the choice anyone thinking rationally will make between the two rights is just as clear. Indeed, in the long run, even a bully is better off under civil liberty than under natural liberty.

Passage 6

First, clarify the meaning of *estate*. Rousseau is not conceiving of estate in the sense of a large manor house with spacious grounds and liveried servants; rather, *estate* means simply one's property, regardless of its extent. Then explain the relevant sense of *sovereignty*. *Sovereignty* refers to the source of power legitimizing a form of government. It is important to note here that

Rousseau distinguishes sharply between sovereignty and government. The subtitle of the *Social Contract* is *Principles of Political Right*. For Rousseau, the people provide the source of power, or sovereignty, but they can delegate this power of political right to a government that can assume various forms—republic, aristocracy, monarchy. Although the seat of power is democratic for Rousseau insofar as it emerges from the consent of all the people acting in concert with one another, the particular form of government they select may or may not be a democracy in the modern sense, depending, for example, on historical, cultural, or geographical factors. It is crucial to keep in mind, however, that the government is the agent of the people, that is, what they have adopted in their "corporate capacity" to see to the establishment and preservation of their best interests when they form a community. Thus, even a king is beholden to his "subjects" in terms of the source of legitimacy for his rule.

In the passage at hand, Rousseau's claim is that the right an individual has to his or her property is superceded by the right of the community to all such estates. Without the priority of rights established in this way, sovereignty would be rendered meaningless. To illustrate the point, consider the following case. A community wants to build a road through your property, thereby disrupting your life because you will have to leave your dwelling and relocate. What should you do? According to the passage, your obligation is clear: You must allow the community to build that road. The community has rights that supercede the rights of any one member of that community.

Students frequently balk at this consequence. If so, ask: (a) Who benefits from the road built? The answer: everyone in the community! Then ask: (b) By what right do you own this property? The answer: by virtue of the fact that the community has been established as a community and, therefore, as a social entity with a legal system guaranteeing the right to own property. How, then, can you consistently refuse to consent to the community's wishes if the community is the very reason why you enjoy owning the property now in dispute? Obviously, in some cases, the community can overextend itself in its relations with individual citizens, but if the community is acting for the common good as expressed by the general will, then the priority of rights must be preserved according to the order stated by the passage.

Passage 7

Some people are artistic, some not; some people are athletic, some not; some people are skilled in business matters, some not. Rousseau recognizes the obvious fact that people are unequal by nature in these and countless other respects. Despite these differences, however, we are all equal "by convention and legal right" insofar as we embrace the social compact and its protective force. Thus, if a student has a grievance against another student, the former can seek redress from the teacher, the representative of sovereignty in the social compact of the classroom. And, more generally, if a person has a grievance against another person, the former need not seek redress by challenging the latter to a duel. The law in its various forms and agencies is available to seek equality and moral justice.

Passage 8

Ask the students, "What does this passage remind us of?" Some classes do not establish the relevant historical and doctrinal connection without a nudge or two. But, students who are adept at seeing relations between abstract contexts will quickly say, "The Declaration of Independence!" And they are correct. Thomas Jefferson read Rousseau—the *Social Contract* appeared in 1762, more than a decade before the Declaration was penned—and was influenced by Rousseau's ideas concerning equality

before the law. Note, however, that enjoying rights under the social compact goes hand in hand with binding the participants in the compact to "observe the same conditions." For Rousseau, rights and duties are interdependent and commensurately so, a fundamental relation that has apparently been forgotten by individuals who trumpet their self-asserted "rights" without acknowledging corresponding obligations.

Curricular Integration

The position developed in the *Social Contract* falls readily under social studies. The following three areas contain questions and discussions that illustrate the relevance of Rousseau's thinking to standard curricula and that also excite interest among younger students. The first two areas begin with topics of direct concern to students since their context is the classroom, a world of rules and implicit social compacts that has defined their educational existence from its inception. These topics are then widened within the context of society, with students invited to extend their thinking from the classroom into the world at large.

A. Law and Rule

The Classroom: It is often observed that gifted students have a heightened sensitivity to justice as fairness. If a classroom rule has been instituted more for the teacher's self-interest or personal convenience than for the overall well-being of the class, it is reasonable to expect resistance to the implementation of this rule on the grounds that "it's not fair."

- *In such circumstances, should the teacher be willing to justify the introduction of this rule?*

Students who react to the alleged unfairness inherent in the imposition of such a rule are displaying an inchoate awareness of the kind of sovereignty that underlies Rousseau's version of the social compact. It may be taken as a given that the teacher is the de facto head of the class and thus the primary rulegiver in terms of the class as an ordered (if numerically small) society. However, the general will has been ruptured in a sense if the teacher has taken advantage of his or her position with respect to sovereignty to institute a rule that satisfies the interests of the teacher at the expense of the well-being of the class as a whole.

Teachers may say to their charges, especially under duress, "This is not a democracy!" Thus, once the teacher has instituted rules or instructions for the classroom, the students are not free to discuss or debate their status. But, from a more abstract perspective and with Rousseau in view, the sovereignty of the classroom is in a sense precisely democratic in origin. After all, the teacher serves the students and must function on behalf of their overall best interests since the very presence of young people as students in a classroom (and, by proxy, their parents) provides the source of legitimacy—the power—that makes the school what it is, a type of social compact. Children are learners, and, as such, they require teachers in order to be taught so they can function as adults within society. However, teachers do not require students in order for teachers to learn—as adults, teachers can teach themselves whatever they need to know in order to assume their role within society. But, society maintains that children cannot do the same for themselves. Hence, the need for schools. It may be concluded that, if a rule has been instituted that is truly for the common good of the class as a whole, then it should be possible to explain and justify that rule to the members of the class.

Society: When a teacher decrees a rule for the classroom, it may be assumed that this rule serves the common good of students and thus aptly manifests the social compact. But, now consider a government enacting a law. When a particular law is decreed under the aegis of the general will, is this law based on the interests of everyone under the jurisdiction of the social compact or only on the interests of a minority or special interest group? Consider the following cases:

- *If the government decrees war on another country, is a citizen required to go to war regardless of personal considerations?*

- *If, less dramatically, the government imposes a tax on an activity many of its citizens enjoy (e.g., smoking), does this tax reflect the general will and, if so, how?*

B. Freedom

The Classroom: The frustrated cry of the student whose self-interest in a particular case clashes with the preferences of the class as a whole serves as the motto for this chapter. It doubtless seems obvious to the individual so affected that his or her freedom has been restricted, and in a way that produces discontent, if not something more anxiety-producing.

- *What can be done when a student faces this kind of situation?*

To reduce the degree of unhappiness produced by the group's decision, the student in question can make a sincere attempt to reflect on the interests of the class and to determine, if possible, why their interests are in conflict. This attempt should improve understanding in two directions: outwardly, toward the other members of the class, and inwardly, toward the individual student's own interests and desires. If the class decision is indeed a reflection of the general will as embodied in this miniature society, then Rousseau's position suggests that it is ultimately in the best interests of everyone participating in this social compact that the decision of the class be adopted and carried out—by all concerned. If I don't want to go on the field trip, perhaps I should ask myself what advantage will come from the trip for me even if I am initially disinclined to participate in the venture. Also, and just as relevant to my feelings and attitudes, what good could I produce for the class by redirecting my interests so that they correlate with the interests of the general will?

Society: On the larger scale of society, if a person belongs to a democracy, he or she implicitly agrees to accept whatever the majority says on an issue. Thus, the freedom to express oneself on given issues will override, or at least to a certain degree compensate for, whatever inconvenience occurs if the majority institutes policies or rules not directly coinciding with one's interests. Furthermore, one is always free to attempt to alter the instituted policies by working "within the system" to change the way people think. Rousseau has promised that membership in the type of association he is advancing will offer freedom to whoever participates in it. But, surely those individuals comprising a minority in a democracy can be compelled by the majority to act against their wishes or interests—in effect, becoming subject to the "tyranny of the majority."

- *How are these individuals "free" in such circumstances?*

It is relevant to indicate the parallel between the student struggling to understand the common good of the class as it seemingly interferes with his or her self-interest and the mature adult thinking of one's place in the society and how one's interests, even if they clash with those of society, might best be understood and, if necessary, revised so that they cohere with, or at least are not opposed to, the common good.

Such understanding is, of course, far more easily stated in the abstract than achieved in actual fact. The key to understanding is the appropriate perception of the common good and how it pertains to the interests of particular individuals.

C. Democracy and the General Will

For Rousseau, sovereignty derives from the consent of the people, whether explicitly or tacitly given. The expression of sovereignty can take the form of a democracy, although Rousseau would have had reservations about the question of realizing the general will when the democracy has a large population. Consider, then, the present state of affairs in the United States:

- *If, as Rousseau maintains, the general will is the underlying source of sovereignty and the general will seeks the common good, then is the United States, as a democracy, successful in satisfying the common interests of all its citizens?*

- *If a significant percentage of the eligible voters in a democracy chooses not to vote in government elections—as is presently the case in the United States—do the results of such elections represent and manifest the "general will"?*

- *Finally, in a democracy as large and complex as that in the United States, does the notion of a general will aimed at the common good have any real significance in the first place?*

These are important questions well worth debating in the classroom using particular examples of governmental decisions introduced by students or teachers. Reflection on the meaning and scope of Rousseau's concepts of the general will and the social compact will foster a greater appreciation of the related concept of the "common good." The number of factional disputes triggered by local cultural, religious, and economic differences remains high, resulting in hardship and suffering for millions of people. The suspicion lingers that a significant percentage of these disputes arise at least in part from a kind of inbred tribalism, an attitude that could be altered if the undeniably real differences among the peoples of the earth were tempered with what people share, with what is the same or "common" to all of us. The common good might differ in some respects within the various sections of a city, state, or nation, and it might also differ from nation to nation. But, at some level, all human beings are one, and on this admittedly high plane of generality it should nonetheless be possible to determine a common good such that all, or at least the majority of, our interests as human beings can be satisfied.

Younger students often face the same type of problem on a personal level when the diverse interests they embody as individuals conflict with the common good of a class in such matters as academic projects, field trips, and volunteer work. Yet, the source of this problem is in a way its solution. Students often display keen self-awareness, and it is one of the merits of Rousseau's thought to show that one's sense of self-interest is defined, in part, by the connections one has with other members of the society. Thus, part of what I know is good for me and my self-determined interests includes taking into account what I know is good for my neighbors. If my neighbors and I differ in some

respect as individuals, the burden is on us as individuals to see ourselves in light of our individuality and also how we are both members of a larger societal whole. The more awareness students have of the presence of the common good—the principle underlying Rousseau's notion of the general will—the more readily they will grow and develop in such a way as to integrate their own individual interests with those of the society in which they will eventually reside.

Rousseau's fertile reflections on the meaning of freedom and the social means to realize such freedom offer profound lessons on one of the most important contemporary issues: How should the citizens of a nation think and what should they do in order to get along? And, if that noble goal is attained, how should the nations of the world think and act in order to get along with each other? Students cannot solve the world's ills, but they can make a small, yet significant beginning by training their thoughts and attention on that dimension of the common good available to them.

Reference:

Rousseau, J-J. (1970). *The social contract*. New York: Hafner.

Web address for online text:
http://www.constitution.org/jjr/socon.htm

CHAPTER 7

Freedom and Responsibility: Existentialism and Younger Students

Rules. Rules are everywhere. "Do this." "Don't do that." All students are surrounded by and coexist with a plethora of rules. Their lives in school are, in large measure, defined by rules. Most younger students choose to obey these rules—but why? To avoid punishment? To curry favor with teachers? To pursue their best interests? To do the right thing for its own sake? It might then be asked—would these students choose to be so obedient if they were completely and absolutely free?

The concept of freedom has been, in one form or another, a pivotal ingredient in philosophical reflection since the time of the ancient Greeks. In Chapter 6, we examined Rousseau's attempt to integrate freedom within a theory of society. An especially dramatic evocation of reflection on freedom arose from the recent philosophical movement known as existentialism. This type of philosophy began in the late 19th century with the radically different positions of the Danish philosopher-theologian Søren Kierkegaard (1813–1855) and the German philosopher-poet Friedrich Nietzsche (1844–1900). Also crucial to the germination of existentialism were some of the pivotal events of the 20th century, primarily the ravages wrought by the two world wars. Thoughtful people began questioning the seemingly sacrosanct trio of reason, logic, and the systematic philosophy of such thinkers as Aristotle and the German Georg Hegel (1770–1831), and they sought new ways to express what was thought and felt about the world and our place in it. As a result, some of the major principles and concepts of existentialism became much more visible because they were developed in novels, short stories, and plays—literary media with a much wider audience than typically accorded to works of systematic philosophy. Although existentialism is not as dominant a movement among philosophers now, at the beginning of a new century, as it was during the middle of the 20th century, its legacy was significant, if not profound. The primary exponents of existentialism remain a source of insight and discovery for contemporary students of philosophy.

Jean-Paul Sartre

One of the most important and influential existentialists was Jean-Paul Sartre (1905–1980). Sartre wrote in virtually every form—novels, short stories, plays, literary criticism, all in addition to philosophical works on many topics. In 1965, Sartre was awarded the Nobel Prize for Literature, but he rejected it. In the period after World War II, Sartre had become increasingly interested in Marxism, and he felt that accepting this award (and its monetary prize) would be inconsistent with his Marxist beliefs. Around the time existentialism was beginning its ascendancy, Sartre, observing the considerable influence existentialism had exerted on the popular mind and hearing much wayward criticism of its principles and consequences, gave a lecture in 1945 (published in essay form a few years later) in which he responded to this predominantly negative reaction. The essay, "L'Existentialisme est un humanisme" ("Existentialism Is A Humanism), was written in an informal, non-technical style so that Sartre's general position would be accessible to anyone who had an interest in the philosophy of existentialism. But, as we shall see, this approach to the defense of existentialism resulted in important and revealing logical tensions.

Since the concept of freedom pertains primarily to the behavior of human beings, its analysis has been the concern of that branch of philosophy known as ethics. The first chapter of Part I analyzed the concept of friendship (Aristotle), a foundational instance of ethical inquiry. However, Sartre's approach to a properly philosophical dimension of freedom combines ethical concerns with basic concepts in metaphysics, the branch of philosophy that articulates the structure of reality through the use of general or abstract notions. Previous chapters devoted to metaphysics included St. Augustine on the nature of time and Thomas Aquinas' proof of the existence of God based on the design of the universe. Jean-Paul Sartre, combining the ethical and metaphysical dimensions of philosophy, produced an essay embodying an especially vibrant and varied discussion of freedom that continues to be pivotal to the Western mind.

The following excerpts are taken from Bernard Frechtman's translation of "L'Existentialisme est un humanisme." Although all the excerpts are accessible and provide a reliable statement of Sartre's version of existentialism, we shall confront several terms that, although relatively common in philosophy, nonetheless require brief explanation. The overall position developed by these excerpts will help students to reflect on the meaning of being human—and also on what it means to be free as a human being. As a result of this reflection, the reality of and rationale for rules, whether in the classroom or in life, may take on additional significance for students—and, of course, for anyone interested in following Sartre's argument.

1. I should like on this occasion to defend existentialism against some charges which have been brought against it.

2. …what can be said from the very beginning is that by existentialism we mean a doctrine which makes human life possible and, in addition, declares that every truth and every action implies a human setting and a human subjectivity.

3. What complicates matters is that there are two kinds of existentialism: first, those who are Christian, among whom I would include [Karl] Jaspers and Gabriel Marcel, both Catholic; and on the other hand the atheistic existentialists, among whom I class [Martin] Heidegger, and then the French existentialists and myself. What they have in common is that they think that existence precedes essence.…

4. Atheistic existentialism, which I represent, is more coherent. It states that if God does not exist, there is at least one being in whom existence precedes essence, a being who exists before he can be defined by any concept, and that this being is man.… What is meant here by saying that existence precedes essence? It means that first of all, man exists, turns up, appears on the scene, and, only afterwards, defines himself.

5. Thus, there is no human nature, since there is no God to conceive it. Not only is man what he conceives himself to be, but he is also only what he wills himself to be after this thrust toward existence.

6. Man is nothing else but what he makes of himself. Such is the first principle of existentialism.

7. But if existence really does precede essence, man is responsible for what he is. Thus, existentialism's first move is to make every man aware of what he is and to make the full responsibility of his existence rest on him. And when we say that a man is responsible for himself, we do not only mean that he is responsible for his own individuality, but that he is responsible for all men.

8. In fact, in creating the man that we want to be, there is not a single one of our acts which does not at the same time create an image of man as we think he ought to be. To choose to be this or that is to affirm at the same time the value of what we choose, because we can never choose evil. We always choose the good, and nothing can be good for us without being good for all.... Thus, our responsibility is much greater than we might have supposed, because it involves all mankind.

9. Besides, if it is impossible to find in every man some universal essence which would be human nature, yet there does exist a universal human condition.... What does not vary is the necessity for him to exist in the world, to be at work there, to be there in the midst of other people, and to be mortal there.

10. Man makes himself. He isn't ready made at the start. In choosing his ethics, he makes himself, and force of circumstances is such that he cannot abstain from choosing one. We define man only in relationship to involvement. It is therefore absurd to charge us with arbitrariness of choice.

11. Before you come alive, life is nothing: it's up to you to give it a meaning, and value is nothing else but the meaning that you choose. In that way, you see, there is a possibility of creating a human community.

—From "Existentialism is a Humanism" by Jean-Paul Sartre

Passage 1

Sartre forthrightly states his intention: He will defend existentialism (or, more precisely, his version of existentialism) against objections brought to bear against it by academic philosophers, as well as by representatives from the media and even the general public.

Passage 2

Ask students to identify the term that appears three times in this sentence: *human*. This repetition signals one of Sartre's most fundamental themes, that the goals and demands of our existence are defined strictly and exclusively by human beings themselves, not by anything that exists beyond the limits of humanity.

Passage 3

Two vital and quite distinct points should be made concerning this passage:

a. "Existentialism" as a rubric covers very different approaches to philosophical concerns. Sartre's existentialism is atheistic, and he is never shy about emphasizing this fact. By contrast, Gabriel Marcel (1889–1973, a French contemporary of Sartre) develops existential principles and themes in the course of which God plays an essential role. Thus, to call someone an "existentialist" hardly identifies conclusively that person's philosophical beliefs since one can be an existentialist without necessarily being an atheist. The dangers of typecasting a philosopher or a movement in philosophy because of a shared or generic name are very real and testify to the inherently misleading aftereffects of names. It may also be observed that the important German philosopher Martin Heidegger (1889–1976), cited by Sartre in this passage, will be considered in

Chapter 10, although the topic of that discussion—the nature of technology (a favorite topic among students!)—is not normally considered a particularly existentialist theme.

b. After distinguishing types of existentialism, Sartre indicates what these types have in common: the conviction that "existence precedes essence." The terms *existence* and *essence* have long and varied careers as fundamental philosophical concepts in metaphysics. Typically, *essence* refers to *what* something is, while *existence* refers to *the fact that* something is. To specify the essence of something is to state properties or characteristics that that something must possess in order to be an instance of this kind of thing and not some other kind of thing. This type of inquiry differs from recognizing that the something in question is there, existing, in the first place. Thus, the primary metaphysical concern that the distinction intends to highlight is that a thing's nature and its existence are distinct from one another.

Passage 4

The link Sartre sees between God and human beings should be noted; a more precise determination of this relation will be discussed in the next excerpt. For now, Sartre clarifies how essence and existence pertain to human beings. As Sartre says, think of human beings "appearing on the scene" without any prior essence—or nature—dictating what each human being must be in the course of a lifetime. It is important not to misunderstand the direction of Sartre's thinking here. He is not denying that human beings have a collective history, a record of past events that in some sense we carry with us into the present. Nor is he discounting the scientific possibility that evolution and genetic factors may contribute significantly in making human beings what they are today. His point is merely that each individual person is unique when that individual appears on the scene (i.e., begins to exist and to make decisions). History, evolution, and genetic makeup (among other elements) are present to the brute fact of an existing human being—but what that person *chooses to do* with his or her life is entirely up to that individual person. In this sense then, the existence of an individual human being is, for Sartre, more fundamental than any dimension of essence that we might want to impose on that human being.

Passage 5

The first sentence of this passage is an excellent candidate for applying principles of critical thinking. Is there reasoning in this sentence? Yes, Sartre is moving from a premise, "There is no God to conceive it [human nature]," to a conclusion, "Thus, there is no human nature." After students have identified the logical structure of this sentence, ask whether the conclusion follows from the premise. Almost invariably the answer is that it does not! Ask, "Could there be a human nature even if there were no God to conceive and create such a nature?" Yes, is the reply. At this point, discussion can move in various directions, for example, that evolution forms the nature of human beings or that over time we implicitly structure our own nature simply by interacting with one another. Such discussion is relevant to the general philosophical point concerning the existence of a human nature, but in the interests of brevity and topical focus, all that needs to be said now is that Sartre's conclusion does not necessarily follow from his premise. As an aside, this is probably one of the places in the essay where Sartre cut corners in order to establish a point by omitting what he doubtless felt would be excessive and unnecessary argumentation.

His intention in this sentence is to move from the nonexistence of God to the lack of a human nature, and he accomplishes this end, although without explicitly considering other possible alternatives that might establish a human nature or something very close to it apart from whether or not God exists.

It is also important to note how Sartre connects the need *to conceive* what a person will be with the need *to will* what that person is to be. Thought and action are intimately related. If I conceive myself to be of heroic stature, but do not will myself to act heroically, I am hardly a hero. In this respect, Sartre shows that his position is in no sense an ivory-tower intellectualism—the truly free human being must be aware that individuality rests on conceiving a goal and then acting in the world in order to achieve that goal.

Passage 6

What we choose to be is what we are—the first sentence of this passage neatly and concisely summarizes Sartre's existentialism in terms of thought and action. And, with the utterance of this philosophical epigram, we may now begin to evaluate Sartre's position as a whole.

Ask the students whether, given Passages 1–6, Sartre has said anything that limits the range of choices open to us as individual human beings. Is there any limit on the freedom of a human being to define himself or herself? To dramatize this point, I ask the students whether, according to the principles and conclusions Sartre has laid down so far, I am allowed to choose a seemingly outlandish form of behavior (e.g., bullying anyone and everyone I see) as a way of defining my individuality. "Yes!" is the standard response. "If you want to be a bully, go for it!" In general then, Sartre appears to have produced a radical sense of freedom, this in conjunction with the denial that human beings have an essence. The first principle of Sartre's version of existentialism seems to open a door to virtually any choice, as long as it is my choice, freely chosen. But, if choice is completely open-ended, if freedom means license to perform every conceivable kind of action, how would such freedom affect human beings insofar as they exist socially with other human beings? If I somehow enjoy and am fulfilled by being a bully, what about the people who are on the receiving end of my bullying? Sartre has recognized the problem—and at precisely this point the purely theoretical dimension of Sartre's defense of existentialism becomes highly dramatic by virtue of an emergent logical tension.

Passage 7

Now we are told, clearly and decisively, that freedom entails responsibility. But, even this consequence would not limit freedom in a theoretical sense. For according to the opening phase of the passage, I could choose to be a bully or to cheat my way through life (or to make a variety of other, far less palatable choices)—as long as I were also willing to assume responsibility for such a choice. However, Sartre proceeds to develop this sense of responsibility. His contention is that, when I am responsible for my own individuality, I am also responsible for *everyone.*

Students tend to take this claim very literally; thus, a frequent reaction to this part of the passage is to question how such a responsibility is possible given the obvious fact that so many people exist in the world. How could any one individual be "responsible" for all these other people? Sartre's position in this regard receives additional development in the following passage.

Passage 8

This is an especially fertile passage. First, note the important shift Sartre introduces from creating the image of what we "want" to be to creating an image of what we "ought" to be. The "ought" introduces an evaluative, if not decidedly moral, dimension into the discussion. Thus, if I choose to cheat on an exam, does the image of humanity-as-cheater square with what I want to accomplish for myself by this choice? Does my decision to cheat implicitly sanction the decision of all human beings to cheat? If an individual were to find such an extension of a given choice distasteful or even potentially chaotic, then the inference Sartre suggests is that this individual would not in fact make such a choice.

The second noteworthy aspect of this passage concerns the pronouncement that we always choose the good and never choose evil. This claim is reminiscent of a similar position argued in Plato, that a human being always construes a choice in terms of what is good for that person at that time. In short, we never choose evil for the sake of evil—we always choose what we think (or tell ourselves!) is good. If I choose to cheat, I justify this choice on the basis of what I think will be good for me as a result (e.g., getting a high grade on a test or essay, avoiding the wrath of parents, etc.). Of course, what I conveniently overlook is the fact that the good comes at the price of passing off the work of others as mine, a blatant form of dishonesty.

The third and final aspect of this passage to be noted is that, when we make an individual choice for what is good, nothing that we choose to be good can truly be good for us as individuals unless it is good for everyone. At this point, however, Sartre's position faces a serious objection. As a young student in class discussion put it, to claim that there is a "good for all" looks suspiciously like an essence that is common to each and every human being. A fundamental logical crux suddenly emerges: If Sartre emphasizes radical freedom as a consequence derived from his denial of a human nature, then his position is threatened with the implication that humans can do whatever they want to do whenever they want to do it—a virtual invitation to social chaos. But, if he wants to block the imputation of such chaos by appealing to a good that is common to all people as the source of our collective and individual responsibility whenever we make a choice, then his position is threatened with internal inconsistency since he has denied that such a universal value exists and can be binding on everyone. It seems, then, that Sartre must choose: radical existential freedom or social responsibility? If radical existential freedom, then social responsibility vanishes; if social responsibility, then a human essence slips back into the picture and radical freedom vanishes. The dilemma is logically severe and, it would seem, unresolvable.

It should be recalled that this tension has been generated from an essay that, admittedly, was written in a popular mode. It is also important to keep in mind the general point that the ordinary language we employ in order to think about our lives is rife with vagueness and multiple meanings, hence the need for a refined, technical language in which a philosopher might develop ideas more clearly and coherently. Thus, to be fair to Sartre, we should also study his mammoth work *L'être et le nèant* (*Being and Nothingness*), sometimes described as "the principal text of modern existentialism." Of course, whether this massive work (almost 800 pages in English translation) affords Sartre the room to balance coherently the divergent concerns of the essay we are currently examining is a project for another occasion.

Passage 9

Passages 2–4 deny that there is a human essence. But, later in the essay, Sartre insists that some aspects of our situation are indeed common. He calls these aspects "a universal human condition," thereby distinguishing between a human essence and a human condition. The latter includes the fact that we must spend our lives in the world (e.g., we have a body and must coexist with other bodies, whether natural or human), we must work (even those born into wealth must exert effort to retain it), we must be with other people (for Sartre, the solitary hermit—a rare individual—has shunned the human condition), and we must die (everyone dies, although recent technology suggests that life may be extended far beyond what has always appeared to be its natural termination). Everyone faces this quartet of circumstances, although we confront the details as unique individuals. It is the individual's confrontation with the human condition that interests Sartre in this essay.

Passage 10

Here Sartre addressees the charge, frequently made by unsympathetic critics, that the typical existentialist is enamored with arbitrary actions, purely random behavior, and a philosophical free pass to pursue all manner of excess. Permeating this criticism is the popular image of the existentialist-as-Beatnik—bearded, wearing a beret, sipping absinthe, and plotting subversive actions against the established order. This is a cartoon, of course, although various Left Bank habitués looking and acting such a part fueled this image and thus fired the imagination of ordinary people on both sides of the Atlantic regarding what existentialists were and how they behaved. For Sartre, such a barren and impoverished existence is impossible simply by virtue of the fact that a human being is alive. After all, if one were to abstain from involvement in a given cause, or indeed in any cause, this itself is a decision, albeit an implicit one. In this case, the chooser's values are defined solely with regard to self-interest walled within a kind of virulent narcissism that is difficult even to imagine, much less attempt to actualize. By contrast, the Sartrean existentialist is involved with the world, shaping his or her own identity through the ways the individual seeks to become active in that world. For the later

Sartre, such involvement meant embracing Marxism. But, this was his choice—and, of course, it was only his choice.

Passage 11

Apart from the key logical tensions that emerged after a critical evaluation of Sartre's reasoning, there nonetheless remains a core concern that is important for all students: the emphasis on individual choice and the fact that life becomes meaningful for us only if we make our own choices and are responsible for those choices. The student as an individual must realize that choices confer value upon the object of choice. Thus, if a student obeys a rule in school, then such obedience possesses an important sense of value to that student, its precise nature as a value being determined by that student.

But, self-interest is not sufficient to direct individual choice properly. Students must, or at least should, make choices in which other people are essentially involved; hence, Sartre's point concerning the possibility of meaningful choices creating a community. There are, of course, many communities defining the existence of an individual student: classroom, school, family, neighborhood, city, country. From the existentialist perspective, then, the individual student is responsible for choosing freely. If, however, we heed Sartre's injunction concerning the link between responsibility and what is good for everyone, then it is also vital for the student to realize that free choices must be made only in terms of how they balance individual self-interest with the collective well-being of others—classmates, teachers, parents, friends, neighbors, citizens—in the various nested communities in which that student exists.

If asked, "Why did you obey that rule?," a younger student's first response might be little more than "Well, it's the rule." But, reflection on Sartre's essay has brought to light that a more articulated answer would encompass not

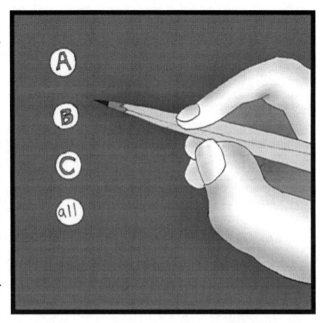

just the student's immediate self-interest, but also the connections between this choice and what is good for the various communities this student partially defines. From this perspective, then, Sartre's existentialism provides a philosophical framework that can help illuminate the reality of rules and the rationale behind a student's choice to obey them.

Curricular Integration

There are two areas in standard curricula in which Sartre's thoughts on freedom and responsibility may be usefully applied. One is fairly obvious, while the other may not be quite as evident. Consider the latter first.

A. Science

Sartre has denied that an essence defines human beings. Of course, the larger, more inclusive question is whether *anything* can be said to have an essence. For if the concept of an essence is only a philosopher's dream, then it should not be surprising that human beings lack an essence; after all, under this hypothesis, nothing has an essence!

Contemporary philosophers are generally leery of trying to determine the essence of something. Many philosophers now prefer to discuss operational or functional properties of things rather than to assert—and defend by demonstration—the claim that the "essence" of those things can be determined. Furthermore, even philosophers who continue to insist that essences do in fact exist will maintain that the structure of these essences is difficult to discern and describe.

To appreciate the rationale for this hesitation, ask the students whether they can give an essential definition of something in nature (e.g., a tree). Remember that an essence, under the interpretation discussed here, represents properties that are unique to an individual type of being. Thus, the essence of a tree will encompass all and only those properties that distinguish a tree from all other types of things, whether living or nonliving. In class, any student's definition of the essence of a tree will be quickly criticized (see whether a dictionary definition of tree helps in this quest—it will not!), and after a series of attempts, the result will be a kind of general skepticism about the possibility of such an inquiry. The teacher may vary the example to fit the scope of different sciences—botany, biology, chemistry—but, the discussion of these alternate examples will inevitably lead the class to the same inconclusive results.

This exercise illustrates the importance of the concept of definition in the sciences and also the apparent limitations of human knowledge in the face of the complex universe in which we exist. If it is part of the purpose of a science to provide definitions of the basic components of that science, then reflection on the meaning of an essential definition suggests that we must be equally clear on what we can and cannot know at the point when we begin our quest to unlock the secrets of the natural order. Perhaps operational or functional definitions are the best that we can produce.

B. Social Studies

Although Sartre denies that human beings have an essence, he insists that we are responsible for our choices and that these choices aim at "the good." If Sartre's notion of the good is identical to what we now call "values," then the question arises whether it is possible to identify values that are "essential" to human beings, both as individuals and as members of society.

Is it, for example, essential to the nature of an individual human being to be honest? Published reports indicate that the incidence of cheating continues to increase in American high schools and universities. Is this increase good for the individuals who choose to cheat? If so, then on what grounds are these individuals responsible to themselves and others? Discussing these questions with students will illustrate how values cohere with students' conceptions of how they intend to lead their lives once they have emerged as players in "the real world" beyond the rule-bound arena of formal education. My experience in this regard suggests that the teacher (or parent) should be prepared for discussion marked by a rather severely pragmatic approach toward the supposed "value" of such virtues as honesty. But, despite what may be a sobering experience on the part of the teacher, discussing the justification for such a pragmatic approach can only be fruitful in eliciting what students hold to be truly valuable as they see life and its demands.

From a social context, is it essential that human beings as members of groups obey rules established by those groups? As the world continues to shrink through technological advances (the Internet, cell phones, etc.) and resulting interpersonal immediacy, there nonetheless remain significant differences between and among the various cultures that populate the Earth. Furthermore, within a given culture, certain rules have been recognized as essential for the stability and well-being of people existing as members of that culture. In parallel fashion, within a given culture, widely various groups of people agree, tacitly or explicitly, to follow rules that limit and control their behavior as members of these groups. One such group is the society of a school. If a student, gifted or nongifted, chooses to obey the rules laid down by the authorities of that school, has this individual sacrificed something integral in his or her individual freedom by making this choice? Or, from another perspective, has this student chosen to maximize individual possibilities by allowing the school to direct behavior along lines that will be most effective for the student as both an individual and a member of a group, all of whose members share the same set of goals?

Pursuit of this question in a social science context will instigate discussion of values that define a society, rather than an individual. If Sartre is correct, then these values must be justified in terms of some broad sense of "what is good for all." As such, the values chosen will constitute the bases for law and social policy within a given society. In discussing these values, students will be required to defend their choices of essential social values by analyzing the relevance of these values for the common good.

It is perhaps ironic that a popular criticism of existentialism—that it engendered a species of virulent nihilism and lack of concern for values—led Sartre to respond to this criticism by developing an array of concepts that fosters an awareness of the meaning of choice and the need to guide our choices not only for the purpose of satisfying individual self-interest, but also to establish the well-being of those around us. If applied in this way, even and perhaps especially to the rule-bound situations in which students find themselves, Sartre's existentialism represents a fruitful and practical blend of ethics and metaphysics, rather than a somber exercise of dark, if not lurid, themes played out far from the concerns of everyday life.

Reference:

Sartre, J-P. (1947). *Existentialism*. New York: Philosophical Library.

Web address for online text:
http://www.marxists.org/reference/archive/sartre/works/exist/sartre.htm

CHAPTER 8

On Social Justice in a Violent World

I t does not take a philosopher to appreciate the fact that people do not always treat each other justly. What, then, is the best way to improve this troublesome and complex situation?

This vitally important question has received an important answer by an individual—the focus of this chapter—who would not typically be classified as a philosopher, at least not of the same order as Plato, Aquinas, or Rousseau. The legacy of Martin Luther King, Jr. (1929–1968) is securely enshrined in his leadership and example in establishing basic civil rights for African Americans. However, King also intended to promote the well-being of his people by making the United States a country that was more just in terms of the way individuals of color were treated in the social and economic spheres of society. The following excerpts, drawn from King's speeches and writings, represent a unified position that explains and justifies what, for King, is the best way to call attention to the need to increase social justice in America.

The purely literary dimension of these excerpts tends to conceal structures of thought that are definitely philosophical in intent and execution. We shall see King appeal to figures in the history of philosophy to support points he wants to make. In addition, the position is developed by the use of definitions and distinctions and also by reasoning introduced to support them. In these respects, then, King, although primarily known as a man of faith and religious belief, took advantage of the techniques of philosophy as a rational exercise whenever it was time to solidify his thoughts in language that would appear in print and, as a result, be available for inspection and scrutiny by anyone who wanted to appreciate the quality of his mind and the relevance of his message.

1. Now there are three ways that oppressed people have generally dealt with their oppression. One way is the method of acquiescence, the method of surrender; that is, the individuals will somehow adjust themselves to oppression, they adjust themselves to discrimination or to segregation or colonialism or what have you. The other method that has been used in history is that of rising up against the oppressor with corroding hatred and physical violence. . . . But there is another way, namely the way of nonviolent resistance. This method was popularized in our generation by a little man from India, whose name was Mohandas K. Gandhi. He used this method in a magnificent way to free his people from the economic exploitation and the political domination inflicted upon them by a foreign power.

2. This movement [nonviolent resistance] is based on the philosophy that ends and means must cohere. Now this has been one of the long struggles in history, the whole idea of means and ends. Great philosophers have grappled with it, and sometimes they have emerged with the idea, from Machiavelli on down, that the end justifies the means. There is a great system of thought in our world today, known as communism. And I think that with all of the weakness and tragedies of communism, we find its greatest tragedy right here, that it goes under the philosophy that the end justifies the means that are used in the process.

3. This is the whole idea, that the individual who is engaged in a nonviolent struggle must never inflict injury upon another. Now this has an external aspect and it has an internal one. From the external point of view it means that the individuals involved must avoid external physical violence. So they don't have guns, they don't retaliate with physical violence. If they are hit in the process, they avoid external physical violence at every point. But it also means that they avoid internal violence of spirit.

4. There is something else: that one seeks to defeat the unjust system, rather than individuals who are caught in that system. And that one goes on believing that somehow this is the important thing, to get rid of the evil system and not the individual who happens to be misguided, who happens to be misled, who was taught wrong. The thing to do is to get rid of the system and thereby create a moral balance within society.

5. Now, it is very interesting at this point to notice that both violence and nonviolence agree that suffering can be a very powerful social force. But there is this difference: violence says that suffering can be a powerful social force by inflicting the suffering on somebody else: so this is what we do in war, this is what we do in the whole violent thrust of the violent movement. It believes that you achieve some end by inflicting suffering on another. The nonviolent say that suffering becomes a powerful social force when you willingly accept that violence on yourself, so that self-suffering stands at the center of the nonviolent movement and the individuals involved are able to suffer in a creative manner, feeling that unearned suffering is redemptive, and that suffering may serve to transform the social situation.

6. And so the nonviolent resister never lets this idea go, that there is something within human nature that can respond to goodness. So that a Jesus of Nazareth or a Mohandas Gandhi can appeal to human beings and appeal to that element of goodness within them, and a Hitler can appeal to the element of evil within them. But we must never forget that there is something within human nature that can respond to goodness, that man is not totally depraved; to put it in theological terms, the image of God is never totally gone.

—From *Testament of Hope* by Martin Luther King, Jr.

Passage 1

As we have seen throughout the readings in Part I, the use of a distinction to elucidate and identify circumstances is a typical strategy for the philosopher. In this case, King sketches three options available to an oppressed people in order to deal with injustice, options that set the scene for what follows. King's explicit debt to Gandhi should also be noted, both for the substance of nonviolent resistance and for Gandhi's heroic application of that doctrine in the successful liberation of India from Great Britain.

Sadly and tragically, the first two of the three options that King has presented here have often been put into practice in the history of humanity's inhumanity to itself. Therefore, although it may not be immediately apparent from the first passage, King will argue for the third approach as the only one that is morally justified. This argument rests on taking a stand concerning a question that has long exercised philosophers attempting to deal clearly and correctly with moral conflicts.

Passage 2

The related concepts of ends and means go back to the Greeks. Both Plato and Aristotle developed significant sections of their moral teaching by determining how an end—the purpose or goal of an action—relates to the means employed to achieve it. One approach cited by some philosophers—neither Plato nor Aristotle, by the way—is that the end justifies the means, that is, if we determine that we want to achieve some goal, then the means we use to realize that achievement is immaterial. King cites the important Renaissance philosopher Niccolò Machiavelli (1469–1527), perhaps best known for *The Prince*. Machiavelli was interested in showing rulers the best way to attain rule and, once secured, the best ways to preserve

Martin Luther King, Jr.

it. In general, Machiavelli's recommendations derive from the belief that, if ruling is good, then the ruler must not be squeamish about whatever means are necessary to maintain that rule, including deception, destruction, even murder. The moral question—*Should* such actions be done?—typically does not arise. Thus the end—ruling a state—justifies the means, whatever works to establish and preserve that rule.

King then connects means and ends in this context with communism. Although communism is no longer as vibrant or "great" a political force now as it was when King wrote these lines, the example nonetheless remains sharp and relevant. Thus, Josef Stalin executed tens of millions of dissidents in the former USSR who refused to follow the communist system because, as far as Stalin was concerned, the end justified the means. In order to preserve the communist system, the individual in charge of the government eliminated opposition by simply eliminating those people who opposed the system. King points out that the pivotal weakness of communism is subscribing to this principle, since it is adherence to the idea of achieving a given end by any means available that justifies the kind of wholesale slaughter that Stalin perpetrated against his own people.

This horrific example of the end justifying the means is of epochal and profoundly tragic dimension, and I have found it useful in class to mention other examples of a more mundane, but nonetheless real sort to illustrate the point. Thus, a student might feel that plagiarism and cheating on a test are acceptable means on the grounds that getting a good grade is an end that justifies any means for attaining it. In general, students quickly appreciate the force of the distinction between means and end, and it is vital that they do so since the importance of this distinction in King's argument cannot be overemphasized.

Passage 3

Again, King's use of a distinction to make his point in the manner of a philosopher should be noted. Furthermore, the content of the distinction between *external* and *internal* violence is of paramount importance. Assume that we are on a peace march, making a public statement against some form of oppression. A crowd has gathered, and someone hurls a rock at a marcher. According to King's argument, the advocate of nonviolence will not retaliate by throwing the rock back at the assailant even if there is a strong natural urge to do so. This is to control external physical violence. But, the individual struck by the rock also contains the often explosive desire to act in this way, what King refers to as "internal violence of spirit."

Which type of violence is easier to control: external or internal? Discussing this point is engaging and important to understanding the full import of King's argument concerning nonviolent resistance. First, clarify for the students how, in general, external violence is controlled. My experience has been that some prodding

may be necessary before students ascend to a level of generality sufficient to recognize that laws have been instituted for the control of external violence. People cannot just haul off and attack other people, and if they do act in this way, laws exist to curtail such violence. Once the control of external violence has been identified, then students readily recognize that internal violence cannot be controlled in the same way. Internal violence is based on something having gone askew within a person who feels the need to react to another person in this harmful way. Internal violence is controlled by the individual's own understanding and the resultant decision—perhaps established with difficulty and after a struggle—to banish any upsurge of negative and unjust feelings and emotions aimed at other people. If this kind of description of the two types of violence is made clear, the resulting consensus among students is that internal violence is much more difficult to control than its external counterpart. For how is it possible to get inside a person's mind in order to demonstrate that the desire for violence is misplaced because the thinking of that individual is confused?

King has responded to this question, but before considering that response, it is well to note that discussion of this passage frequently raises the question of self-defense. Does King's position mean that, if one is attacked, one is morally forbidden to defend oneself with physical violence? If the discussion moves in this direction, my response is that King's thinking addresses situations that involve groups of people, rather than one individual interacting with another individual and also that it is intended to apply to groups of people who are systematically oppressed. Whether the position he is developing in this arena of public affairs can be applied to self-defense is not easily answered, but since the general context of discussion is removed from this situation, it seems legitimate to request that the problem be put to one side, at least for now.

The connection between self-defense and physical violence is typically difficult to interpret, at least from a strictly philosophical and moral perspective. Furthermore, this question is timely in many circles of American education if the conflict in question is a more localized arena of injustice (e.g., that between a bully and the object of the bully's taunts). Should the individual being abused by the bully respond in kind or attempt to cope with the situation by following, perhaps in some modified way, the path of nonviolent resistance? A thoughtful examination of King's principles in this regard may have much to offer in dealing with this difficult problem and, by extension, in coping with the dangerous increase of many sorts of violence in schools.

Passage 4

Once again adopting standard philosophical technique, King introduces an important distinction, which might be illustrated by considering, for example, a racist and the racist's beliefs as instances of an unjust system. Thus, it is the systematic presence of racism that is evil, not the individual who has been ensnared it. Ask whether people are born racist. The answer is invariably "no." King suggests that racists are made by circumstance and are not born into this pattern of prejudice. Those individuals have received misguided information, have been impressed with the beliefs of others (perhaps from their elders who were racist) have been indoctrinated in modes of thinking and attitudes that are racist (perhaps in ways that are endemic to the surrounding culture). Whatever the source for the unjust system, the appropriate response is to re-educate the person afflicted with these beliefs so that the beliefs are eradicated, not so the individuals are harmed or defeated. King's position in this regard implies that doing physical violence to a racist is no less immoral than doing such violence to a saint.

Passage 5

In this passage, King offers different perspectives on the effectiveness of suffering. His argument against war is not that it will not achieve its end, but—following the principle and its applications asserted in Passages 2 and 3 above—that the end does not justify the means. If violence must be used in order to achieve a morally good end, then according to King's argument, such a means is not morally justified. By contrast, the approach King argues for embraces suffering as an effect willingly endured by the individual seeking a certain end, rather than inflicting such suffering on another party in order to achieve that end. This self-suffering is "creative" and "redemptive," and it is worth asking students what they think King means by using these words to describe suffering that the protester brings on himself or herself.

Pose this question from the standpoint of someone watching a peace march on television in the '60s (as I did at the time). What if a viewer sees marchers retaliating in kind against those who had attacked them (e.g., by throwing rocks). What would such a viewer think? The students answer, "The marchers are hypocrites!" After all, a sincere peace marcher would not become violent even if provoked. Then ask, "If you were watching a peace march on television and the marchers did not retaliate in kind, what might you think?" There is a brief period of reflection, then someone nearly always says, "I might think that the marchers are right, and that they really do believe in what they are marching for." In other words, the self-suffering becomes "creative" in the sense that it instills in the minds of observers the impression that this is a serious issue, that the marchers themselves are serious people—to the point of willingly accepting pain, jail, or even worse—and that I, as someone watching from the outside, should become seriously involved with this issue, as well!

It is important to appreciate the point that, in this context, King is arguing the moral question, not the psychological one. Students frequently comment, "If someone throws a rock at me, I'd throw it right back at them!" and "Very few people would act in this nonviolent way if they were provoked." Precisely. King is urging us to think of what we *should* do, not what we *would* do if we were involved in this kind of situation. The difficulty of achieving and maintaining such self-control is one of the principal reasons why the resulting self-suffering is so creative and so redemptive. Adopting and following the practice of nonviolent resistance requires a certain kind of person and a certain kind of character. King realized that the general public observing such individuals acting peacefully could not help but be impressed by their example and, it may be hoped, that, as a result of such observation, the beliefs of the marchers would become viable principles in the minds of a much wider and doubtless more socially and economically influential audience.

Passage 6

For King, not only are the nonviolent resister's actions morally good, but also spectators observing the behavior embodied in such resistance are thereby put into a position where they can appreciate its goodness and, as a result, take it upon themselves to recognize that the point of the resistance—the implementation of social justice—should animate their own lives and dealings with other people. However, King's examples of goodness should be noted since (with the exception of the appeal to Gandhi, a Hindu) they depend on the Christianity of which King was both practitioner and advocate. The question then arises: Can the point of nonviolent resistance be established without appealing to religious figures or to God as the source of the goodness that ultimately grounds the nonviolent resister's admittedly difficult actions?

Pose this question: Can an individual act in accordance with the principles of nonviolent resistance while not believing in Christianity or, even more fundamentally, not believing in God? Discussion of this question will enhance students' understanding of what it means to be a human being and also why, given this understanding, it is incumbent on them to respect their fellow humans. The reasons King presents in this passage for such respect depend on a supreme being. However, the goodness that inspires the nonviolent resister in the drive for justice can be based on reasons derived from the simple fact of human beings coexisting on the same planet and the intrinsic value that we all as individuals enjoy simply by virtue of this shared existence.

As a subsidiary topic for discussion, ask this question: Which of these two justifications—that based on God and religion or that based on the intrinsic dignity of being human—presents the stronger rationale for accepting the principles of nonviolent resistance? Students who are religious tend to support the first alternative (effectively agreeing with King), but not all students are religious and not all religious students are Christian. The question is useful to pursue, especially with a class characterized by wide cultural diversity, since it sets in relief the function of religious belief in this context. It also shows students that it is possible to justify something as fundamental as an adherence to nonviolent resistance in order to achieve social justice by appealing to a basic feature of their experience—interaction with other humans—which they tend to take for granted as obvious and lacking any deep significance. The world of individual human beings constitutes (as the great German philosopher Immanuel Kant put it) a "kingdom of ends," and if students can grasp that each human being is worthy of respect and justice, then King's principles will have been established, although for reasons other than those he himself asserts.

In the last analysis, the practice of nonviolent resistance is open to various forms of philosophical justification, but however this matter may be resolved, we must be grateful to Martin Luther King not only for the example of his life and leadership, but also for the thoughtful development of his beliefs, especially regarding the implementation of social justice according to means that accomplish this end and at the same time reduce the extent and degree of violence that so pervades contemporary American society.

Curricular Integration

Perhaps the most dramatic arena for discussing the philosophical relevance of Martin Luther King's position on nonviolence is to pit it against the counterposition embodied in Malcolm X's oft-quoted slogan "By any means necessary." For King, it is a matter of principle (see Passages 2 and 3) that the end does not justify the means. Thus, even if an end—social justice—is clearly good, certain means—violence—are inappropriate to achieve that end. Therefore, King's position apparently implies that, if violence is the only way to produce social justice, then social justice is impossible to justify on moral grounds. By contrast, Malcolm X's position assumes that the end, if socially desirable, certainly does justify the means regardless of the character of the means so employed.

Question: Which is the best approach for achieving social justice? The most compelling—and heated—discussions of this question have occurred in classrooms with an approximately even racial mix. However, I have observed energetic and perceptive discussions in classrooms composed almost exclusively of one race. Furthermore, the division of sides on this issue has never been according to strict racial lines even when the classes are equally divided racially. Thus, the given racial makeup of the class will have no essential bearing on the direction in which debate of this issue will follow.

The subject in which to pursue this discussion is social studies, but as a subject area broadly defined. In the discussions that I have observed since the outset of my adventures with younger students, the range of topics emerging from this dispute has been considerable. Here are three:

Areas of Analysis

Psychological: Students have observed that an individual living under oppression and accepting King's principles of nonviolent resistance becomes tantamount to a boiler under continually increasing internal pressure. At some point, the pressure must be released, and when this release occurs, the individual will explode. Since such an explosion will doubtless produce harmful actions, either to other individuals or to the person undergoing the pressure, students arguing this point infer that on psychological grounds the theory of nonviolent resistance is faulty and potentially damaging to given individuals. It would follow from this line of argument that the expression of frustration through violence would, in fact, be "healthy."

My practice in the face of this point is to admit that such intense frustration could occur, but insist that it can be controlled if the person is thinking clearly and keeps his or her eye directly on the end to be achieved (i.e., social justice following nonviolent principles). The point here is that, even if such intense frustration is produced, (a) it will dissipate over time once the reason for enduring the frustration is firmly kept in view, and (b) on an even more fundamental level, our rational good sense has the power to control our emotions. The issue is important, since how people behave in social settings depends at least in part on their own individual psychological constitutions. But, the

teacher will determine the value of pursuing this kind of discussion.

Historical: A different approach to the question is to ask whether, if King had not lived, social justice in the country would have reached its present state. A variation on this question: If more people had followed Malcolm X's principles than followed King's, would the degree of social justice in the country be greater, less, or the same as it is at present? Strictly speaking, questions of this sort do not admit rigorous answers since the justification of answers depends on what would happen if a counterfactual claim about history were true. Nonetheless, analyzing these possibilities is worthwhile because students will introduce reasons explaining why they think that either King's or Malcolm X's position is stronger and would produce greater positive effects if implemented. As a footnote, although it has not happened on every occasion, it is fascinating to see students appeal to Passage 3 while discussing this question. They then argue that, if Malcolm X's approach is followed, the result admittedly might be a greater degree of social justice or the same degree of social justice achieved in less time, but at the high price of having produced residual ill will, if not something stronger, and that, as a result, internal violence of spirit would remain even if external violence had been curtailed. Furthermore, they say, since internal vio-

lence often leads to external violence, it is not clear that, in the long run (a phrase often used in this context by especially perceptive students), a quick solution (Malcolm X's approach) is better than a slower, but more thorough solution (King's approach).

Philosophical: The nature of justice has been a concern of philosophers since Plato's *Republic,* and a thorough philosophical analysis and critique of the thinking outlined in the passages quoted from King would have to take a stand on the meaning of justice, both in individuals and in society. Here are two more circumscribed topics that nonetheless require adopting a decidedly philosophical standpoint as a prelude to discussion:

• *Question 1: If violence is the only way to achieve social justice, does the end justify the means in this case?*

In a recent discussion of King, an African American 8th grader who had been generally reticent to speak in prior sessions of the philosophy program raised her hand and said that, although she agreed with King's approach as a matter of principle, if all types of nonviolent resistance had been tried and none of them had succeeded, then it was her belief that "by any means necessary" made sense and that violence was justified. But, and she emphasized this point on her own, only if it were clear that all nonviolent courses of action were exhausted would she side with the Malcolm X approach. The young lady presented this case with considerable feeling and thoughtfulness, and I was quite moved by the position (and also by the fact that she had conquered her reluctance to speak in order to contribute her thoughts to what was, for her, obviously an important issue).

Of course, being moved by a student's sincerity is one thing; accepting the reasoning that resides within that sincerity is something else. The question here is whether King's position allows this kind of argumentative end-run, as it were, or whether—as claimed above—he would say that under no circumstances is violence allowed in order to achieve an end, regardless of how just and noble that end may be and how strapped we are in terms of the available means. As philosophers are want to say in such situations, the point is vexed! And, as happens more often than my vanity would like to admit during my philosophical discussions with kids, I am not certain of the answer.

- *Question 2. Should reparations be made to African Americans in the present given that injustice toward them (i.e., institutional slavery) has occurred in the past?*

This is a "hot button" issue that is a natural topic to pursue in light of what has been introduced above in our review of King's thinking. Because of time limitations, I have never had an opportunity to pursue this issue with younger students, but I am positive—in part because I have had these discussions often with college students—that it would be both worthwhile and thoroughly energizing for all concerned. Note that to answer this question in the affirmative implies that one's understanding of justice rests on a certain understanding of the relation between justice and history. If I must contribute to reparations because of something my ancestors may have done, then it would seem to follow that I am in some essential sense responsible for my ancestors' behavior. In effect, the implementation of social justice would then span the movement of historical time; it cannot be restricted to a certain epoch or period if reparations from current citizens are deemed justified for something done by citizens who lived in the past. This is only one aspect of the topic; many more will become evident once discussion has begun.

These two questions represent a small sample of the issues that arise when the topic of social justice is at hand. It may be hoped that a thoughtful and careful examination of Martin Luther King's speeches and writings on this topic might inspire students to be more sensitive to the question of justice writ large, as well as more aware of the importance of guiding their individual relations to other human beings—all human beings—in accordance with fairness and fundamental respect.

Reference

King, M. L. (1990). *Testament of hope: The essential writings and speeches of Martin Luther King* (James Melvin Washington Ed.). New York: Harper.

CHAPTER 9

Feminism and Social Justice

Important philosophy is not always produced by philosophers—a claim that is not as paradoxical as it might initially appear. The discussions in previous chapters have concentrated on figures such as Plato, Aristotle, Augustine, Aquinas, and Rousseau. These individuals devoted their lives to thinking and writing about the classic issues of philosophy, hence their designation as "philosophers." But, philosophers have hardly cornered the market on philosophy's etymology: love of wisdom. Indeed, anyone who takes an intense interest in serious issues and is willing to spend the requisite time and energy thinking and writing about these issues can produce work that is philosophical in character, even if the author may not have devoted his or her life to philosophy in its canonic sense. A good example is Martin Luther King, Jr. on justifying the principles of nonviolence, the subject of the previous chapter.

Another exemplary case in point is the individual who serves as the centerpiece of the present chapter: bell hooks, the pseudonym for Gloria Watkins. Born in 1952, Watkins holds a doctorate in English literature and has taught at the City University of New York. In addition, she is an important and influential social commentator, lecturer, and author of a spectrum of publications, including a number of works on feminism and social justice. Gloria Watkins uses the pen name "bell hooks," first, to honor the memory of her maternal great-grandmother, an outspoken social critic in her own time, and second, to direct attention toward the writings she has produced, rather than to the persona of their author, whose name, if the convention of written speech were followed, would be written with upper-case letters.

The following excerpts are taken from *Feminist Theory: From Margin to Center*, published in 1984. The views developed in this work have been reexamined and developed in later writings by bell hooks, but they represent a core position that remains worth careful examination. The title of the work is indicative of its main argument: We will move from the margins of feminism (i.e., from a position that

bell hooks

runs around the external limits of its concerns) into the center of what, for bell hooks, is the true goal of feminism once that term is properly understood.

My experience has been that students in their middle school years are keenly aware of questions and problems pertaining to feminism and social justice in general. Issues in these areas are framed and developed in *Feminist Theory* in a way that affords young students expansive opportunities to enhance their understanding of a variety of basic philosophical concepts and positions, all of which revolve around questions concerning values that human beings display— or, perhaps, should display—when they interact with other human beings. Furthermore, the process of reflecting on the concepts embedded in the passages appearing below will introduce a number of considerations pertaining to the practice of critical thinking (the relevance of which will also be noted in what follows).

Passage 1

The importance of having reliable definitions in hand when attempting to understand the implications derived from fundamental philosophical concepts has been emphasized throughout the chapters in Part I. In this introductory passage, bell hooks announces that feminism, taken as a label or rubric to name a range of issues and positions, is characterized by such heterogeneous viewpoints that even those working from within that group cannot fully agree on exactly what that label should be taken to represent. As we shall see, it will be part of the burden of her discussion to argue for a certain interpretation of feminism that is decidedly broader in definitional scope than that held by many individuals who refer to themselves as "feminists."

Passage 2

The phrase "women's lib" became in the 1960s a sort of slogan—or, perhaps, war cry— to embody a movement that was aimed primarily at liberating women from long-standing, but artificially imposed social constraints. For contemporary kids, the '60s may verge on ancient history, so it is doubtless a prudent exercise to ask them to identify some of the social conditions and problems that faced women during that decade and beyond, since, in many important respects, these problematic constraints remain even to this day.

A "liberated" woman was typically thought of as an individual who had been emancipated from what often were the domineering attitudes and restrictive actions of men, whether in the family or, more widely, in formal education, business, or the workplace generally. This woman was liberated if she had secured a social position, including educational and work opportunities, which allowed her to compete with men for the same desired ends. Such a sta-

1. A central problem within feminist discourse has been our inability to either arrive at a consensus of opinion about what feminism is or accept definition(s) that could serve as points of unification.

2. Most people in the United States think of feminism or the more commonly used term "women's lib" as a movement that aims to make women the social equals of men.

3. It is now evident that many women active in feminist movement were interested in reform as an end in itself, not as a stage in the progression toward revolutionary transformation.

4. Particularly as regards work, many liberal feminist reforms simply reinforced capitalist, materialist values (illustrating the flexibility of capitalism) without truly liberating women economically.

5. Feminism is a struggle to end sexist oppression. Therefore, it is necessarily a struggle to eradicate the ideology of domination that permeates Western culture on various levels as well as a commitment to reorganizing society so that the self-development of people can take precedence over imperialism, economic expansion, and material desires.

6. . . . our own analysis would require an exploration of all aspects of women's political reality. This would mean that race and class oppression would be recognized as feminist issues with as much relevance as sexism.

7. As a black woman interested in feminist movement, I am often asked whether being black is more important than being a woman; whether feminist struggle to end sexist oppression is more important than the struggle to end racism and vice-versa. All such questions are rooted in competitive either/or thinking, the belief that the self is formed in opposition to an other. . . . Most people are socialized to think in terms of opposition rather than compatibility. Rather than see anti-racist work as totally compatible with working to end sexist oppression, they are often seen as two movements competing for first place.

8. Defining feminism as a movement to end sexist oppression is crucial for the development of theory because it is a starting point indicating the direction of exploration and analysis.

—From *Feminist Theory: From Margin to Center* by bell hooks tus is commonly considered a laudable goal and, if attained, a worthy accomplishment for a given society. However, for bell hooks, liberation characterized by these concerns marks only the beginning of feminism understood in its most important and socially effective sense.

Passage 3

This passage serves a number of purposes, both as critique and also as prelude. First, clarify the notion of an "end in itself." If I want to become educated, then I might seek that end *for the sake of something else* (e.g., to become wealthy or powerful). However, I might also want to become educated as "an end in itself," simply from the belief that education is a worthwhile goal, quite apart from any potentially practical purpose that it might serve in my life. In the present context, reform should be understood in terms of the limits tacitly imposed on feminism as a movement defined solely by economic concerns. The point is not that the pursuit and attainment of this goal is unworthy—only that it has been sought as an end in itself and, for bell hooks, this end is incomplete, existing only as a partial triumph on the way toward what the feminist movement should be seeking to attain once it has reached its proper destination.

A hint to the scope of this mission is contained in the phrase "revolutionary transformation." It is well to make certain that students have a firm sense of the connotation of the adjective *revolutionary*. References to the Revolutionary War in American history are obvious; less obvious, perhaps, is the revolution in Russia in the early 20th century. It will become apparent that the philosophical aftermath of this pivotal revolution, although understated at this juncture, is essential to the perspective on feminism bell hooks is developing.

Passage 4

This passage is subtle and can be used as a paradigm case for a certain type of critical thinking. For example, ask the students to "read between the lines" and identify bell hooks' attitude toward capitalism, the theory of economics that defines the American way. The intimate juxtaposition of "capitalist" with "materialist values" suggests that a proponent of the former also accepts, more or less uncritically, the latter. Although capitalism may or may not be wedded to materialism in the direct sense conveyed in this passage, bell hooks admits that the facility with which some of the practical desires and goals of women can become readily assimilated to the structure of capitalism attests to the "flexibility" of that economic system. This flexibility is, by itself, advantageous to women, as well as to the advocates of capitalism as an economic system. The danger, as she sees it, is that such flexible satisfaction of the range of immediate desires fueled by capitalism may blind women, and anyone who believes in feminism, to the relation between capitalism and "true" economic liberation for women. In other words, economics properly understood will connect the narrow concerns for material goods to a broader base of values. We are about to see what these values are and to whom they pertain.

Passage 5

As a prelude to discussing this complex passage, it is worthwhile to ask students to state the general meaning of *therefore*. This word is crucial to reasoning, whether philosophical or otherwise. *Therefore* signals that what follows is a conclusion, presumably a statement or assertion concluded from a series of premises that, collectively, support that conclusion. Note, then, the sequence of bell hooks' reasoning. She claims that feminism "is a struggle to end sexist oppression." She concludes that this struggle is therefore "necessarily" a struggle to "eradicate the ideology of domination that permeates Western culture," as well as a commitment to "reorganizing society" in a certain way. The inferred transition, if examined with care, is quite dramatic. The argument is that feminism, properly understood, is a struggle of a much vaster scope than simply seeking the end of sexist oppression, the avowed purpose of the movement in the eyes of so many of its proponents. How, then, does the reasoning in the passage justify the introduction of this broadened treatment of feminism?

Clarify for the students that the phrase "ideology of domination" refers to a system of ideas that drives those who hold these beliefs to dominate or control other peoples or cultures. According to bell hooks, this ideology permeates Western culture. In other words, it is inherent in the Western mentality to control others in different parts of the world. The question that arises: What is the connection between this ideology and oppression understood strictly as sexist in intent and practice?

The global implications of this passage should be emphasized: bell hooks sees the oppression that is part of sexism to be similar or identical to the kind of oppression resident in other forms of control. Because of this much broader sense of oppression, the "self-development of peoples" is hindered or blocked altogether. The Western approach to culture and society is so pervasive and dominant that peoples in other parts of the world—a world becoming increasingly smaller by virtue of rapidly spreading forms of technology—are no longer able to develop their own cultures as an expression of their individual history and social concerns. For bell hooks, such a limitation is a form of oppression and, importantly, is of a piece with the oppression found in the interaction of men and women and the domination of the latter by the former. Her assertion is that the ultimate goal of feminism is a reorganization of society ordered in such a way that these

oppressed peoples will be liberated from dominating Western influences and thereby be allowed to establish their own culture and destiny. The question that remains, however, is how she has justified the shift from feminism understood as an attempt to end sexism as one form of oppression to the conclusion that feminism should be broadened to include all forms of oppression.

Passage 6

This is perhaps the key theoretical passage in this adaptation of bell hooks' position. First, ask what the students understand by "women's political reality." In context, political does not refer to whether a woman votes Republican, Democrat, or Independent. "Political" here is closer to the ancient Greek conception of the *polis*, or city, encompassing everything characterizing a member of the city's social life and environment. This more pervasive reality is what must be explored. Once we venture into this larger sphere, then we will recognize the kinship between sexism—which has been the dominant concern of the feminist—and racism, as well as all forms of class oppression (i.e., class understood primarily in an economic sense). In sum, the political reality of women encompasses all forms of social injustice, not merely that based on gender, since women live in a society that necessarily includes all forms of social interaction.

Passage 7

This is also a pivotal passage, and from a variety of perspectives. I gradually realized that the conclusion established in this passage would serve as an excellent "leading" question to initiate a session. Begin the class by asking, without preamble or explanation of any sort, "Which is the more important issue in social justice: sexism or racism?" A variety of responses will be offered. Most students answer that racism is the more important problem. But, a discussion ensues almost immediately, and disagreement—occasionally becoming quite animated—is frequent.

From a strictly philosophical perspective, the answer chosen to this crucial question bears critical scrutiny only in light of the reason or reasons given to support it. The justification for racism as the more important issue is typically based on the severity resulting from oppressive conduct. Thus, students will cite the fact that racism can, and tragically often has, resulted in death for those who are oppressed, whereas sexism does not, at least as a rule, have such fatal consequences. Therefore, they argue, since the results of racism are more severe than the results of sexism, racism is the more important social problem. By contrast, those who select sexism argue that there are more oppressed women in the world than there are oppressed peoples, since women constitute at least half of the human population. Therefore, these students respond, since more human beings are oppressed by sexism than by racism, it follows that sexism is the more important social problem.

These answers are informative from the standpoint of critical thinking. Two very different kinds of answers have been given to the original question: *qualitative*, that is, that racism is more important because of the type of consequence that oppression of this form can cause; *quantitative*, that is, that sexism affects a greater number of people than racism. Thus, the students are responding to the question from different perspectives. (If pursued, the issue becomes one of deciding whether the number of people involved is more or less important as a reason than what might happen to a certain group of people if racial oppression becomes as drastic as it can—and has—become.)

From a more theoretical perspective, this is the juncture where bell hooks has effectively justified the claim made earlier, in Passage 5,

that feminism properly understood entails the elimination of all forms of oppression, not just the restricted oppression men have forced upon women. The attempt to divorce racism from sexism rests on the tacit assumption that working to end one form of oppression precludes working to end another form—indeed, all forms—of oppression. As bell hooks points out, the tendency is to dichotomize when we think—either this or that, x or y, but not both. However, reflection on the realities under scrutiny will reveal the compatibility of racism and sexism as equally virulent forms of oppression. We will then discern that the problem is oppression, not simply this or that form of it. Once this realization has become concrete, our resolve should be to eliminate oppression by attacking its corroding presence whenever and wherever it appears.

Passage 8

The approach to feminism taken here may appear, initially, to be inconsistent with the thinking developed in Passage 7 since the burden of that passage was to extend the proper scope of feminism to its edges, as it were, to the boundaries of oppression wherever and in whatever form it may occur. However, the point to be emphasized is that feminism considered as a movement to end sexist oppression is only a starting point. For bell hooks, consideration of this minimal characterization of feminism, even though it is only partially accurate, introduces the thoughtful person to the question of oppression in all its myriad forms, whether blatant or subtle. To introduce students to this kind of concern at a young age is surely one small, but significant way to reduce the destructiveness of oppression.

Curricular Integration

The context of bell hooks' discussion falls readily into the area of social studies. A number of questions relevant for student discussion have already been raised in the commentary on the passages examined from feminist theory. The following list outlines additional topics students will find engaging and informative to debate.

1. *Is it possible to define terms such as "feminism" or "justice" in ways that, even if not commanding universal agreement, will at least facilitate meaningful discussion?*

The larger question here concerns the nature of definition as such: How is it possible to define terms that appear to be as slippery and contentious as those animating bell hooks' position? This inquiry is especially pertinent for issues arising in social settings since the discussion and resolution of these issues require at least some consensus on the meanings of the words and concepts employed in the discussions. But, the question extends to the physical sciences, as well, which must eventually come to grips with problems of definition even as technological advances for studying nature become more and more sophisticated. Some analysis or review of principles of definition

may be worth discussing as an introduction to the issues raised by bell hooks.

Another dimension of critical thinking also often emerges in this and related discussions. Do the answers to such questions depend on gender? Would we expect a young man to answer in one way and a young woman to answer in another way (perhaps the opposite) just because the former is male and the latter is female? For example, responses to the racism/sexism question (raised in discussion of Passage 7 above) tend to fall, at least initially, along gender lines: Females think sexism is more important, males think racism is more important (or, perhaps, that sexism is not as important as the females believe it to be). But, do females answer in this way just because they are females and males just because they are males? If so, then it may be useful to review the relevance of *ad hominem* argumentation in these kinds of discussion. An argument *ad hominem*, or "to the person," aims at the speaker, rather than what the speaker says (or writes). Although it is certainly reasonable for females, regardless of age, to feel the pressure of sexism, the question of which form of oppression is more important should be addressed according to its own merits, rather than according to its effects on one individual. The same considerations hold, of course, for males.

Gifted students tend to be as prone to this kind of argumentative bias as anyone. However, my experience has been that additional discussion of the question at hand establishes for the students the realization that their individual interests must be assessed in light of their place within society as a whole. In other words, even if I may be oppressed racially (or by sexism), I must attempt to see the problem in the largest context possible in order to arrive at a conclusion serving the best interests of everyone in society. My concerns are important to me; that goes without saying. But, I share my concerns with those of others, and our concerns will, on occasion, be in conflict with one another. The

recognition that such conflict is common amidst the welter of the world's affairs will be an invaluable aid in formulating ways to resolve or at least defuse such conflict.

2. *Is capitalism as practiced in the United States an essentially materialistic economic system?*

The purchase of goods is essential to capitalism, and if "goods" refer predominantly, if not exclusively, to material goods, then the connection between capitalism and materialism necessarily follows. If so, the question that must be asked is whether the materialistic dimension of capitalism can be—or, more basically, *should be*—limited by other considerations. bell hooks' position establishes a relation of deep intimacy between the two phenomena, so much so that, in her mind, the resulting materialism makes it difficult for the protagonists of capitalism to recognize other, more fundamental realities, such as the forms of oppression that are rife around the world (and, unfortunately, still in many regions of the United States).

If students take the time to reflect on capitalism and on what they may perceive to be their inherent need to acquire "things"—whether of fashion, technology, or what have you—then it is possible that they might realize the need to attend to the nonmaterial dimension of the world. Of course, demonstrating this dimension to students and their obligation to heed its demands is not readily accomplished. Is it possible to establish a system of minimal needs that every citizen of a capitalistic society should possess? If so, is it then relevant to suggest that, until every member of this society achieves these minimal needs, even a capitalistic society must restrain its desire for acquisition of additional goods? Discussion of these questions will be energetic, if not heated!

3. *Is the United States in any sense an imperialistic society?*

One might immediately answer this question with a resounding "No!," at least if imperialism means actively attempting to acquire political control of neighboring or even distant lands. However, ask the students whether more subtle forms of imperialism exist. For example, if a country has a powerful capitalistic system, does that country inevitably exercise a kind of cultural imperialism via its capitalistic prowess, not only on neighboring countries, but, especially in a world defined by a global economy, on nations everywhere? bell hooks refers to the domination of other peoples by Western culture "on many levels" (Passage 5). Is it good if American popular culture—films, music, fashion, etc.—becomes so dominant that the counterpart expressions of less economically viable cultures begin to vanish from the pressures of U.S. advertising and sales?

This question leads to sustained and serious discussion of culture in general and of the importance of respecting and sustaining cultural differences as they exist around the world. Indeed, these concerns arise within the United States itself as the number of immigrants from a variety of nations continue to seek a better life in a democratic setting. Ask whether the students think that a cultural balance among the various nationalities and ethnic groups residing in the United States is a good thing and, if so, whether they believe that such a balance is a foreseeable goal.

4. *If I am apolitical—not caring about political issues, not taking part in political discussions, even perhaps not voting in elections when eligible to do so—can I still consider myself a good citizen?*

Recent national elections have drawn approximately 50% of eligible voters, implying that half the American population is sufficiently apolitical not to participate in the process that decides who governs the country. How essential is it to the well-being of the country—and, by extension, to that of each individual citizen—to be active in political affairs? The answer depends on the meaning of "good citizen," and determining the characteristics that go into good citizenship will provide a worthwhile forum for student discussion. Ask: What defines a good citizen of a country?

5. *In order to secure social justice, which problem is more important: racism or sexism?*

The discussion examined in this chapter (presented in the commentary on Passage 7) contends that racism and sexism are two sides of the same problem and that both are equally fundamental. In fact, bell hooks contends that an individual addressing either problem is logically required to work to eliminate, or at least to mitigate, both problems. However, this position is open to discussion by considering the possibility that either racism or sexism is, in fact, more serious and therefore more morally pressing. One gambit to initiate discussion is to ask students whether they have personally witnessed or been the subject of oppression in some form. Students may then be invited to offer reasons either to justify one form of oppression as more urgent or to reinforce bell hooks' position that forms of oppression are all of a piece and require unified attention.

6. *How should society be reorganized in order to reduce, if not eliminate, the reality of oppression?*

This question can serve as the culminating inquiry for this reading. Ask the students what they would change in society in order to increase the possibility that human beings will not be tempted to oppress other human beings. This question may be pursued in at least two directions: (a) nationally, within one's home country (e.g., the U.S.), and (b) internationally, between countries. The teacher should be prepared for a wide variety of answers, each of which, if deemed material to the problem, should be subjected to critical evaluation by the rest of the class. If, for example, the appeal is made to increase education on the grounds that oppression is ultimately rooted in forms of ignorance, then follow-up questions may ask (a) what kind of subjects would such education include to distinguish it from current educational policy? and (b) as a subsidiary and practical concern, how would this kind of change be funded from the current society?

According to bell hooks, revolutionary change is required in order to address this situation. But, just how "revolutionary" would these changes be? Is she intimating that some socialist reforms will be necessary in order to eliminate, or at least reduce, the reality of oppression? And, even if such revolutionary changes could be effected in the U.S., what would have to be done in parallel fashion to the regimes in other countries that, from our perspective, are oppressive in one way or another? Is a change in education a feasible avenue to follow in order to produce the kind of extensive reformation of human conduct that bell hooks is envisioning? If not, then what additional aspects of society would have to be changed in order to have a positive effect on reducing oppression?

The teacher should not expect the class to reach full agreement concerning any of the alternatives raised in response to such fundamental and all-pervasive questions. The discussion of points made in the process of seeking revolutionary change will, however, be both spirited and illuminating. In general, it is a singular virtue of the readings discussed above that they help make students aware of aspects of the concept of social justice that they either tend to overlook entirely or relegate to a level of secondary importance with respect to their own personal concerns. A heightened appreciation of the reality of oppression, and of connections that link different forms of oppression, stands as a laudable result from consideration of bell hooks' decidedly philosophical approach to the nature of feminism as an active agent in the promulgation of social justice.

Reference

hooks, b. (1984). *Feminist theory: From margin to center.* Boston: South End Press.

CHAPTER 10

Technology: Servant or Destroyer?

What would our life be like without cars, appliances, televisions, and computers? In fact, what would life be like without axes, saws, shovels, and wheelbarrows—not to mention knives and forks? What if all we had between our bare skin and the wilds of nature was . . . whatever our hands could somehow manage to control?

Technology is everywhere. Its products thoroughly permeate the fabric of contemporary life, more or less so depending on where we are in the world, but with virtually all societies characterized by at least some technological artifacts. Technology is, in many ways, a study in opposites: Thus, atomic power produces much for the public good, yet the awesome energy of the atom can also be released to such a frightful degree that the cataclysmic destruction of the earth remains a continuing possibility. On a somewhat less dramatic scale, the burdens of daily life have been eased by the creation of a wide variety of labor-saving machines; but, if, as many members of the scientific community believe, the ozone layer is being depleted as a consequence of the operation of these machines, then it is not clear that the amount of labor saved would justify the eventual denuding of the planet. The emergent question then: Is technology the savior of humanity, or is it the tool of humanity's ultimate destruction?

Chapters 8 and 9 have considered questions of social justice (Martin Luther King, Jr.) and gender equality (bell hooks). These questions are clearly important, and to some degree they concern virtually everyone on the planet. However, the question of technology is arguably, from a logical standpoint, more crucial than either of these questions. For if the doomsday scenario resulting from technology gone berserk and wreaking cosmic destruction is a real possibility, then whether or not people treat each other justly and whether or not the genders treat each other equally become moot for the simple reason that, if the Earth can no longer sustain life, *there will no longer be any people*! Issues of social justice and equality presuppose the existence of people capable of treating each other in these ways. But, the attendant problems of technology, if not resolved, will eliminate the relevance of these issues by virtue of eliminating their necessary condition: human beings. In that respect, the problem of technology is *the* most pressing practical—and philosophical—issue we face today.

Technology is derived from the Greek word *techne*, which also provides the root of the word *technique*. Technology began as soon as humans began to make tools, to fashion nature in ways so that the products of human technique became capable of controlling nature to suit our ends. However, technology as a subject of philosophical concern and analysis is of much more recent vintage. The German philosopher Martin Heidegger (1889–1976) was one of the first major thinkers to address the question of technology and to reflect on the meaning of this world-spanning phenomenon. Heidegger is often categorized as an existentialist, and although some of his earlier writings do consider problems and questions that became the subject of philosophers such as Jean-Paul Sartre, Heidegger preferred not to be associated with that label. Heidegger considered himself as, simply, a thinker, someone who attempts to meditate on issues that are important not only to philosophers, but also to any responsible and thoughtful person living in our time.

The passages given below are drawn from a pair of thematically related essays Heidegger wrote in the early 1950s: "The Thing" and "The Question Concerning Technology." These essays are the result of many years of reflection and therefore exhibit a certain dense-ness of texture as Heidegger renders his thoughts into language. Furthermore, as part of his philosophical strategy, the language Heidegger uses to express these thoughts is intended, in part, to reorient our approach to the concept of technology by the use of words that are in some way unusual. It is fair to say

Martin Heidegger

that Heidegger's style, especially in his essays, is often elliptic and elusive. However, the passages introduced here are relatively straightforward in form and content.

It should also be mentioned by way of pre-amble that kids find the topic of technology to be of great interest to discuss, especially in light of the central problem that Heidegger's approach brings into the open. Some of the most fiery disputes I have witnessed during my years of philosophizing with young students were ignited in the context defined by the Heideggerian treatment of technology. Answers to the questions that arise in these disputes are, as one might expect, not readily established. But, the effort involved in understanding the problem of technology can only enhance our appreciation of the fundamental importance of one of the defining phenomena of our time—indeed, perhaps, as already noted, the most important dimension of contemporary exis-tence.

1. All distances in time and space are shrinking. Man now reaches overnight, by plane, places which formerly took weeks and months of travel. He now receives instant information, by radio, of events which he formerly learned about only years later, if at all.... The peak of this abolition of every possibility of remoteness is reached by television, which will soon pervade and dominate the whole machinery of communication.

2. Near to us are what we usually call things. But what is a thing? Man has so far given no more thought to the thing as a thing than he has to nearness.

3. When we pour wine into the jug [*Heidegger's example of a thing*], the air that already fills the jug is simply displaced by a liquid. Considered scientifically, to fill a jug means to exchange one filling for another.

4. These statements of physics are correct. By means of them, science represents something real, by which it is objectively controlled. But— is this reality the jug? No. Science always encounters only what its kind of representation has admitted beforehand as an object possible for science.

5. We shall be questioning concerning technology, and in so doing we should like to prepare a free relationship to it. The relationship will be free if it opens our human existence to the essence of technology. When we can respond to this essence, we shall be able to experience the technological within its own bounds.

6. The current conception of technology, according to which it is a means and a human activity, can therefore be called the instrumental and anthropological definition of technology.... Even the power plant with its turbines and generators is a man-made means to an end established by man. Even the jet aircraft and the high-frequency apparatus are means to ends. A radar station is of course less simple than a weather vane.... And certainly a sawmill in a secluded valley of the Black Forest is a primitive means compared with the hydroelectric plant on the Rhine River.

7.   But suppose now that technology were no mere means, how would it stand with the will to master it?

8.   Technology is therefore no mere means. Technology is a way of revealing. If we give heed to this, then another whole realm for the essence of technology will open itself up to us. It is the realm of revealing, i.e., of truth.

9.   It remains true, nonetheless, that man in the technological age is, in a particularly striking way, challenged forth into revealing. That revealing concerns nature, above all, as the chief storehouse of the standing energy reserve.

10.   . . . essential reflection upon technology and decisive confrontation with it must happen in a realm that is, on the one hand, akin to the essence of technology and, on the other, fundamentally different from it.

11.   Such a realm is art. But certainly only if reflection upon art for its part does not shut its eyes to the constellation of truth concerning which we are questioning. . . . the more questioningly we ponder the essence of technology, the more mysterious the essence of art becomes.

—From "The Thing" and "The Question Concerning Technology" by Martin Heidegger

Passages 1–4 are taken from the essay "The Thing." These passages set the philosophical scene for a more concentrated pursuit of technology by reorienting the common-sense understanding of technological things toward a more fundamental, and therefore more revealing, account.

Passage 1

It is a good idea to reinforce the sense in which time and space are "shrinking." Kids are quick to realize that he does not mean the shrinking of time and space literally, but rather our ability to traverse these basic realities. Thus, one could ride a horse from Chicago to New York, but it would take weeks, while one can drive this distance in less than a day (going non-stop), and one can fly there in 2 hours. The distance in miles is a constant, but the time it takes to cover this distance decreases as technology advances. Similarly, whereas it took approximately 2 months before Londoners learned that they had lost the American colonies in the Revolutionary War, now anything that happens in the world can be known throughout the globe in a matter of seconds. Finally, Heidegger's point about the dominance of television was prescient when it was written in 1950, since at that time the future of television as a rival to radio was not at all certain. Heidegger saw clearly that it would not be long before television became completely entrenched throughout the world as the dominant form of media communication. And so it has come to pass.

Passage 2

The move made in this passage is vintage Heidegger—simple on the surface, but with profound implications if one follows his lead. Ask whether the students can determine why Heidegger initiates the problem of technology by posing the question, "What is a thing?" As a supplemental question, ask about the referent to "thing" (i.e., to what can this word refer?). Students immediately observe, "Anything!" This abstractness and generality is precisely the way to begin to reflect on technology, since any object that is technological is also a *thing*. For Heidegger, just as what is "near" to us in nature or the world generally has never been the subject of thoughtful inquiry, so also is the fact that what exactly we mean when we call an object of any sort a "thing" has not been given its due attention. Heidegger intends to rectify that philosophically relevant omission.

Passage 3

A jug is, at least at first glance, a simple thing. It is used to carry a liquid from one place to another and to dispense that liquid. Students know that an empty jug is not really empty—it contains air. They also know that, if a liquid is poured into the jug, then the fluid air is displaced by a more cohesive liquid. A rudimentary scientific analysis of the reality of a jug would concentrate on these data and then move on to other matters. Heidegger's question: Does the scientific approach to the jug give us an exhaustive account of what the jug truly *is*, that is, the ultimate reality of the jug as the product of human artifice? Yes . . . and no.

Passage 4

Heidegger's point in this passage is perhaps not readily seen. The pivotal concept is that of control. Science controls the determination of the reality of the jug by approaching this entity from well-defined assumptions. An object, such as a jug, can be controlled scientifically if what is said and, apparently, known about that thing can be encompassed within measurable parameters. In this case, the reality of the jug emerges into tangible existence for science to the extent that what a jug does—contain something by way of displacement—enters a dimension such that this function of the jug can be measured according to publicly observable standards. This dimension of publicity, of measurable configurations open to anyone equipped with appropriate instruments to verify them, renders the jug accessible to the language and methods of science. Heidegger's point is not that the scientific approach to the reality of the jug is incorrect; rather, it is that science reduces things such as jugs—and everything else that comes under the purview of scientific inquiry—to modes of reality conditioned by empirical, or measurable, means. For Heidegger, the "thingness" of things, such as the way a jug displays its underlying reality as a technological device, must be determined by other considerations. How can this hidden reality be brought into the open?

Passages 5–10 are from the essay "The Question Concerning Technology." Although it will become evident that these passages do not provide a neatly capsulized definition of technology—Heidegger is not the kind of thinker who operates according to such a rigid rubric—Heidegger does offer to the careful student a thoughtful awareness of what must be considered in order to win a more penetrating understanding of the roots of technology.

Passage 5

The key term in this passage is *essence*, a word with an ancient heritage in the language of philosophy. The contrasting concept of essence is *existence*, and the fundamental distinction between these two dimensions of the reality of a thing goes back to the ancient Greek metaphysicians—and, as we saw in Chapter 7, it is fruitfully employed by the contemporary existentialist philosopher Jean-Paul Sartre. In brief, the essence of something is *what* makes that thing to be what it is; its existence is simply the fact *that* it is. Thus, whatever is the chalkness of chalk represents the essence of

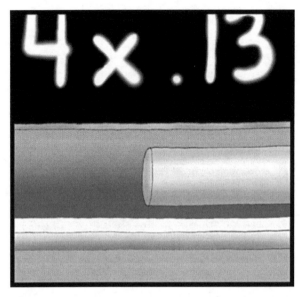

chalk; the fact that a piece of chalk rests on the chalkboard awaiting use illustrates the existence of chalk. The two concepts stand for basic and distinct approaches to the metaphysical analysis of things. In this case, Heidegger seeks to liberate, or to make free, the essence of technology; that is, he hopes to show, if possible, whatever makes technology to be what it is at its most basic level. If so liberated, then it may be possible for human beings as thinkers to experience technology at a depth sufficiently appropriate to understand its nature and limits.

Passage 6

This passage sets up the common approach to technology, an approach that Heidegger thinks is immediately attractive, but which, after careful reflection, becomes naive and simplistic. First introduce the relation of "means to an end" with an example or two. The piece of chalk provides a ready case: end = writing on the board, means = piece of chalk. Thus chalk is a means to an end: getting something written on the board. Another example: end = moving from point A to point B, means = automobile. Thus, a car is a means to an end. (It may be noted that the relation between means and end functions in the same fundamental way here as it does for Martin Luther King, but, in a very different context.)

Heidegger's examples at the end of the passage offer an opportunity for a simple, but useful instance of critical thinking. Ask the students to extend the sequence that Heidegger introduces: (a) sawmill; (b) hydroelectric plant; (c) . . . Not much coaxing is required before students answer "nuclear power plant," the next phase in the technology of producing power that Heidegger, writing in 1950, could not have known. Then ask, "What is the difference, in principle, between a sawmill, a hydroelectric plant, and a nuclear power plant?" Students quickly see that the best answer is "In principle there is no difference—all three produce power."

The relation between means and ends is so common and inbred in our thinking about everyday necessities that it probably is the primary conceptual core for what Heidegger has labeled the "instrumental" understanding of technology in general. We tend to think of technological devices, whether as simple as a piece of chalk or as decidedly complex as a nuclear power plant, as *instruments*, as means to achieving a certain end. Thus, if there is a problem to be solved, then we appeal to the capacity human beings possess to make a machine in order to solve that problem. Once the machine is in place and operating, whether jug or power plant, the end has been achieved. Thus, in essence, technology is nothing but instruments, means to ends. The question Heidegger wants us to consider is: Should technology be understood as *nothing but* means to ends?

Passage 7

Popular wisdom has it that technology can be used for either good ends or questionable (if not morally dubious) ends. The cloning of human beings is one of the most recent, and also one of the most dramatic, technological advances handled according to this bromide. It

seems evident that scientists will continue to work in this area until the cloning of human beings is achieved. But, as popular wisdom has it, whether this technology will then be employed for good or questionable ends—providing replacements for damaged or diseased organs in contrast to producing genetically customized offspring for picky prospective parents—is independent of the mechanical processes comprising that advance. The relevant philosophical point is that the distinction between means and ends completely saturates this popular belief about the essence of technology. For Heidegger, it is at precisely this juncture where the relevance of the means-ends distinction vanishes—if, that is, we approach technology from a more thoughtful direction.

The following question helps introduce this kind of thinking, and it always throws students into a tizzy. Ask: "Do we control technology, or does technology control us?" The initial response is overwhelmingly in favor of the former—we control technology. But, then, the glories of reflection set in and, almost without exception, an adventurous and courageous student will go against the majority view and begin to describe senses in which it appears that technology controls us. In effect, a position is established according to which technology has a life of its own, quite apart from those individual human beings who create technological devices and the masses of humans who expect, and then demand, these devices for their increased comfort and convenience.

Passage 8

Heidegger assumes that the essence of technology will not emerge if we look at its productions, simplistically in his eyes, merely in terms of the means-ends relationship. Our burden as thinkers is to ask, "What does technology reveal about human beings insofar as we derive the 'stuff' of technology from the world of nature about us?" It is this derivation from nature that,

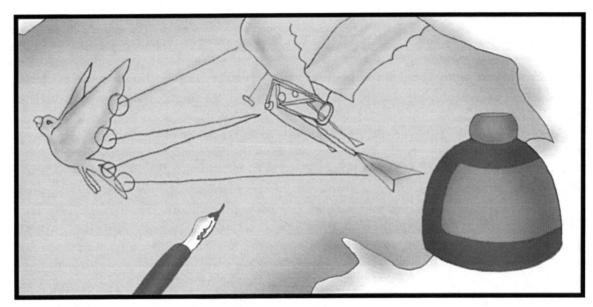

for Heidegger, provides the framework for eliciting the essence of technology, that characteristic or mode of being that all technological things share making them what they are.

Passage 9

What, then, does due reflection reveal about the essence of technology? Human beings, the instigators of technology, may now be seen not as stewards, but as exploiters of nature. Technology at its most basic level shows that human beings look at nature merely as a storehouse of possible energy and materials to be used for producing things that, in our estimate, will satisfy a broad gamut of needs and interests. Heidegger shifts the philosophical emphasis from the side of the thing, the technological device created, produced, and employed to serve our concerns, to the side of the human origin of that thing. How, then, should we proceed if we want to think more clearly and resonantly about the "thingness" of technology?

Passage 10

I preserved the paragraph break in quoting this passage because the reader should be aware of the emphasis Heidegger places on art in the context of continuing to reflect at an essential level on the question concerning technology. Heidegger claims that the realm of art is "akin" to technology and yet "fundamentally" different from it. Ask the students to explain this relation—how is technology like art and how does it differ from art? The former sense can be readily determined: Both result from human action and both make things. The complicated sense of the relation comes from the other direction, that is, determining how technology and art differ from one another. This question, which Heidegger raises, but leaves unanswered (he discusses art in other essays, although not in relation to technology), offers hope of penetrating the essence of technology more fully than has been done so far. Heidegger's approach to technology opens up a number of possible routes for additional reflection and for an increased understanding of what is, as noted, perhaps the most urgent issue before us today—and in the future.

Pursuing this topic with students discloses a number of thoughtful possibilities for a richer appreciation of both art as a distinctive form of human activity and technology, which, as the previous discussion has perhaps indicated, is a complex phenomenon in its own right. The following suggestions, arranged under two large subject headings, may be useful to point to the question of technology in contexts that are circumscribed within standard areas of study.

Curricular Integration

A. Science

The kinds of questions that can be introduced in the context of science cover a broad range, from issues that allow at least some form of empirical measurement as part of the context of analysis, to questions of a more speculative nature. Students enjoy discussing these issues, although it should be noted that these discussions may test the teacher's ability to keep the flow of ideas within a strictly scientific context. In that regard, the three topics outlined in this section show that the ultimate significance of science as a distinctively human pursuit cannot be divorced from other important activities that define the human condition.

1. It seems evident that many technological advances based on science simultaneously improve and harm, or at least in some way diminish, the quality of life. Television and the computer are obvious examples, among many others. Is it possible to measure or evaluate the benefits and harm produced by a given piece of technology? If so, and if the negative effects outweigh the positive, should this piece of technology be restricted or even eliminated?

2. There is an apparently inevitable transformation from (a) scientific knowledge pursued for its own sake to (b) the application of that knowledge to form technological things for practical purposes. Can this transformation be halted? In other words, is it at all feasible to envision the ongoing quest of science to expand our knowledge of nature without the consequent adaptation of the results of scientific inquiry toward what we perceive to be practical ends? If the answer to this question is negative, that is, that science inevitably and perhaps necessarily leads to technology, then it seems to follow that the potential and actual negative effects of technology indicated in (1) above will always be with us, since it is difficult to see how the negative and positive dimensions of technology can be separated from one another.

3. Finally, an even more fundamental question: If science leads necessarily to a wide variety of technological applications, then is it possible to halt scientific inquiry? The answer to this question seems to be an unequivocal "No!," and the response of students, even those not especially keen on science, has always borne out the certitude of this response. Human beings are, it seems, curious by nature, therefore science, if understood as little more than organized (and, frequently, mathematicized) curiosity, is an essential feature of the human drama. But, of course, this conclusion, if sound, clearly reestablishes the intimacy between science and technology, with all that follows from this intimacy in terms of the medley of effects from the pervasive presence of technological things in our world. One wonders about the kind of world that our descendants, both immediate and long-range, will inhabit.

B. Language Arts/Art

The conclusion of Heidegger's thoughtful pursuit of technology raises the possibility that understanding art will afford insight into technology. Discuss by attempting to define or characterize art so that what makes art to be what it is can be appreciated for its own sake and also as a catalyst for inquiry into the differences between art and technology. A jug is one thing; a Van Gogh painting of a jug is quite a different thing. What can be generalized about these differences to illuminate the essence of art and, eventually, to shed light on the essence of technology?

It should be emphasized in discussion that art in this context does not refer only to painting, but to any of the fine arts: music, dance, poetry, sculpture. This broad-based approach to art will make critical analysis more difficult since the obviously significant differences between, for example, a painting and a poem mean that characterizations of art that pertain to art as such will become necessarily general and abstract. However, the complexity of this discussion can only assist in sharpening our awareness of technology since the clearer we are about art in general, the more readily it should be possible to get closer to the essence of technology by identifying those characteristics that artistic things possess—and that technological things lack.

Encourage students to think about art from the broadest possible perspective, not simply in terms of this or that piece of art. This discussion should proceed to the point where a set of properties that seems to characterize art in general has been secured. This set is doubtless, by the nature of the inquiry, tentative. For example, students will frequently say that a characteristic that sets off a work of art is the fact that it is beautiful. However, someone is usually quick to respond that not all art is beautiful, and, on occasion, an especially acute younger thinker will note that beauty can perfectly well belong to nonartistic things (e.g., a sunset). So, the connection between beauty and art is not as firm as the investigator might want it to be, although there is a sufficient link to justify approaching art with beauty in mind since many, perhaps most, technological things are not considered to be beautiful. The point is

that, once a set of properties accruing to art has been established, then it will be possible to compare art with technology and attempt to discover what technology has in its essence that art in its essence does not possess. And, even if the desired set of properties cannot be established, the exercise of thinking through the various candidates students put forth provides an excellent arena for critical thinking.

Students will appreciate the difficulty, as well as the importance, of seeking a definition of such fundamental realities, especially when their influence concerns all of us. Furthermore, and from a more global perspective, the attempt to define technology and to determine its effects may recall Chapter 1, where definition as the vehicle for expressing a clear and accurate understanding of fundamental concepts was introduced and discussed. The problems that philosophers now consider are at times different from those that inspired the ancient Greek thinkers, but philosophy as a form of analysis and speculation continues to be one of the most compelling and enriching pursuits practiced by human beings. It may be hoped that the future of technology will not unduly interfere with, much less terminate, this pursuit, or of course everything else "noble and fair" (Plato, in the *Phaedrus*) that defines the human condition.

References

Heidegger, M. (1971). The thing. *In Poetry, language, thought* (pp. 165–186). New York: Harper.

Heidegger, M. (1977). The question concerning technology. In *The question concerning technology* (pp. 3–35). New York: Harper.

PART II

Education as Applied Philosophy

CHAPTER 11

Critical Thinking and Artistic Creation

Anumber of the suggestions for curricular integration offered in Part I revolved around the concept and practice of critical thinking. However, an educator with a serious interest in incorporating critical thinking into a school curriculum might feel the need to be an expert in critical thinking simply to evaluate the many existing approaches that bear that name. Furthermore, this problem would seem to be compounded if critical thinking and the creation of art were asserted to be intimately related to one another—so intimate that doing the latter incorporates essential dimensions of the former. But, these initial reservations, although noteworthy, need not deflect inquiry into the possibility of juxtaposing artistic creation and critical thinking in a middle or high school curriculum.

In fact, the following discussion describes an approach to curricular arts integration—indeed, the very making of art—that, when viewed from a certain broad-based, philosophical perspective, concurrently accomplishes three important educational ends. If the method of critical thinking outlined below is accepted as one possible paradigm of this process, then students who make art within academically defined subjects will not only acquire first-hand experience with artistic creativity, but will also become more adept at the art of critical thinking while they broaden and enhance their understanding of these subjects. In addition, the hands-on approach to thinking through philosophical questions and problems illustrated in the readings from Part I will contribute to students' ability to master critical thinking when applied to any of their more traditional subjects.

Critical Thinking: A Model

As noted above, exponents of critical thinking vary considerably concerning its precise structure. The following four-step model of critical thinking is a position that, both in philosophical scope and detail, can stand against other competing and divergent models. This approach is especially relevant for the types of thinking found in the humanities, but its principles are sufficiently expansive to accommodate adaptation to other disciplines, as well. The following outline states the structure of critical thinking in broad strokes. Note by way of anticipation that the example of arts education analyzed after this outline will illustrate the power of these principles in a way both practical and well suited to younger students.

I. State the Problem

The first step in critical thinking is that the student must have a clear understanding of what is expected and must be able to demonstrate this understanding by articulating this expectation.

II. Formulate a Hypothesis to Solve the Problem

Here the student embraces a broad selection of his or her experiences and focuses on those aspects that pertain to the problem. The aspects relevant to addressing the problem are then stated in a suitably general form.

III. Infer a Conclusion From This Hypothesis

Once the hypothesis has been established, the student infers a conclusion that pertains to, and ostensibly resolves, the problem at hand. This conclusion will usually take an "if . . . then" form, not perhaps in a consciously aware sense, but at the level of reflective inquiry. Thus, the student may think, "If things happen in a certain way, then this kind of event or conclusion will usually follow." The particular content of the "if . . . then" depends on the discipline that is being studied. When inquiry has reached this level, then following the rules of formal logic

and avoiding logical fallacies are key elements for success during this phase of critical thought.

IV. Evaluate the Strength of This Conclusion

At this juncture, critical thinking becomes an art. In order to determine the strength of the reasoned conclusion, the student must situate it in a broader context, often against competing conclusions drawn from other possible hypotheses. Plato's terse description of thinking as "the dialogue of the soul with itself" aptly evokes this internal process.

The student must then decide whether or not to accept this conclusion as reliable and, if reliable, whether or not to think and act in the world based on that conclusion. The formal canons of logic and right thinking must here be integrated with the flux of life as lived, which involves much more complexity than logic can cover by the essential inclusion of a learned sense of value. Thus, evaluating the conclusions drawn from the first three steps of the schematic outlined above for critical thinking includes reflecting on the transition from merely *thinking* about aspects of the world to *acting* in the world. Such complexity is why Aristotle speaks of "practical wisdom" as an essential prerequisite to complement the more structured and abstract aspects of critical thinking.

An Example of School Arts Integration

The following example illustrates how an arts context can be an occasion for the concurrent practice and development of critical thinking. More general thoughts about the pedagogical intersection of artistic creativity and critical thinking will be offered after discussion of this language arts example has been completed.

An English teacher is using a method called "Neutral Dialogue" to instill in her students an understanding and appreciation for the ways characters interact in a play. Here is one such dialogue:

> A. Hello.
> B. Hi.
> A. How was your day?
> B. Fine. And yours?
> A. Okay. The bus was late.
> B. Is that so?
> A. Yes.
> B. Did you get to school on time?
> A. 10 minutes late.
> B. Too bad.
> A. Well, I'm off to . . .
> B. 'Bye.

It should be evident why this exchange is called "Neutral Dialogue"—the language is very simple and what has been said is open to an enormous range of interpretation. The central purpose of this exercise is to invite students to *think* about what this dialogue might mean—depending on the personalities of the characters involved and the way in which they interact—and then to *perform* their thoughts by engaging in this dialogue as a sort of mini-drama. This is art in a very real sense: The student has taken a script, understood and interpreted its significance, and then transcribed that significance into a performance.

Presentation of and preparation for this exercise may be divided into five main steps as listed below. After stating this outline, we will then briefly examine each of these steps and show how students learn critical thinking while they are preparing this exercise.

1. Present the dialogue.
2. Define the characters.
3. Determine their intentions.
4. Determine their physical gestures.
5. Rehearse.

Depending on the type of drama being studied, the teacher can concentrate on Step 2 (defining characters), Step 3 (determining the characters' intentions), or Step 4 (determining the characters' physical gestures). Such shifts in focus allow the teacher to emphasize different aspects of dramatic action with correlative effects on students' awareness of these aspects in their reading and appreciation of dramatic literature, regardless of whether that literature is experienced as staged or in a purely literary setting.

How Artistic Creation Incorporates Critical Thinking

In the following analyses, those elements of the four-part model of critical thinking that provide the controlling feature in each step are designated (in brackets) as I–IV and have been placed at the head of each discussion.

1. *Present the Dialogue [I]*

The statement of the dialogue should make clear to the students that they are to study and reflect on what has been said—however spare it might be—and to interpret the content of what has been said in ways that will dramatically justify their understanding of the sense of the dialogue. Thus, the purely dramatic elements of the assignment depend on those aspects of critical thought that contribute to the students' understanding of the original text.

2. *Define the Characters [II, III]*

To define something means to set up limits so that the object or idea defined is seen as, ideally, "other than" everything else. In this case, the students are asked to define the characters of two people given a brief and neutral set of linguistic exchanges between them. The student must first have some understanding of character as the name for the traits and characteristics of a person involved in a dramatic situation. This step isolates the problem. Then, the student must be able to determine—from the text of the dialogue—what properties each character possesses.

Abstractly stated, human beings are ensembles of sameness and difference. One way in which we indicate these differences is (a) what we say to each other and (b) how we say it. Since no one person has all possible human attributes, students must decide which attributes to assign to the characters of A and B. This decision is based on and derives from what A and B say to each other. But, the amount of information disclosed in the exchanges is so scant that the student is compelled to situate each exchange—and also all the exchanges insofar as they form a set—in light of that student's understanding of human possibilities "writ large," as it were.

The result is a kind of induction, the first formal step in critical thinking. Here the student gathers together each exchange and then situates them against a backdrop of that student's awareness of forms of human interaction, comparing and contrasting the fund of experience relevant to the dialogue as a whole. The student then formulates a hypothesis: "If two characters meet and talk to each other as illustrated by this dialogue, then A is this type of person and B is that type of person." Thus, the student must generate an inductive approach to discerning the personal characteristics of each character based on that student's grasp of the meaning of the language constituting the dialogue. A subtle interplay emerges between the extreme brevity of the text and the immense richness of the student's individual experiences. From this interplay—especially vibrant perhaps

for the gifted, but common for kids generally—the student must decide what kind of personality A and B would display when they interact in a conversation of this sort.

3. Determine Their Intentions [II, III]

Once the student has broadly conceived of the character of A and B, then the student must move *from* a general sense of the types of personality A and B evince *to* the particular discourse they have directed toward each other. This transition in thought may be stated in a way that emphasizes its abstract or logical form: "If A was in a certain mood or situation, then A would say [this] to B." But, the student continues to think, and another hypothesis appears: "But, if A were in a different mood or situation, then A would say [something else] to B." Furthermore, upon additional reflection, the student would realize that the mood or situation also determines *how* A says something to B and, of course, *how* B responds to A.

For example, if A had had a terrible day, then the initial "Hello" might be said in a hollow and barely audible whisper, as if it were A's final living word. And if this day had been one of undiminished triumphs for B, then the "Hi" in response might be delivered with great gusto and zest. Reverse the day's situation for each character, and the way each character says these lines would also be reversed. Furthermore, if A and B are friendly—or unfriendly—rivals, then the elements of irony and sarcasm also become potential dramatic engines. And, of course, these are only a handful of an extremely large set of possibilities.

Assume that the student notices that B interrupts A at the climax of the exchange, and abruptly ends the conversation. Armed with this observation, the student concludes that B's attitude toward A is defined by only a superficial interest in A's world. The student then reasons as follows: "If B is really uninterested in talking to A, then B's attitude toward A will tend to be ironic." As a result, B will probably be conversationally clipped with A. Thus, the student concludes that the line "Is that so?" should be delivered with a faintly rising inflection, thereby suggesting that the lateness of the bus is merely a contrivance on A's part to make A look blameless for his or her own lateness. It is important to observe that this kind of thinking may fall prey to logical fallacies. If, for example, our hypothetical language arts student were to reason that the line "Is that so?" would be said by someone *either* (a) moderately interested in the conversational partner *or* (b) whose attitude was riddled with sarcasm, as in "Who do you think you're kidding?," and that these were the *only* possible alternatives, then this student would be guilty of the fallacy known as "false dilemma" or "black and white" thinking. It is a fallacy because, in this case, other alternatives are clearly available. For example, "Is that so?" might be a perfunctory comment indicating awareness of a certain social custom, but without any real interest in the other individual one way or the other.

There are additional decisions to be made. Thus, if B's intentions toward A are ironic, does it follow that B will say *everything* to A in an ironic tone? In other words, does an intention defined by irony require a character to be consistently ironic in everything that character says? Human beings are not always consistent in their thoughts and actions, and believing that they would be so consistent in a given situation requires careful thought and justification on the part of the student who embraces such an interpretation.

In the *Poetics*, Aristotle tells us that a character, if assumed to be inconsistent, should be consistently inconsistent. In other words, if B fluctuates in ironic comments, then B should continue to fluctuate in this regard, or at least so says Aristotle. The student may or may not be aware of Aristotle's injunction in this con-

text; having this classical factoid in one's dramatic bag of tricks is hardly essential to the exercise. The point is that the decision to have the character consistently display an attribute or to vary with regard to that attribute is important and must be decided and justified through critical examination of the possibilities. In general, then, as students review their thinking on the decisions concerning the dramatic content of their characterizations, they must be aware of logical guidelines—and pitfalls—that must be obeyed or avoided in order to ensure a reliable reading and interpretation.

4. Determine Their Physical Actions [II, III]

The student has interpreted the characters' intentions by formulating hypotheses based on the language spoken as a set of "givens" and then drawing inferences from these hypotheses. Once the intentions have been determined, then the question becomes how to realize these intentions in terms of physical action.

In general, the same kind of critical thought process applies here, only now the student is dealing with hypotheses that apply to the transition from intention into action, rather than with hypotheses that apply to the transition from language into intention. Here again, the student is confronted with multiple possibilities, as many as a perceptive student is capable of engendering. For example, when A says "Is that so?," the student who has accepted the premise that A is ironic might infer that delivering this sentence should be accompanied with a slightly lifted eyebrow; this gesture is one way of indicating physically that our mind—as our body testifies—does not quite jive with our words as far as believing what has just been uttered by one's conversational partner. Finally, since the connections between intention and physical action are also complex and rife with possibility, the student must exercise the same

thoughtful control in discovering and selecting these possibilities as in determining the intentions of the character (Step 3). Critical thinking is equally important in this phase of preparing and performing the neutral dialogue.

5. Rehearse [IV]

Critical thinking is not separated from critical action, that is, actions chosen and done as a direct consequence of critical thinking. After the student has thought through an approach to the personalities, intentions, and gestures of A and B, the student puts such applied critical thinking into practice by rehearsing this interpretation. When thought, feeling, and action all merge in the concrete immediacy of performance, the student may receive validation of the "rightness" of thought that has funded this performance. But, on the other hand, the merger of these three components may reveal to the student that something does not quite "work"; as a result, there must be a reexamination of the principles and inferences that have grounded this performance.

Only when the critical thinking that animates the student's artistic vehicle has been applied in the "real" world of dramatic action will the critical reliability of that thought receive its ultimate justification. From this per-spective, then, rehearsing is not merely part of the job of the student as a performer; it also provides a laboratory for testing whether the thinking of that student has been sufficiently critical and relevant to justify serious attention on the part of the audience. In this regard, the student is in a sense rehearsing for his or her role as a key player in the drama of life itself.

Pairing Artistic Creativity and Critical Thinking: Prospects and Proposals

In order to establish the effects of critical thinking in language arts, as well as other subject areas, it may be asked whether it is necessary to make the critical thought process described above *explicit*, to both the student and teacher. One may contend that it is sufficient for the teacher merely to be aware—without knowing why in a "textbook" sense—that, in actively participating in such an arts-related exercise, the students are concurrently learning how to think critically. But, if a student is in fact thinking critically in one subject area, can it be assumed that this student has understood the principles of critical thinking to such an extent that he or she will be able to apply them to situations or problems in any, perhaps all, other subjects?

If assuming such transference turns out to be unwarranted, then it is necessary to make the principles of critical thinking explicit and to translate these principles into the vocabulary and structure of other subjects. This transformation would seem to be an especially fertile area for investigation and additional reflection. But, whether or not this prospect ever reaches full fruition, it may nonetheless be confidently asserted that the concurrent learning described above is a strong point in favor of arts-related education for younger students, especially in language arts. Instead of looking at or listening to the works of other artists, often from long ago and far away, students are examining and reflecting on the art that they themselves have executed. There would be more incentive to become reflective and analytical about something immediate and tangible—indeed, something of their own creation—than if students were merely placed in the presence of the works of others and invited, perhaps compelled, to become interested in them.

Judged from the standpoint of sheer technique, the quality of student-made art will vary widely, and this range of variation will doubtless hold in the case of dramatic performances of neutral dialogues. But, how "good" this art is does not matter; what matters is that students have been successfully creative and have also created in such a way as to reinforce their natural abilities to think critically. The point is not to exclude art appreciation in the usual sense; students must study and analyze the great art of the past and present. The point is that introducing the student production of art into a language arts curriculum in intimate conjunction with the richness, complexity, and relevance of student thinking about that art will not only encourage all students to enter the world of art in general, but will also enhance their abilities to understand the particular subject they are studying—here language arts, but in theory *any* subject presented in an arts-related setting.

It may be concluded that, if as many arts as possible are incorporated into the standard academic subjects, those students enjoying this integration will also display a correlatively thoughtful increase in the appreciation and understanding of these subjects. The possibilities for such integration and development are without limit—as, of course, is the very activity of art itself. The gifted student will benefit especially from this approach to critical thinking.

CHAPTER 12

The Oldest Cave Art: On Giftedness and Excellence

On the last day of his life, Socrates discussed with some friends (as described in Plato's *Phaedo*) a number of crucial philosophical questions, not the least of which was whether the soul, especially his own, would exist after death. In the course of his deliberations, Socrates tells us that he always has believed that all things, including human beings, are naturally defined by and drawn toward "what is best" (*Phaedo*, version 1955). This vital thought is echoed by Plato's student, Aristotle, who begins the *Nicomachean Ethics*, one of the seminal works in the western philosophical tradition (and often cited in *The Examined Life*), by asserting that all human activities are aimed "at the good" (*Nicomachean Ethics*, version 1941).

Here we see Plato and Aristotle laying down the principles that ground society's current concern for values. Something of value is perceived as whatever an individual believes is good for that individual, whatever will be conducive to his or her best interests. There are, of course, vast and often violent disagreements concerning the nature of the good; Plato and Aristotle knew and appreciated this fact since such disputes were just as common in ancient Athens as they are today. But, these great thinkers reflected on the fact that, in one sense, all values depend on our conviction that we must aim at what we consider to be best for us. Thus, teachers who exhort their students to do their best are appealing to a fundamental principle that subtly invokes a pronounced and potent philosophical tradition.

Excellence and the Gifted

These reflections are relevant to gifted education. It is a characteristic of the gifted to be exceedingly curious concerning the world about them. Furthermore, this curiosity is not defined solely by quantity, but by the breadth and scope of the

many different things and events that attract their attention. There is also a qualitative dimension. The gifted are especially sensitive to superlatives, that is, to whatever is best in any area of human endeavor. If, for example, someone holds a record in a certain kind of activity, then the gifted child will often become intrigued by the limits described by this record. The child also wonders whether these limits can be surpassed and, perhaps, whether he or she might be the one to surpass them.

The philosophical standpoint sketched in the opening paragraphs suggests that this interest has a sound and important theoretical foundation. For what the gifted child has recognized—doubtless subliminally, but nonetheless in a way that has struck deep, resonant chords—is the indirect presence of what Plato and Aristotle would call "the good" (i.e., what is or appears to be best for human beings to strive to achieve). This abstract sense of the good is embodied in concrete forms of human activity, to be sure, but an essential ingredient in what has attracted the gifted to this reality is the fact that they are in the presence of a superlative—the defining limits of a certain sort of human endeavor. The

point here is not to elevate such sensitivity so that it becomes a response enjoyed only by gifted children—all children are thrilled by the presence of what is best in this or that activity. But, it is fair to assume that the gifted feel and react to excellence in special ways that must be acknowledged and, if possible, pedagogically guided so that they can realize their full potential.

Superlatives affect the gifted in various aspects of their behavior. One of the most obvious and also unique aspects is their typical drive for perfection in much, if not all, of what they undertake, a concern often cited in descriptive analyses of gifted intelligence and personality. The frequent inability to be satisfied with a job well done indicates that, for the gifted, it is not sufficient merely to have done a task well. They must do that task, whether academic or otherwise, in the best possible manner.

The fact that they typically fail to reach this goal in their own eyes, and the fact that such self-imposed failure is frequently a source of irritation to them reveals that what drives the gifted in this regard is, in a very real sense, an appreciation of the good—of whatever is the best that can be done. This powerful motivation to actualize the good is real, even if for the young gifted student—indeed, for any person endowed with additional, yet finite ability—such excellence is a goal to be sought for regardless of whether or not it is ever attained. Nevertheless, according to the philosophical perspective authored by Plato and Aristotle, the gifted child's concern, if not passion, for reaching what is seen as the best has, again, a time-honored theoretical foundation.

Cave Art as a Superlative

Superlatives in human endeavors take many forms, some of which occur in areas that, in the long run, are perhaps not worth serious emulation. The *Guinness Book of World Records* lists thousands of superlatives that may well stand the test of time for the simple reason that few people, gifted or otherwise, are concerned enough to challenge them. Superlatives in other areas defining human excellence, such as athletics, are much more popular and attract considerable attention from a wide audience. Of course, popularity by itself does not adequately index the value of a given superlative. However, an especially fascinating superlative was discovered just before Christmas in 1994 in an arena of human activity that is also particularly consonant with the sensibilities of the gifted: the world of art.

While searching for prehistoric caves near Vallon-Pont d'Arc, a town about 50 miles from Avignon in southern France, three French spelunkers made a discovery that would forever change our understanding of the origins of art. After crawling headfirst down a narrow stone shaft more than 30 feet below the surface opening of a crevice, these astonished explorers witnessed a sight that had been concealed by time and natural forces for thousands of years. They had entered a cave (later named Chauvet Cave in honor of the leader of the expedition) the walls of which were covered with nearly 300 paintings of animals in hues of ocher, charcoal, and red hematite. These paintings have been scientifically dated as 32,000 years old—predating the famous art of Lascaux cave by 14,000 years. The Chauvet Cave art is therefore the oldest known art in the world, and its discovery has been widely celebrated, with articles and pictures of the paintings appearing in major U.S. news magazines, *National Geographic*, *Natural History*, and such French publications as *Le Point* and *Le Nouvel Observateur*.

Adorning the cave walls are paintings of prehistoric Irish elk and also a type of deer, now extinct, with enormous antlers. Nearby are paintings of owls, panthers, and a wooly mammoth with mysterious round circles around his lower legs, making him look like a proud show poodle just emerging from the grooming salon. An additional surprise is that more than half the animals represented are predators—lions, rhinos, mammoths, hyenas—rather than their more peaceful counterparts such as deer, horses, ibex, and bison, the animals more frequently hunted by early humans. One of the bison paintings is particularly fascinating from the standpoint of perspective; it occupies three planes—the body seen from the side and the antlers from the front, with the animal's face in a coquettish three-quarter turn toward the viewer.

Technically, the paintings are amazingly diverse. Sophisticated techniques depicting motion and using *trompe l'oeil* produced increased realism. Some paintings are more than flat depictions—they are miniature bas-relief sculptures. The artists who created these works exploited the naturally bumpy shapes in the rocky walls to evoke such shapes as a horse's mane or a pregnant cow's bulging abdomen. There are also instances of multiple images deployed so that they may have seemed to move when viewed in flickering lamplight.

The artistry displayed in Chauvet Cave includes shading, layering, fore-shortening, and staggering the representation of animals to achieve perspective. Furthermore, the economy of line in the paintings is seen today only in the most deft cartoon artists. And, of course, it should be kept in mind that the basic materials for creating such art—now readily obtainable—were unknown then. Colored paint had to be mixed from what was available: egg whites, blood, saliva, animal fat, and mineral powders. Thus, the wonderful excellence in artistic technique practices by the Chauvet painters was executed with what, for us, are primitive tools and materials.

Two Senses of Superlative Art

The art in Chauvet Cave is a superlative in both an obvious quantitative and a not-so-obvious qualitative sense. Gifted students will be immediately attracted to such art simply because, having been produced 32,000 years ago, it is the oldest art known in the world today. But, what is even more fascinating about this art it its manifest excellence. The range of content, the variegated colors, the diversity of technique, the scope of emotional response— all these characteristics will connect the gifted student not only with the demonstrable superlative of vicariously beholding the oldest art, but also with the far more subtle superlative of experiencing great art.

One can only imagine the sense of wonder and adventure evoked when this pair of superlatives coalesce. What was it like to live at that time? How did these people think about and react to their world? Were they really primitive in their outlook on life, or were they just different from those who possess a modern mentality? Would it be possible to recreate some of

their experiences in contemporary forms? If so, then gifted students would be inspired by the oldest art to seek out and express their own visions of what is good for human beings to think about and do when they respond artistically to the concerns and demands of the world about them. In sum, the Chauvet Cave art can serve as an intersection of superlatives and therefore provides an opportunity to direct gifted intelligence and its inherent concern for the best toward a variety of worthwhile educational objectives.

Curricular Integration

The gifted students' pursuit of excellence through the various superlatives embodied in Chauvet Cave art can be initiated in the following four areas. These areas represent an ensemble of experiences and activities that will challenge the gifted in a variety of ways.

A. Language Arts

Students can explore the psyche of prehistoric cave dwellers through writing journals. By adopting a cave dweller persona, a student can imagine and then list the hopes, fears, and daily activities of a typical cave dweller. The events that the student considers worth entering will circumscribe what he or she believes is best or most important in the course of daily life. Students may then be requested to justify their choices concerning the nature of the good in this eminently practical context—a justification that can be expressively contoured according to the principles of critical thinking outlined in Chapter 11.

B. Social Studies and Sciences

Creating a prehistoric picture zoo will allow students to study the effects of time on the animals depicted there. With cave pictures from periodicals, more general information from library books, display boards, and marking pens, students can devise a chart showing differences between animal life in the time of Chauvet Cave and the present. Students can select prehistoric animals from pictures of cave art, determine the nearest equivalent animals alive today, and then indicate which animals are now extinct and attempt to analyze why they became so. In this way, students will win an appreciation of what is good for animals and how certain animals (and humans) have succeeded or failed to satisfy the demands of the good in this regard.

C. Visual Arts

Can students produce their own cave art for classroom display? Yes, by making a three-dimensional replica of a decorated cave (i.e., painting three sides of a display box). Supplies needed: shoe boxes, papier-mâché materials, tempera paints, paint brushes. The students study the designs of the Chauvet Cave paintings, then create their own designs on the walls of their miniature caves. Their appreciation for the excellence of the Chauvet artists' "primitive" technical skill should be enhanced considerably by this exercise.

D. Science and Mathematics

Challenge the students to devise a timeline that will display the vast span of time represented by 32,000 years. Butcher paper or cash register paper 16- to 32-feet long should be used for a timeline of this dimension, as well as pictures of events in history and of cave art. Marking pens, sticky tab labels, glue, rulers, and measuring tapes will also be useful for this project. After discussion, students can compute the length of paper required to represent 32,000 years, and the length of equal segments to represent periods of 100, 500, or 1,000 years. Labels and pictures are then attached at appropriate points on the paper.

While such a history line illustrates the vast difference of time between the cave dwellers and their modern counterparts, the artwork represents a remarkable similarity of spirit displayed in factors that influence and inspire gifted children today: fascination with the natural world around them, creativity, and a driving need for excellence in self-expression.

From a contemporary vantage, Plato and Aristotle are considered "ancient" philosophers, although they remain historically much closer to our own time than they are to the Chauvet Cave artists. But, recognizing the importance of the pursuit of excellence is a characteristic shared, each in their own way, by both these nameless artists—their identities forever shrouded in true antiquity—and our two illustrious philosophers. Students should also be given every opportunity to participate in this kind of ultimate quest. Perhaps the above discussion has opened a few perspectives on such an educational and artistic endeavor.

References

Aristotle. (1941). *The basic works of Aristotle.* New York: Random House.

Hughes, R., & Bjerklie, D. (1995, February 13). Behold the stone age. *Time*, 52.

Plato. (1955). *Phaedo.* Cambridge, England: Cambridge University Press.

Cave Art Classroom Activities

1. Cave Dweller Diary

Project: Write a journal describing the life of a cave dweller.

Materials: Blank notebooks, perhaps with student-drawn cave designs on the cover.

Procedure:
- Use a page per day for entries.
- Adopt the persona of a cave dweller.
- Imagine and then list the hopes, fears, and daily activities of a "typical" cave dweller.
- Keep the journal for 1 week or 2 weeks, as desired.

2. Prehistoric Picture Zoo

Project: Devise a chart showing differences between animal life in the time of the Chauvet Cave and today.

Materials: Cave pictures, library books, display boards, marking pens.

Procedure:
- Select prehistoric animals from pictures of cave art.
- Find the nearest equivalent animals alive today.
- Indicate which animals are extinct.
- Determine why they became extinct.

3. Great Art Shadow Box

Project: Make a three-dimensional replica of a decorated cave by painting three sides of a display box.

Materials: Shoe boxes, papier-mâché materials, tempera paints, paint brushes.

Procedure:
- Secure a display box.
- Study the design of the Chauvet Cave paintings.
- Have the students create designs on the "walls" of their caves.
- Paint the three sides of the display box.

4. Timeline

Project: Devise a way to display the vast span of time represented by 32,000 years.

Materials: Butcher paper or cash register paper 16 to 32 feet long, marking pens or sticky tab labels, pictures of events in history and of cave art, glue, rulers, measuring tapes

Procedure:
- Discuss and then compute the length of paper required to represent 32,000 years.
- Discuss and then compute the length of each label representing an equal component of this period.
- Attach the labels at appropriate points on the paper.
- Attach pictures of historical events at appropriate points.

CHAPTER 13

The Philosophy of French Funetics: An Essay in Applied Gifted Intelligence

This chapter describes an innovative game for teaching introductory French to younger students and develops a philosophical interpretation explaining the success of this game based on a theoretical approach to gifted intelligence and language acquisition. Although the dominant context for the relevance of these conclusions concerns gifted students, the principles of the game are such that they can readily be applied to any student population. As we shall see, the game's the thing . . . !

The Doodle Factor

An especially intriguing characteristic of gifted students was revealed during my class discussions of primary source philosophy. One day, after several years of teaching philosophy to gifted elementary and middle school students, I noticed two 7th-graders writing notes during class. I was tempted to remark on what appeared to be a manifest lack of attention to the ongoing discussion. But, just as I was poised to chastise the seemingly errant pair, one of the students—while continuing to write—interjected a comment that not only fit the flow of discussion, which was at a fairly high level of abstraction, but was also quite profound. Apparently, this student could follow a philosophical discussion, think independently and creatively about that discussion, and produce notes on (I assume) non-philosophical topics—all simultaneously. How is such multidirectional intelligence possible?

Writing notes is hardly doodling, but with my sensibilities alerted, I noticed shortly after the above incident during philosophy classes for grades 5–6 at Northwestern University's Center for Talent Development that many of these students exhibited similar divergent consciousness by doodling while concurrently discussing abstract ideas. My sense of wonder was piqued still further.

This phenomenon—the doodle factor—was mentioned to International Baccalaureate French teacher Maureen Breen (now retired), who had in fact already exploited it in an interesting and valuable way. She had devised a method, "Funetics," for teaching French to students who had received no prior academic training in the language.

The following is an example of a French sentence "written" (or, perhaps, "drawn") in Funetics:

amis (friends): The logo is a pair of stick figures linked by a heart to show their friendship.

A Brief History of Funetics

For more than 15 years, Maureen Breen employed cartoon logos to present the abstract concepts necessary to understand and learn per-

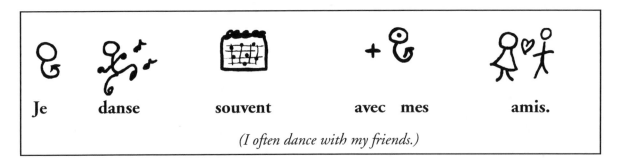

| Je | danse | souvent | avec mes | amis. |

(I often dance with my friends.)

The basic element of Funetics is a *logo*. Here is a "funetical" breakdown of the logos in this sentence:

je (I): First-person singular pronoun; the logo indicates that the speaker is singular and is speaking about himself or herself.

danse (dance): The logo is visually self-explanatory.

souvent (often): A calendar page on which many days are filled in with dots.

avec (with): The logo is self-explanatory, given a basic knowledge of arithmetical signs.

mes (my): The logo is identical to that for the personal pronoun "**je**" ("I"), but with a dot added to convey possession.

sonal pronouns in a foreign language. Thus, the logo for "I" (**je**) in the sample sentence can readily be developed to represent all such pronouns. These pronouns can then be deployed in a schematic that visually and clearly conveys what often requires several pages of textbook prose to communicate to beginning students. Furthermore, students learning pronouns can draw and label the logos themselves while working at the board or on paper at their desks. Breen observed that this activity was more enjoyable for the students, less taxing on the teacher, and more effective as a memory spur for the students' comprehension.

Given the success of this background in using logos to express subject pronouns, Breen gradually began to represent verbs and nouns with logos. Encouraged by her students' enjoyment of the drawings, as well as the rapid understanding the drawings engendered (not to mention their recognition of the possibility of doodling themselves for fun and academic

profit), Breen developed an entire language of more than 600 logos encompassing all the standard parts of speech. From this solid foundation, it was both an easy and enjoyable transition to create a learning game—Funetics—based on these logos.

Funetics in Action

In this game, competing teams vie for the shortest time in producing two distinct, but closely related linguistic results: forming a sentence composed entirely of logos and having that sentence spoken in correct French by their teammates.

How to Play Funetics:
(with 20 students)

The teacher covers the French material in such a way that students know a number of logos and their corresponding words. The teacher then prepares a list of 20 sentences in French to be used in the game. After dividing the class into two teams of 10 and designating one student to be timekeeper (this role should rotate during the playing of the game), the teacher gives one sentence to each student. Students look privately at their sentences and are allowed a few minutes to plan which logos to use in forming the sentence they have been given. The game begins. Player #1 from team #1 goes to the board and draws the logos for the sample sentence illustrated above. As soon as a teammate responds with the correct French sentence, the teacher calls time, and the timekeeper stops the clock and announces the amount of time taken. Then it is the other team's turn. At the end of the game, the team with the shorter total time wins for that day.

Hypothesis

What does this technique for teaching French disclose about gifted intelligence? It is possible that the gifted can rapidly assimilate French as a language with a structure foreign to nonnative speakers by their ability to process and unify, virtually simultaneously, visual depictions exemplifying different kinds of experiences and different forms of intelligence. The following account describes and analyzes this ability.

Basic Concepts

Intelligence. Consider Robert Sternberg's (1988) definition of intelligence: "purposive adaptation to and selection and shaping of real-world environments relevant to one's life" (p. 72). This definition is sufficiently broad to use as a basis for contouring the more restricted domain of gifted intelligence. Sternberg's comment on gifted intelligence—"being intellectually gifted does not mean any one thing, for there are many kinds of intellectual gifts" (p. 74)—is not very helpful by itself. However, in conjunction with his characterization of intelligence in general, this appeal to intellectual multiplicity points the way toward a more restricted and tangible formulation of gifted intelligence.

Gifted Intelligence. It may be suggested that the following matrix of characteristics can be found in academically gifted students:

Divergent Thinking. Divergent thinking differs from its counterpart, convergent thinking, in that the former stresses the ability to generate information "from given information, where the emphasis is upon variety and quality of output" (Storfer, 1990, p. 358). By contrast, the latter, convergent thinking, occurs where the domain of inquiry is so systematic and ordered that there are "rules or principles for converging on the solution" so that "conventionally accepted best outcomes" are produced (p. 358). Thus, the gifted student is not always concerned with getting the right answer—the primary concern of convergent thought—although, of course, gifted students often excel at producing such answers, as on standardized tests. But, such students are frequently concerned with exploring a number of alternate routes originating from a given question—routes leading to destinations that may well diverge from the intended scope of that question.

Integrative Insight. When presented with a variety of widely disparate phenomena, gifted students can discern likenesses and similarities in these realities and can then insightfully integrate the resulting strands of significance.

Creativity. Integrative insight presents data in some semblance of potential order; creativity fashions that potential into something new and different. Gifted students are creative and innovative, often in forms and styles that resist prediction.

Intense Desire for Knowledge. Underlying integrative insight and creativity is a straightforward, sincere, and intense desire to know about the world—desire for knowledge that may require unusual, perhaps even unorthodox, routes in order to be satisfied. The ancient Greeks believed that philosophy began with wonder; the gifted student often lives within a state of wonder and does his or her best to transform that experience into something more tangible.

Divergent, integrated, creative, intense—each attribute in this quartet may not be found in every gifted student, nor even when all four attributes do appear in a given student will each be present to the same degree. But, this categorization adequately expresses my experience with gifted students, and it is offered as a representative description suitable for present purposes and perhaps for other contexts, as well.

Visual Intelligence. When students adapt and shape their environment, *vision* is the avenue of perception that often dominates the channeling of information leading to such adaptation. Philosophers both ancient and contemporary have recognized the general primacy of vision in this regard. For Plato, "sight is the sharpest of the physical senses" (*Phaedrus*, 250d), and his student Aristotle elaborates the point with a pair of significant and useful additions: We naturally delight in our senses, "and above all others the sense of sight." The reason for such enjoyment, he adds, is that "this, most of all the senses, makes us know and brings to light many differences between things" (*Metaphysics*, 980a25–7). In our own time, the art critic and philosopher Rudolf Arnheim reflects this ancient position when he states, axiomatically, that sight is "the most efficient organ of human cognition" (Arnheim, 1969, p. vi). The natural delight associated with sight and the extensive range of differences disclosed through the visual dimension of experience are especially fertile factors in accounting for the success of Funetics.

Furthermore, the observations of philosophers are reinforced by contemporary studies concerning modalities, or preferences for different kinds of information (Pettersson, 1989). Rune Pettersson cites research showing that

30% of elementary school children in the U.S. have visual modality, 25% have auditory modality, 15% have kinesthetic modality, and the remaining 30% have a mixed modality. Although this research indicates that forms of modality other than the visual are preferred by 40% of the children examined, it must be recalled that these results indicate *preferences* in modalities, not exclusive choices. And Temple Grandin's point (duly documented) concerning the overall dominance of the visual must be taken seriously. This professor and accomplished scholar of animal husbandry—who also is autistic—observes that people "throughout the world are on a continuum of visualization skills ranging from next to none, to seeing vague generalized pictures, to seeing semi-specific pictures, to seeing . . . very specific pictures" (Grandin, 1995, p. 28). Thus, what we see constitutes a significant portion of what we think with, and about, in and through our minds.

What does a seen picture mean? The tendency is perhaps to construe the significance of a picture as linear or as "flat" in its two-dimensionality as the plane on which the picture appears—in short, as simply whatever the eye immediately beholds. But, Pettersson (1989) asserts that a "visual" can "possess many different functions and effects or combinations of functions and effects" (p. 142). Thus, a picture may be *cognitive*—conveying knowledge and information; *affective*—providing entertainment, reinforcing an experience, triggering associations and influencing emotions and attitudes; and *compensatory*—making it easier to comprehend, learn, and recall things read. In fact, all three types of effects are present when gifted students respond to Funetics.

Structure

The "Fun"ction of Funetics. A serious student of French desires to know French. In the first sentence of his *Metaphysics*, Aristotle asserts that everyone "by nature" desires to know (980a22). If so, then acquiring knowledge is inherently pleasant, since it is part of our nature to enjoy the activity of learning. Indeed, this is why we *desire* to learn, since the activity of learning is self-fulfilling. Learning produces a unique pleasure, valuable in itself quite apart from its practical benefits. For whenever we see things and discern differences in what we see, the natural delight derived from such recognition fuels our desire to know more about what we have seen.

The matrix of characteristics offered to describe gifted intelligence contains no explicit reference to the pleasure involved in learning, but the intense desire for knowledge displayed by the gifted provides the premise for such a consequence. For it may be assumed that the gifted are particularly sensitive to acquiring and enjoying the unique pleasure that derives from fulfilling the desire to know. When gifted students announce that they want to have "fun" in school, they are not merely displaying another dimension of youthful hedonism; rather, they are indicating that they want their learning experiences to be enjoyable while these experiences retain their function *as* learning. This wish, following Aristotle, seems both reasonable and philosophically perceptive.

But, can learning French be fun? If learning is inherently pleasant, then learning French ought to be made as enjoyable as possible, for then students will assimilate the language more quickly and with increased understanding of and appreciation for its structural intricacies, power, and beauty. The goal of Funetics is to combine the pleasure of learning in general with the particular challenge of learning ways to add new words in order to think, speak, write—and play—in a foreign language.

Principles of Logo Formation. The challenge of Funetics revolves around the experience of the logos that constitute the main elements of the game. *Logos* may be defined as visual indicators of words (usually individual words) that relate the student *from* a certain drawn configuration—a "visual," in Pettersson's vocabulary—*to* a corresponding French word *through* one or a set of experiences. Now it may be observed, as Janet Olson (1992) has pointed out, that "what has been lost in the history of writing is its visual, or pictorial, aspect" (p. 128). In this regard, then, the logo as a visual indicator recoups a small measure of this fundamental and historically vital dimension of linguistic experience. Although the visual figure as such does exhibit this dimension, the figure is named "logo" to emphasize the fact that the picture is primarily directed toward the realm of language—to the spoken or written word (or, in some cases, words), a connection implied by the Greek word *logos*, the etymological root of *logo*. Also, the connotation that *logo* has in advertising contexts, as the name for the visual emblem of a product, is not irrelevant here, since the logos animating Funetics are often clever and amusing, as are the advertising logos for some products.

Logos: Categories of Experience. The following section explores this continuum by introducing descriptive categories to name some of the types of experiences underlying various logos. Although this set is provisional and incomplete, it illustrates the complexity and extent of the experiences that fund the formation of the logos, experiences that animate and excite gifted students whenever they play Funetics.

Representation—Direct, ***poisson*** [*fish*—noun] The logo visually resembles the referent of the logo.

Representation—Inferential, ***tomber*** [*to fall*—verb] In this case, the viewer must infer that the image of the ladder, plus the line representing motion, imply that the stick figure is falling.

Association—Concrete to Abstract, ***pour*** [*for*—preposition] In an age when street demonstrations are fairly common, it will not be difficult to make the transition from seeing the concrete image of the demonstrator's hand waving a sign to recognizing that this individual is "for" some cause.

Association—Abstract to Concrete, ***Chicago*** [*Chicago*—proper noun] The appearance of this logo is spare, almost geometrical, but once the curved line and dot are associated with a certain spatial standpoint, the result is a mapped representation of the Windy City in relation to Lake Michigan.

Association—Abstract to Abstract, ***mais*** [*but*—conjunction] The primary sense of *but* is conveyed by the upper arrow directed *toward* a certain destination in tandem with the lower arrow *reversing* that direction, as illustrated in sentences such as "I was going to the store, *but* it started to rain." The conjunction *but* links, then establishes the complex relation between, these compound thoughts within a single sentence.

Symbolism, *jamais* [*never*—adverb] For comprehension of this logo, there must be prior recognition of the mathematical convention representing the concept of infinity as a sideways eight, with the diagonal bar slicing through this sign, thereby completely negating its sense.

Visual Pun, *il y a* ["There is," "There are," etc.] This common idiomatic expression is represented by an electric eel plugged into a socket and finding this intimacy both illuminating and soothing. Thus, il y a is discerned from a visual depiction of "eel . . . eee! . . . ah. . . ."

Logos and Visualized Experience. In sum, more is happening in Funetics than meets the eye. But, it is the eye that first meets each logo within a purely visual dimension of experience. Furthermore, since one of the primary sensory avenues exercised by all contemporary young students is the *visual*—evidenced by music videos, computer games, photo-snapping cell phones, and multichannel television systems—visual activities often dominate the experiences students utilize to acquire knowledge.

But, of course, the eye, even if dominant, does not do its informative work alone. In fact, some educators insist that vision has not received its full pedagogical due. Janet Olson (1992) has clearly stated the connection in the context of educating the "total" child: "When children are educated with both the visual and the verbal modes of learning . . . they can move back and forth between these domains without effort" (p. 51). Ideally, then, the education of any student should combine both modes of learning.

Pettersson (1989) states this conclusion in a theoretically precise way by asserting that conveying "information through both verbal and visual languages makes it possible for learners to alternate between functionally independent, though inter-connected, and complementary cognitive processing systems" (p. 202). Note, then, that the cognitive systems incorporated in Funetics exhibit a broad spectrum of experience. Indeed, the interplay between the verbal and the visual here is such that an even more expansive canvas than that suggested by Olson and Pettersson may be introduced. To concretize and consolidate the diverse avenues of experience linking gifted students with the panoply of logos, we may employ Howard Gardner's (1983) seven types of intelligence:

Linguistic—*c'est èvident!*

Visual/spatial—*c'est trés èvident!*

Kinesthetic—The students are moving and speaking while they play the game, and their motion is controlled by the desire for extremely rapid yet accurate execution of the relevant logos.

Interpersonal—Each student represents his or her team and must convey a message to assist the team in its performance.

Intrapersonal—This kind of teamwork requires knowledge, self-awareness, confidence, concentration, and internal strength.

Mathematical/logic—Designing the logos and accurate time-keeping.

Musical—French, if spoken with proper rhythm and cadence, is a very musical language.

Thus, students learning to incorporate these elements of the language into their pronunciation patterns are extending their native abilities for appreciating and practicing music in these senses.

The point of this deployment is tactical, not definitive. The suggestion is not that Gardner's system of classification can, by itself, adequately account for the processing of Funetics logos by gifted students. Nonetheless, for present purposes, this system provides a convenient framework for recognizing the breadth of experiences described by logos as the primary element in Funetics.

In sum, the implementation of logos affords students a challenging opportunity to combine learning a foreign language, embryonic—or perhaps more—artistic expression, the pleasure of intelligent humor, and the possibility of creativity—all within one highly fun-filled experience.

Results

Mechanics

Vocabulary and grammar are learned faster and more thoroughly with the assistance of Funetics since it is an artificial or created language (in this sense it resembles Esperanto) and thereby can avoid some of the syntactic pitfalls of a naturally evolving language. These factors also require less rote drill work in order to imprint elementary concepts and facts onto students' memories. In this regard, logos act as compensatory by providing an added visual memory spur, rather than, as in the typical memorization process, having the student learn an unknown French word by somehow linking it to another

English word through the dry reaches of memory.

It is also a happy consequence that less homework is required to help win mastery and what homework is given is more pleasant since its performance includes the fun of drawing the logos. The logo structure of Funetics is also readily applicable for written examinations; thus, the enjoyment inherent in playing the game carries over into the often strained and occasionally nerve-wracking ordeal of taking a test in a foreign language. Students can enjoy being tested in French through Funetics to an extent approximating the pleasure experienced in playing the game itself.

Furthermore, Funetics serves as an anchoring that grounds what the student knows in real words within real experiences (i.e., the student will be less prone to attempt to express ideas in written French if he or she cannot represent that aspect of grammar in logos). Students will be sufficiently busy playing—and, concurrently, learning the mechanics of the language—*via* the logos that have been mastered. Finally, the fact that students have so quickly and competently acquired mastery of the basic elements of the language will give them added confidence and expertise when, in subsequent literary studies, they confront more complex aspects of the language. Learning French fundamentals at an increased rate of speed will help students master this material faster than they would have without the initial propulsion provided by playing Funetics. As a result, students will sharpen their knowledge of French mechanics through the integrative processes inherent in Funetics, enjoy themselves in the process by participating in a continually creative process, and also have more time for other quests concerning the wondrous world in which they dwell.

Speaking

The assimilation and use of the logos, especially in the spoken phase of Funetics, is something that students can practice and learn quickly and actively, as opposed to passively and slowly watching the teacher establish a point or reading about it in a book. Speaking is a *behavior,* and it should be practiced to be learned. With Funetics, the students speak French all at the same time, not by turns. Their contact with the language as spoken is by concentrated social immersion, thus the effects of this contact are increased both qualitatively (students learn to speak more accurately) and quantitatively (they learn more vocabulary faster).

Confidence in pronunciation is also more quickly attained since the beginning student is less self-conscious about speaking a foreign language when saying new words occurs in a game context. A mispronounced word when uttered here carries little of the interpersonal sting that

the same *faux pas* would engender in a more demanding social setting. Although all students benefit from learning a language where there is a decrease in social disapproval of linguistic errors, gifted students would be especially sensitive to its unifying effect since they are often singled out and made the subject of derision simply because they are who they are.

Conclusion

As a game, Funetics is fun to play. But, the tendency with games is not to analyze them for purposes of discovering *why* they are fun. This chapter has offered a reasoned explanation of Funetics' perhaps surprisingly complex structure in order to show why such a game is fun. Furthermore, this account has raised questions concerning the principles underlying Funetics that are intriguing and fundamental to both education and philosophy.

If pleasure can and ought to be essential to learning, then it is worth investigating whether an increase in types of intelligence combined within one educational activity will produce proportionately greater degrees of pleasure. Thus, is it true that the more types of intelligence are combined in one activity, the more pleasant is the learning derived from such combination—with, presumably, a commensurate degree of success in learning? This pleasure is not pursued for its own sake; rather, its presence is only enhanced as a necessary and desirable consequence of learning through the activity of playing the game. But, if the link between increased pleasure and increased learning is true, then Funetics has happily coalesced with the ancient wisdom of Greek philosophers to show us one way to reflect on realizing more completely the possibilities latent in gifted intelligence. The hope is that readers who find the themes introduced here engaging and challenging will continue to pursue such reflection.

If so, then the game of Funetics may have more to teach us than simply an innovative and exciting way to learn French. It may lead to understanding more comprehensively and clearly the diverse intelligence of the gifted.

References

Aristotle. (1941). *The basic works of Aristotle.* New York: Random House.

Arnheim, R. (1969). *Visual thinking.* Berkeley: University of California.

Gardner, H. (1983). *Frames of mind: The theory of multiple intelligences.* New York: Basic Books.

Grandin, T. (1995). *Thinking in pictures.* New York: Doubleday.

Olson, J. (1992). *Envisioning writing.* Portsmouth, NH. Heinemann.

Pettersson, R. (1989). *Visuals for information.* Englewood Cliffs, NJ: Educational Technology Publications.

Plato (1977). *Phaedrus.* Cambridge, MA: Harvard University Press.

Sternberg, R. (1986). *Intelligence applied: Understanding and increasing your intellectual skills.* San Diego, CA Harcourt Brace Jovanovich.

Sternberg, R. (1988). *The triarchic mind: A new theory of human intelligence.* New York: Viking.

Storfer, M. (1990). *Intelligence and giftedness.* San Francisco: Jossey-Bass.

Note: The game of Funetics has been published as *French Through Funetics: Language Learning Through Logos,* by Maureen Breen and David A. White. It is available from Command Performance Language Institute, 1755 Hopkins St., Berkeley, CA 94707-2714; consee@aol.com.

CHAPTER 14

"The Bohemian Life": Opera and Gifted Education

Opera is considered by its devotees to be the highest form of art. Grand opera, to give the art form its more venerable name, is so praised because it represents an especially vibrant intersection of words, music, and stagecraft. In theory, then, opera is a natural artistic medium to present to gifted students (or any student with a sufficiently attuned imagination) since it provides an introduction to an intricately visual and aural experience that will considerably broaden their youthful awareness of how artful words joined with powerful music can enrich their world. The problem, then, is to transform this "grand" pedagogical and aesthetic idea into practical reality.

Prologue

Cynthia Sprague is the Social Studies teacher for grades 6–8 of the Regional Program at A. N. Pritzker School in Chicago. Elementary students in Illinois are assessed in fine arts on state proficiency tests, and although painting as an art form is treated with a degree of thoroughness in American History, the state test also includes questions on music and dance. Sprague was therefore faced with the problem of finding ways to prepare her 7th-grade gifted students for these arts, as well as painting, on the state examination. How should this pedagogical problem be addressed?

Lyric Opera of Chicago, one of the world's premiere opera companies, offers an extensive program in opera education. In the summer of 2001, a teacher education course, "Opera: A Story That Is Sung," was given at the Civic Opera House in downtown Chicago. The week-long course, intended for teachers with or without music, theater, or art background, gave teachers the opportunity to present a mimed version of an opera in the classroom or in a larger venue if available. All aspects of opera were covered—technical, historical, cultural—and the materials necessary for presenting an opera in a school setting were also included: script, cassette and videotapes, a prop and costume guide, and student aids such as crossword puzzles with operatic themes and illustrations to facilitate learning the language of opera and operatic production. The framework of the course incorporated Illinois and Chicago arts standards, plus a variety of language arts and social studies goals. The course was led by Lyric Opera's Manager of Education Outreach, Mary Kurz, a 30-year veteran public school teacher.

Sprague was impressed with the organization and presentation of the course and with the possibilities that were opened up by this approach to opera. In addition to addressing the requirements in several of the arts that appeared on the state examination, Sprague thought that this treatment of opera would foster an appreciation of the art in her students, increase their awareness of the type of music that typically characterizes opera, and, quite simply, be fun for them to do.

One of four different operas is featured each year the summer teacher course is offered, and the opera for 2001 was Giacomo Puccini's classic *La Bohème*. Set in a garret and surrounding neighborhood in the Paris of 1830, the story is an example of the *verismo* movement of late 19th-century Italian opera, depicting in a down-to-earth way "the bohemian life" of six young, eager, but impoverished artists (including a philosopher!). Relationships form, dissolve, rekindle; money is made, spent, borrowed, and owed; moods range from high-flown gaiety to depthless sadness, and the interlocking libretto culminates with the death by consumption (or, as known now, tuberculosis) of the seamstress Mimi, an event punctuated by the anguished cries of her lover, the poet Rodolfo, in the opera's wrenching final scene. (The musical *Rent* is a contemporary adaptation of the same story.) Would a class of gifted 7th-graders be excited to reenact this emotional feast for the ears and eyes?

Preparation [Act 1]

Sprague initiated this project by asking the students whether any of them had ever been to an opera. Some students mentioned that they had seen Elton John's version of *Aida* and several others indicated some experience with musical comedies, but none of them had attended or seen an opera in the full-fledged "opera house" sense. When Sprague then announced her plan to perform an opera with the students, the initial reaction was mixed. A significant number of students (typically boys) were not enthusiastic, but a number of other students (typically girls) expressed a keen interest in the project.

At this juncture, the Lyric Opera cassette tape that included examples of operatic music appearing in various forms of popular culture was very helpful. Many of the hesitant students began to rethink their attitude once they heard that music from opera is indeed common, although in contexts in which its original function has been concealed by other formats. Thus, the "William Tell Overture" (from Rossini's opera of the same name) is famous, if not notorious, from many a cartoon, Bugs Bunny and otherwise, *The Simpsons* wickedly lampoons operatic excerpts, and the grand march from Verdi's *Aida*, as well as a number of melodic moments from Bizet's *Carmen*, also frequently appear in various forms of popular entertainment. Upon hearing these excerpts, the students reacted, "That's from an opera?" Then, in addition to providing a setting for such aesthetic epiphanies, Sprague assigned students to list three times they heard opera while watching several days of television; every student responded with examples such as DeBeers advertisements and references to programs such as *Everybody Loves Raymond*. Indeed, opera is almost omnipresent!

A general air of student receptivity to the project was established, facilitated by playing popular operatic excerpts and identifying for the students what in fact they had been hearing, as well as reinforcing this awareness by having students recognize on their own how frequently they, were in the presence of operatic music. And, when Sprague read the script of *La Bohème* to the students, accompanying the reading with a tape of still photographs of a Lyric Opera production of the work, the students were most intrigued, punctuating their approval with applause at the conclusion of this presentation.

A Philosophical Intermezzo

The next step in the process of preparation involved a series of fortuitous circumstances. I had been doing programs in primary-source philosophy at Pritzker for a number of years. As a keen opera fan, when I heard Sprague's intention to perform an opera with her 7th-grade class, I was very interested in observing the production and participating in some way in its preparation. This 7th-grade class had already done the first year of a 3-year program in primary-source philosophy, so I knew that they had experience in thinking about questions and issues from a philosophical perspective. I felt certain that this background could be relevantly exploited with a view toward broadening the students' understanding of opera.

It has been noted that Greek tragedy can be considered as an ancient precursor to modern opera since these tragedies possessed poetry of the highest order, action, musical accompaniment, and movement (by the chorus). There are, of course, many differences between opera and Greek tragedy, but I thought that there were sufficient similarities to attempt a prelim-

inary discussion of opera based on certain philosophical themes. I therefore adapted a number of positions in Aristotle's *Poetics*, one of the first and most influential works in literary aesthetics in Western thought. I developed a series of questions based on Aristotelian principles and a one-page handout based on this material. Shortly after the students learned that the opera was in the works, I led a discussion of these questions with the students. The following are sample questions from this handout with a brief summary of student reaction.

1. *Which is more important in opera: the words [i.e., the libretto—"little book"] or the music?*

The dominant view was that both words and music were of equal importance, although this compromise position was reached only after several students had spoken in favor of each of the two alternatives. There was a fascinating discussion of this point where it was contended that music without words with characters moving on stage is tantamount to ballet and words spoken by characters without any accompanying music is indistinguishable from drama. An offshoot of this discussion was the students' increasing interest in the importance of dramatic gestures and, as a corollary, how important these gestures would be in an opera.

2. *Do you think you can appreciate an opera even if you do not hear or do not fully understand the words being sung?*

This question is a natural follow-up to Question 1. And a number of students answered that understanding the opera is possible from noting the mood and tempi of the music, and the orchestration used, even if the words said by the characters were unfamiliar or not fully audible. This response is quite sophisticated and all the more surprising since, at this point during the process of preparation, the students had had only minimal exposure to the music of *La Bohème*. It is implicit testimony to the imaginative powers of gifted students that they can thrust themselves into the structure of an opera and then determine characteristics of that art form without firsthand experience of it.

3. *Which is more important to the opera: the characters or the story?*

First, it was necessary to clarify a logical point since several students contended that, if there were no characters, then it would follow that there would be no story. It is true that a story presupposes characters, but it is still possible to reflect on whether, given the details of a plot, the characters involved in that plot or the plot taken as such is more important. (It may be noted that this question is vital for Aristotle's understanding of tragedy, since he argues that the story is more important than the characters.) I found it intriguing that the majority of students were Aristotelians in this regard for they thought that the story was more significant than the characters, although several students offered intriguing reasons to prefer the characters. One line of argument was that characters as elements in the story are more appealing as people; as a result, the observer of an opera will find that the characters resonate in the observer's future human interactions more so than will the flow of the libretto as a sort of disembodied narrative.

4. *How do you feel when Mimi [the heroine of La Bohème] dies? If you feel sadness, do you think that this feeling, occurring as it does at the end of experiencing a work of art, will help you cope better with your feelings when someone you know dies? Or is the death of a character in an opera only just "pretend" and therefore not relevant to what you might feel in real life?*

These questions are derived from the much discussed problem of *catharsis* in Aristotle:

whether the experience of watching a tragedy "purges" our emotions by refining their nature or whether the purgative quality of the experience is only a temporary consequence of witnessing the play. Thus, to what extent is a feeling that is experienced during an opera something that has educational value in real life? Some students thought that the experience of sadness felt while watching the death of Mimi could not be transferred into real life since the observer knows that what he or she is witnessing is not "real"; however, other students pointed out that, since the action in the opera was based on reality, it would be possible to learn from the experience of operatic sadness, as it were, and to apply this type of experience into comparable events when they occur in real life.

5. *If the Pritzker performance of La Bohème does not have elaborate and expensive costumes and scenery, how important will that be to the overall success of the production?*

Given the flash and glitter of many Hollywood films aimed at youthful audiences, it was a surprise (and a pleasant one!) to hear the students almost universally reject the importance of elaborate costumes and scenery to the success of the performance. The only argument against this consensus was that, since opera is visual, there must be some attempt made to reproduce the costumes and scenery of the action as they really were, otherwise too great a strain would be imposed on the audience's imagination. But, many students countered this point by arguing that the audience could perfectly well imagine these externals—what Aristotle refers to as "spectacle"—and that, in fact, the lack of fancy costumes and staging would invite closer attention to the point of the opera defined as the intersection of story and music.

Teachers who wish to employ the slate of questions given in this "philosophical intermezzo" and reviewed above may, of course, do so if they feel the inquiry might be valuable to enhance their students' appreciation of this art form. The questions listed here are general and can be applied to any opera—only Question 4 is specific to the opera performed at Pritzker and its point may be readily modified. Thus, if the intended opera is tragic, as many are, then the point of the question could be transferred to the central tragic event defining the plot; if the opera is comic, then the question can be aimed with the same intent at whatever feelings of gaiety or joy the opera evokes.

Preparation [Act 2]

The students now began preparing the opera. It was mandated that everyone in class had to participate in some way in the production of the work. Initially, all parts, whether in the cast or as supporting personnel, were chosen at random from a coffee pot. However, this chance determination of roles was immediately followed by wholesale trading of parts by those students who thought they could improve their original position. Since these transactions were getting somewhat out of hand, Sprague decided to have a second round of random selection,

with the understanding that, this time, destiny would rule. The student reaction after the second round was one of general consent, although Sprague did notice one swap between an unenthusiastic player and a student with a minor role who wanted to play a larger part. Sprague observed that while, in general, no boys wanted to play female roles, girls not only would, but in several cases avidly desired to play male roles. The reasons for this difference are interesting to pursue; one possibility may be that, if girls at this age have a natural interest in performing, then the particular dramatic outlet for such performance, whether male or female, may not that be significant.

An opera requires a stage, costumes, and props. The A. N. Pritzker School stage was available for rehearsal and performance (Pritzker's principal, Louise Rzechula, was wholeheartedly supportive of this artistic adventure). As for costumes and props, Sprague issued a general call for everyone in class to bring whatever they thought would be appropriate in this regard (as things turned out, Sprague herself was the primary source for these materials). All the students who were in the cast enjoyed donning their costumes, makeshift though they were, as if this element in stage production by itself had ignited their imaginations and made their participation in the performance of the opera all the more real. Props were produced in the same way, with the students ingeniously transforming a cafeteria table into Mimi's bed, a grocery cart into the toy vendor's cart, and a remarkably realistic paper flame for the wood-burning stove in Act I. There is a playful mock duel between the musician and the philosopher in Act IV, and the Pritzker students used loaves of French bread for swords (the only problem with this device was the tendency for said swords to decrease in length by virtue of being nibbled on during slower moments in rehearsal . . .).

The students asked Ms. Sprague whether the auditorium spotlight could be used in the performance. She replied that she had no experience with stage lighting. A student volunteered that he had done the lighting for a number of school productions, and he was placed in charge of this phase of stagecraft. Regarding stage action, the gestures of the performers who were miming the lyrics and the blocking for the dramatic action were suggested by Sprague; discussion involving the principals ensued, and compromises between director and performers were struck. Several creative suggestions by the students were warmly received by all, a kind of interaction that encouraged more discussion and further suggestions concerning technical matters of stagecraft. As rehearsals continued and interest in dramatic detail increased, the girls inquired whether they should wear makeup to enhance their appearance, an aesthetic option that was handled judiciously by the teacher. Rehearsal for the performance comprised one period a day for 5 days, then two periods for 4 days, a block of time that included background (given in class) on the geography and history of France. A final walk-through the morning of the performance concluded preparation for the premiere operatic production at Pritzker School.

Performance

There was a subdued, but palpable air of excitement as the students gathered on the stage. A student equipped with a broom (he would later appear in a crowd scene as a street sweeper) gave the stage floor a final sweep. Parents of the students were invited to the morning school-day performance, as were the 4th- through 6th-grade gifted classes—Sprague wanted Pritzker's younger students to witness the initial performance of the opera to get a feel for what they themselves would be doing in forthcoming years.

Up curtain! The teacher welcomed the audience, gave background for the story of the opera, introduced the characters, and explained the meaning of the title. A small "pit" orchestra with a conductor and score was located immediately adjacent to the apron of the stage in order to provide musical accompaniment to the mimed performance; the orchestral members use recorders and homemade replicas of violins as instruments.

The teacher read descriptions of staging and actions of the performers, the performers acted out what was sung, and music from the cassette player played either between segments of action on stage or during the action. The teacher coordinated the playing of the tape with the on-stage action. The props and costumes effectively evoked the feel of the stage—of special note was a flickering flame drawn on a sheet of fluttering cardboard and used in Act I, which is set on Christmas Eve, to animate the stove that four of the young artists were using in a vain attempt to warm themselves in the midst of their freezing garret. The effect was very realistic and much appreciated by the audience. Also very effective was the use of lighting to contribute to indoor and outdoor locations and the evocation of moods.

The taped excerpts convincingly captured the sonic feel and drama of the opera as a whole, with the work's "big" arias fully represented: *Che gelida manina* ("Your little hand is so cold"), *Mi chiamano Mimi* ("I am called Mimi"), *O soave fanciulla* ("O lovely girl"), and *Quando me' n vo'* ("Muzetta's waltz"). The curtains closed after each act, providing an opportunity to reset the stage and also giving the younger members of the audience an opportunity to unwind. Before the final act, Act IV, the orchestra was asked to take a bow, thus replicating conventional opera house practice. When the performance concluded, the entire class gathered on stage for a bow, and the teacher thanked the stage crew and smaller role players (e.g., the revelers and street band). The produc-

tion ran approximately 45 minutes, a prudently designed duration given the demands of a new art form and the fact that the audience had to be closely attentive to what was happening in order to appreciate the opera in all its dimensions. I noted that all the younger students who attended were rapt in attention throughout the performance, a sign that not only were they captivated by what they were witnessing, but also that they would be equally zealous in preparing and performing when their turn came to stage an opera.

Epilogue

Critical Reviews

From the standpoint of student enjoyment, there was strong evidence that the Pritzker 7th-graders found the experience to be eminently worthwhile. A number of students were heard humming melodies from the major arias after rehearsals and during class changes, suggesting that the music of the opera was not only memorable, but also enjoyable enough to accompany the more work-a-day activities of school. Also, and even more significant, was that one of the most prominent post-production responses from the students was an active desire to do *another* opera, and the sooner the better!

Pedagogical Lessons Learned

There is a fine line between controlling the students and encouraging their creativity.

Sprague realized that the more control given to students, the more they liked the process of preparing the opera, and, correlatively, the more they enjoyed the opera as such. Delegating control in this way not only contributes to the students' awareness of their own maturity in establishing the quality of the performance, but also increases their confidence in their own imaginative insights into the structure of the opera and what can be done to accentuate or enhance the opera as a dramatic narrative.

Another way to grant a greater degree of student control is making a point of requesting student input regarding how to improve the opera after the performance has been given. This exercise, which can be done aloud in class or as a written assignment, further develops the dimension of personal responsibility by presenting to each student the opportunity to act as a managing director and to contribute his or her insights into the actual production with a view toward improvement. Some of the suggestions offered by the initial year's 7th-graders could perhaps have been anticipated (e.g., better props and costumes, as well as additional rehearsal to improve timing and entrances). But, others were more fundamental: to find a complete copy of the music and use that in preparation; to be more specific in terms of technical matters (e.g., not to use green lighting because it makes the performers look ill); and rather drastically revisionist (e.g., to use the lines from the libretto and make the opera into a play). It seems evident from the range of suggestions that little in the way of constraint will limit student critical response to their own work.

The second lesson is to anticipate changes in attitude toward the production of an opera, if not opera in general, during the process of preparation. Thus, students who initially displayed little interest in participating in this project wanted at the end to be on stage in the marching band and as members of the crowd milling around the marketplace. This shift in attitude could result from simple peer pressure and the natural adolescent desire to belong, but it could also indicate at a deeper level a recognition that the other students were actively involved in the opera because it was an informative—and fun—thing to do. A related phenomenon was the noticeable difference between the initial male and female student reaction. At the beginning of preparation, the girls were generally much more enthusiastic than the boys. However, this difference leveled off as the process of preparation continued, suggesting that, once boys become comfortable with the demands of an opera, their perhaps natural social reticence to become part of something "artistic" will recede.

A third lesson is of a more specific nature: It is desirable to invite a student to be stage director for the performance. This organizational move has two advantages—first, the teacher can concentrate on timing music with libretto (since this operation involves manual operation of a cassette player) without also having to be concerned with the flow of activity on the stage. And second, a student stage director provides an additional tapping into youthful creativity and does so for a position that can yield considerable positive results. If the director is prudently selected and displays the requisite maturity in dealing with his or her peers, then catalytic exchanges between the performers may produce an even higher degree of insight into the work to be performed and assist in energizing the students' capabilities to realize what they, in concert with the director, have seen in the work.

Fourth, and again practically speaking: Procuring props and costumes became problematic when materials promised by students failed to appear (due to forgetfulness, etc.). It is well to involve parents in this respect during the early planning stages of the production in order to increase chances that these materials will indeed arrive in time for rehearsals and the actual performance.

The final consideration, given the student enjoyment of the production, was whether to include the neighborhood 7th-grade in the next year's opera, an opportunity that could only be good for these students in a variety of ways. Also under consideration was the possibility of having subsequent operas as collaborations between the 7th and 8th grades, an option that would take advantage of the next year's 8th grader's experience with the premier production, thereby improving the overall performance.

Opera and the Curriculum

Social Studies

A general introduction to opera and its history as an art form will necessarily include references to the social aspects underlying the human desire to sing and dance, whether alone or in groups. The extent to which opera emerged as an artistic outgrowth of certain social and economic divisions reflects the general assumptions and influence of these groups in society. Furthermore, a given opera happens at a certain time and place, thereby positioning an inquiry into the historical and geographical circumstances that underlie that setting. How much of this background material is pursued for curricular purposes may, of course, be left to the discretion of the teacher.

Language Arts

The classroom gambit of asking students to write ways to improve the opera is a straightforward, but useful application of combining firsthand experience with works of art and expository prose to record the students' thoughts and suggestions. Another avenue to consider during preparation of the opera is for the students to keep a daily journal of their experience with the opera, noting both the positive and negative aspects of this pedagogical and artistic drama.

Additional possibilities for development in this area revolve around the components of an opera. A libretto is a story and, as such, an example of literature. However, the libretto as a form differs from the more common literary genres analyzed by younger students, usually by being highly compressed, with its poetry more pronounced and immediately engaging. Students who take a libretto seriously as literature will increase their appreciation for the way words can work to tell a story and to evoke feelings. Finally, although the libretto is literature, it is literature wedded to music, and those students who appreciate this symbiotic relation can broaden their understanding of both arts taken individually and of opera as a type of art in which sung words and music are united to accentuate different aspects of each constituent art.

Music

The history of opera will include references to the history of music, the instruments used, and their development over time. Of course, the experience of preparing for and performing the opera will introduce students to a type of music that may be new to many if not most of them. It is not necessary in this regard to have the project become an exercise in learning the lexicon of technical musical vocabulary; but, during the process of preparation the students will absorb a number of aspects that pertain to the aesthetic details of this type of music.

Content Specific to Opera

In unfolding a narrative, the libretto of an opera will contain references, whether incidental or essential for the development of the plot, to a variety of useful items of knowledge that can be discussed in their own right, as well as integrated with more general areas in the curriculum. An obvious example from *La Bohème* is the pivotal importance of tuberculosis, the disease that carries off the heroine Mimi at a tragically tender age. This virulent lung disorder was once widespread, especially in Europe (although rare now, it has been reappearing in various places around the world). An informative unit could be developed focusing on the disease and describing the social and economic conditions of those groups of people most seriously affected by it. In general, virtually any opera contains references of this sort that, depending on the interest of the teacher and the makeup of the curriculum, could be used as points of departure for a variety of engaging and informative educational activities.

Educational Opportunities in Opera

The format in which opera was produced at Pritzker is an especially lively instance of Lyric Opera of Chicago's outreach programs. This approach—an abbreviated, mimed, and staged version of a major opera via a recording in the original language—is, of course, only one of various formats in which opera can be produced as both an educational and aesthetic experience for gifted students, indeed, any students endowed with the requisite interest.

Educators interested in pursuing opera might begin with Opera America's Database of Opera Education Programs http://www.operaamerica.org/education/programsearch.asp, a site useful as a starting point for general information on educational programs relating to opera and children. Educators should also be aware that nearly all regional, state, and city opera companies have programs in opera education.

The Metropolitan Opera of New York has an extensive educational program; it can be found on the Web at http://www.metguild.org/education. Entering "Atlanta Opera—Education," "Sacramento Opera—Education," "Edmonton Opera—Education," etc., on a standard search engine will provide access to an appropriate regional site. For example, the Indianapolis Opera has a disarmingly witty Web site to announce their highly diversified programs in opera education (under the supervision of Patty Harvey); it can be found at http://www.indy-opera.org.

Conclusion

Younger students may or may not choose to embrace a slice of the bohemian life once they embark on the adventures of adulthood, but the diversified educational experiences that surround them while preparing and performing *La Bohème* (or, of course, an equivalently appropriate work) will broaden and deepen their receptivity to the arts as they uniquely coalesce in the world of opera. Although opera is often considered to be a predominantly European medium of artistic expression, the recent past has seen a renaissance of opera in America to such an extent that the current scene in this country has sometimes been referred to as an impending operatic "golden age." William Bolcom's *A View From the Bridge*, Carlyle Floyd's *Of Mice and Men*, John Harbison's *The Great Gatsby*, Andre Previn's *A Streetcar Named Desire*; these are some of the prominent contemporary composers who have written operas that have been both popular with audiences and critically well received and are perhaps potential candidates for inclusion in the repertory alongside Puccini's *La Bohème* and other standard operatic fare. From an educator's standpoint, it is perhaps more than merely interesting to note that all the operas listed above are also based on classic American works of fiction, texts often found in curricula for gifted students. It may not be pedagogically utopian, then, to conclude with the thought that the more the education of gifted students incorporates opera in accessible formats, the more likely that this and succeeding generations of students will grow into maturity with an active appreciation for an art form that has been and continues to be one of the most vibrant and engaging in the world.

PART III

A Philosophical Postlude

CHAPTER 15

Gifted Education: The Event—and Advent—of Theory

Was Mozart gifted? Dickens? Einstein? It seems safe to say that any definition of giftedness would readily accommodate these three individuals. Indeed, perhaps they were what is referred to in the literature as "highly gifted." Or should we just shrug our psychological shoulders, call them geniuses, and be done with it?

There is an interesting and important issue in classification here, and we shall return to such matters in a moment. But, for present purposes, the more relevant question is: From the standpoint of gifted education, what experience did Mozart, Dickens, and Einstein have in common? The answer: When they went to school, gifted education did not exist. In their formative years, these three humanistic titans would have been taught in the same way as their youthful contemporaries. It is perhaps encouraging to realize that, if an individual is transcendentally great in some form of human endeavor, as these three certainly were, then such greatness will presumably manifest itself regardless of any inhibiting or systematically stultifying educational environment. But, what about the many doubtlessly gifted young people schooled with Wolfie and Charlie and Alby who never had an opportunity to display their abilities because their educational systems were not organized to allow for, much less encourage, realizing such abilities? It would be the world's loss, then and now and for posterity, if during these centuries other figures endowed with similar spirit and vision as Mozart, Dickens, and Einstein were in fact somehow crushed by a monolithic and unresponsive educational structure. But, it is also more than sobering to realize that, throughout this period (and, of course, long before), the world doubtless lost many exemplars of giftedness, albeit on a less sublime scale, because the *idea* of gifted education had not yet been envisioned.

It seems to me, then, that a truly epochal event in gifted education—although it may appear initially too obvious to affirm in this regard—was its origin in history and its subsequent entrance into the public arena. This is the occurrence that inspired the following reflections.

According to Jim Delisle (1997), the concept of giftedness arose in the early 1900s—among psychologists, not educators—and the advent of institutional programs for gifted education emerged in the 1950s. One might object that, since these two happenings are separated by roughly half a century, they can hardly be designated as "an" event. However, I suggest that the historical distance between them does not materially affect the fact that, as soon as gifted intelligence became a subject of serious scientific and reflective study and programs for the gifted were instituted in schools, then what might be called the dimension of giftedness became ineluctably intertwined with both theory and practice. Furthermore, at the point when educating the gifted became a public concern, it also assumed, necessarily, a political vesture. Thus, gifted education was and is (a) theoretical, (b) valuational, and (c) practical—in the sense of requiring decisions based on thought and implemented in the "real" world (i.e., in schools where gifted students are often being educated next door to regular students). And finally, once it penetrated this broad spectrum of human activity, gifted education also became a full-fledged candidate for philosophical inquiry.

A brief autobiographical interruption: As is evident by now for anyone who has seen something of the present volume, my primary area of academic interest is philosophy. Also, I am a late arrival to gifted education via a rather circuitous route (I have been blessed with two extremely bright sons, both of whom are much smarter than I am and whose inherent abilities have been strengthened by a steady diet of gifted education). Although I cannot claim anything close to an adequate control of the literature on gifted education, whether in books or journals, I have done the best I can with available time to become acquainted with the issues and positions that animate this branch of education. With this cautionary proviso in mind, I ask the reader's indulgence to accompany me

on what might be a voyage—albeit brief—of discovery with potentially useful relevance for gifted education as it enters the new millennium.

By way of introduction, consider the following exchange between Richard Ronvik, formerly (now retired) director of gifted programs for the Chicago Public Schools, and John Feldhusen, Robert B. Kane Distinguished Professor of Education at Purdue University. In an article, Ronvik (1993) had claimed that educators who wished to substitute "talented" for "gifted" were risking confusion, since "no one seems to know what it [talented] means, or perhaps more accurately everyone thinks it means something else" (p. 8). Feldhusen's (1993) rejoinder was that "it is almost incredible to say no one knows what 'talent' means," and he cited several sources—including a work by Mihalyi Csikszentmihalyi—to substantiate this claim (p. 14). Ronvik (1994) replied to Feldhusen's rejoinder by citing four other definitions of "talented" drawn from "the literature and common usage in the field of gifted education," concluding that "each definition would yield a different population of children" (p. 15).

One might be tempted to dismiss this colloquy as just another instance of authorities politely sparring in print. However, this hasty and negative assessment overlooks what is instructive and vital about the exchange. Ronvik's conclusion accentuates the point that, if indeed the concept of "talent" is disputed and not yet amenable to clear and satisfactory definition, then the presence of four different accounts of the term will yield four different populations of children so designated. It may also be observed (Ronvik leaves the following point implicit) that, if pedagogical policy were implemented strictly in accordance with the definition of foundational concepts, then it is entirely possible that three of these four groups of children would not be provided with educational opportunities to exercise and expand their talents. The reason is straightforward: In fact, they were *not* talented, that is, not as (hypothetically) determined by the lights of the one account of "talent" that had been adopted as decisive by the administrative powers that be.

The point is not to root for Ronvik and hoot at Feldhusen. What should be observed in this exchange is the way in which the challenge to the original claim was handled. Ronvik recognized the import of that challenge, cited sources that demonstrated and reinforced his position, and then—importantly—drew a logical conclusion from that demonstration that would have serious and presumably objectionable consequences if it were made a principle for decision and action.

Furthermore, let us consider the other side. For even if it should turn out that Feldhusen is correct and that the nature of "talent" is indeed accessible to educators, then its accessibility is not merely because an authority in the field has pronounced "talent" to mean this or that, but because the justification and evidence cited by this authority is more credible than that provided by other investigators working in the same area.

The issues and problems driving gifted education since its inception are complex and often subject to dispute. The Ronvik/Feldhusen exchange helps to teach us what we should be looking for to put us in a better position to clarify, if not to resolve, such disagreements. We do not just look for someone who claims, whether aloud or in print, to know the answer to a question and then dutifully follow that individual's answer. We must examine how we respond to and evaluate such claims, and we should proceed with this type of examination by expending at least as much vigor as that used in the original consideration of views presented by others.

I suggest, therefore, that the principal lesson to be learned from the above discussion is *respect for the theoretical dimension* in both the professional discourse and applied classroom activity of gifted education. The point is not

that educators concerned with the gifted should embrace the highly diverse—and often frenetic—world of academic philosophy, their discourse drawn from, contoured by, or punctuated with judiciously selected passages from the philosophical giants of the past or present. Rather, it is that educators, and of course parents, as well, should be aware of the fact that (a) their practical decisions are only a manifest outgrowth from theoretical positions with deep-seated philosophical roots, in some cases from a heritage of thought that goes back several thousand years, and (b) these positions are themselves based on assumptions and beliefs concerning the structure of knowledge, the range of values, and the nature of reality. Every time an article is written, read, and then acted upon, every time a decision is made by an administrator selecting a gifted curriculum or by a teacher exercising a "practical" pedagogical option, the decisions and actions rest on a complex and typically tacit theoretical foundation. Even apparently simple descriptions of the behavior of individual students or specific classroom situations, not to mention recommendations for curricular strategies, definitions of fundamental terms, (e.g., *gifted*, *talented*, etc.), are all inherently laden with theoretical elements.

It is evident to anyone seriously involved with the subject that there is a burgeoning body of literature concerning gifted education—books, journals, magazines, conference proceedings. The following list is not intended to be exhaustive, but it details some of the main types of material found in published discourse devoted to gifted education:

- reports on and conclusions drawn from empirical research;
- discussions of theoretical issues and questions of definition;
- descriptions of programs and projects intended for the gifted; and

- anecdotal accounts of experiences with gifted children, including subsequent generalizations intended for a wider population.

Theory is variously present among all these types. The problem is to appreciate the presence of this foundational dimension and to become as aware of its structure and import as possible.

What, then, is the most practical way to interact with the theoretical dimension of discourse on giftedness? Educators of the gifted can be philosophical simply in being aware of the presence of the theoretical in everything they do, whether describing and reflecting on a particular experience, reflectively planning a program, or actively executing that plan. Thus, the practices involved in *critical thinking*, so often urged as essential to the teaching of the gifted (a version of which drives the discussion of Chapter 11) should also become second nature to educators of the gifted. Here are several parameters that incorporate the primary avenues of critical evaluation philosophy offers in this regard. These parameters provide useful guidelines regarding the process of formulating and applying policies pertaining to gifted education.

A. Look for Assumptions

Much literature in gifted education intends to establish a definite goal, or at least to recommend that a certain goal be taken seriously as an option. But, the tenability of that goal is only as strong as the assumptions that underlie the explicit argumentation and discussion leading to this conclusion. It is vital, then, to identify pertinent assumptions relevant to the issue under scrutiny that might affect a decision regarding its disposition. Here one must "take a step back" from the immediate context of the discussion and reflect on (a) what has not been said in the discussion that might be relevant to its point and (b) what has been said that might be vague, incorrect, or premature. Recalling

details from the full range of one's personal experience is essential in becoming aware of assumptions that might affect the reliability of the conclusion advanced.

B. Check for Consistency

Does the discussion maintain a position that, upon due examination, yields incompatible consequences? If so, then logically the discussion is flawed and its apparent merits must be re-examined to determine the extent to which they are affected by this incompatibility. Such formal incompatibility can emerge in at least two ways: first, internally, *within* the discussion itself when the author makes claims that do not cohere logically with one another, or second, *between* something said in the discussion and aspects of experience not considered in the discussion as such, but that the reader or listener accept as facts. In either case, it is the responsibility of an appropriately aware observer to note any such problem and to determine its effect on the point of the discussion as a whole.

C. Search for Implications

Adopting either a specific recommendation on a limited matter or a fully developed position on a curriculum is a decision with consequences. It is important, first, to be aware of this fact, and then to recognize as many of the consequences as possible. Theoretical positions are often seductive at first glance, especially if these positions have been developed in the relatively brief confines of journals or magazines. Educators should be reminded that an account that sounds good coming off the printed page or heard at a presentation actually may not *be* good once its assumptions and consequences—typically unstated—have been brought into view and examined with care. The question that should always be posed in this regard: What follows if the point of the discussion, whatever that point may be, is adopted as a plan of action?

It has been argued that we should respect the broad boundaries and underlying importance of *theory* in addressing the many questions and problems that face gifted education as it embarks on its second century. However, it also goes without saying that adopting the recommendations sketched above will require patience, persistence, some practice perhaps, and close attention to detail. But, the effort is eminently worthwhile. Although the world may never again see the likes of a Mozart, there are nevertheless an untold number of gifted children who deserve our most persevering efforts in maximizing their opportunities to realize their potential. A first step in such assistance is recognizing our responsibility to be as thoughtful and careful as possible in preparing, implementing, and assessing the programs, both formal and informal, that help contour their young lives. Gifted education can solidify its foundations and extend the remarkable advances that have already been made for so many children by embracing and respecting the dimension of theory as an essential element in its origin and development.

References

Delisle, J. (1997). Gifted children: The heart of the matter. *Understanding Our Gifted, 9*(3), 3–6,

Feldhusen, J. (1993). Foundations of talent: A rejoinder to Ronvik. *Understanding Our Gifted, 6*(2), 14.

Ronvik, R. (1993). Re-examining the foundations of giftedness. *Understanding Our Gifted, 5*(6), 1, 8–14.

Ronvik, R. (1994). A response to John Feldhusen's rejoinder. *Understanding Our Gifted, 6*(3), 15.

CHAPTER 16

"Edutainment": Gifted Education and the Perils of Misusing Multiple Intelligences

James Delisle—*Gifted Child Today*'s unofficial resident curmudgeon—offered in his regular column "Au Contraire" (November/December 1996, pp. 12–13) a series of sharply etched criticisms concerning the relevance of the concept of multiple intelligences when applied to gifted education. This chapter develops the position Delisle staked out by showing that care must be taken before applying the useful perspectives offered by multiple intelligences (MI) to practical matters of education and curricula, especially for gifted children.

It is a well-known fact that some children are multiply gifted—they excel, for example, in academics, art, and athletics. It would seem, then, that the concept of multiple intelligences would be eminently suited to accommodate the multiply gifted complexity of such individuals. In his 1983 book *Frames of Mind*, Harvard psychologist Howard Gardner argued that there are seven distinct intelligences. He elaborated this fundamental division in a more recent work: "we are all able to know the world through language, logical-mathematical analysis, spatial representation, musical thinking, the use of the body to solve problems or to make things, an understanding of other individuals, and an understanding of ourselves" (1991, p. 12). What does this principle reveal about an especially gifted human being?

One of the most important questions confronting the multiply gifted is simple: What should they do and when should they do it? But, although the question is simple, the answer is not. Does MI provide assistance in resolving this all-too-real dilemma?

For example, what aspect of a multiply gifted child's personality tells her *when* she should play music and when she should play soccer? Clearly it is not her ability as a sensitive and skilled musician that informs her when she should practice a Mozart sonata; just as clearly, it is not her ability as an agile athlete that informs her when she must practice her dribbling and passing. Such "intelligences" are dumb in these matters; they do not speak to her when she must make a decision about how to spend her time. It is, rather, her ability to think and reason and evaluate that allows her to make these decisions.

Furthermore, it is possible that she might let her natural excellence in these other "intelligences" usurp her good judgment. If this were to happen, then in the long run the best interests of this multiply gifted child might not be served. Although it is good for a gifted musician to be the best musician possible, it might be better for a given individual to balance the degree of excellence obtainable in music with comparable competence in other forms of human endeavor. Glenn Gould, one of the most accomplished pianists in the second half of the 20th century, was by many accounts a social misfit. Thus, it is not clear that his acknowledged excellence in one intelligence should stand as a paradigm for the pursuit of excellence in intelligences generally.

These observations are not offered as blinding insights, but only as an account that has the minimal virtue of being rather obvious. If so, then important lessons can be drawn for understanding the relevance of multiple intelligences in gifted education. These lessons may be grouped around a pair of questions: (a) Why are these abilities called "intelligences"? (b) Even if these abilities are justifiably designated as intelligences, do they all have the same value in a gifted child's life and education?

Gardner uses one word—*intelligence*—to name a group of distinct abilities. The fact that a single word is used is important and the fact that this one word is *intelligence* is even more important. The word *intelligence* has what philosophers call a normative, as well as an empirical or factual, sense. The empirical sense is measurable: Gifted children are intelligent and can be recognized as such because, for example, they achieve high scores on standardized tests. The normative sense of *intelligence* is more shadowy, less easily described, but no less real. Someone who is described as and known to be *intelligent* is usually accorded a certain measure of respect; for example, his or her views tend to be taken with a greater degree of seriousness. There is, of course, another normative side, the brunt of which is all too often experienced by those who are gifted. In certain situations, intellectually gifted children are subjected to teasing and even worse by their age peers. It is important to note, then, that the word's normative sense is not always positive. Unfortunately, quite the opposite is often true: The appearance and usage of the word can elicit cruel responses from those who view individuals with high intelligence as strange or even threatening.

The immediate concern is, however, not with the empirical or valuational aspects of the word *intelligence* as such. Rather, the intent is to indicate certain features of the word that are crucially important when *intelligence* becomes part of "multiple intelligences."

The fact that one word—*intelligence*—is used implies that there must be something in common between and among *all* the multiple abilities that have been named by that one word. For if there is no common element in all these abilities, then using one word to describe all of them is misleading, perhaps seriously so. If a particular ability has been described as an "intelligence," it is reasonable to think that there must be something in common between that ability—whatever it may be—and intelligence in the usual and narrower sense of the term.

What property, then, do all Gardner's diverse abilities share? To begin, note that the way the gifted child understands and displays excellence in music involves a correlation between the mind and certain motor skills. Note also that this correlation is absent in the way a gifted child understands and displays excellence in mathematics. The motor skills involved in writing out a problem in mathematics are hardly essential to mathematical understanding; indeed, in the age of calculators, the gifted young mathematician is required only to have the ability to press the correct buttons. To carry the point to extremes, the physicist Stephen Hawking, preeminently gifted in mathematics, is virtually immobile, yet this handicap does not hinder his excellence. It would seem then that logico-mathematical intelligence is predominantly mental, whereas the ability to excel in music is an indivisible blend of mental capacity and motor skill.

If the point is to establish the common property in all the intelligences, then it becomes essential to isolate and identify the strictly mental functions involved in logico-mathematical intelligence. Once this identification is made, the next step is to establish correlations between and among equivalent mental functions in the other "intelligences" in order to show that the intelligence exercised in doing mathematics is the same as, or even similar to, as the intelligence involved in making music or playing a sport. Furthermore, even if all these mental functions can be determined as identical, the intelligence activated when making music or playing a sport requires that these mental functions must be intimately connected with motor skills. This connection undoubtedly complicates those intelligences in interesting and important ways. Thus, the intelligence of an exceptionally gifted athlete such as Michael Jordan or Tiger Woods may be, in its own way, no less complex as the correlative intelligence of either a Glenn Gould or a Stephen Hawking.

In sum, it may be suggested that, although it is possible that the ways gifted children understand how to do mathematics, how to play music, or how to be athletic may be similar or perhaps even identical to one another, the identification of those specific mental and motor skills that would confirm this belief is not easily secured. If this conclusion has even marginal merit, then it is not clear what has been gained by naming *all* these abilities as "intelligences." The common name seems to conceal important differences even as it elevates nonacademic abilities to the honorific level enjoyed by intelligence understood in a predominantly academic sense.

Another problematic aspect of MI should be brought into the open. Gardner (1991) asserts as a matter of principle that individuals "possess varying amounts of these intelligences and combine and use them in personal and idiosyncratic ways" (p. 81). Thus, when a multiply gifted child decides that she must do homework rather than play Mozart or soccer, she combines the following intelligences: (a) linguistic—in clearly and precisely formulating in her mind the alternatives she faces; (b) logico-mathematical reasoning—in identifying her goals and then reasoning from these goals to the resolution of the immediate alternatives at hand; and (c) intrapersonal—in assessing how she feels about these alternatives and then drawing on her inner resources in actively making her choice.

If this description accurately portrays the mechanics of such decisions in terms of the intelligences laid down by MI, then it may be contended that the real motive power actualizing this choice is an indivisible intersection of *all three* of these intelligences. Much is incorporated in this intersection: the child's ability to formulate principles expressed linguistically, the machinery of her reasoning, and her sense of values to know how to apply those principles in relation to what she has learned about her world.

Only this intersecting function of intelligence knows and decides when and how to employ the other intelligences. Furthermore, only this aspect of intelligence can gather and control the kind of information required so that an informed decision can be made for the usage of *all* other intelligences. Aristotle would have called this intersection "practical wisdom." And one could make the case that practical wisdom should be considered as a candidate for status as yet another distinct kind of intelligence since such wisdom cannot be reduced to the simple addition of language skills + logical skills + intrapersonal awareness.

These reflections have important consequences for gifted education. It is clearly essential to do everything possible to realize the vast potential of not only all gifted children, but also all multiply gifted children—those who combine excellence in academics with excellence in music or athletics or other forms of human endeavor. To the extent that MI has increased awareness of the importance of all these endeavors as legitimate avenues of education, it has provided an inestimable service not only to the cause of gifted education, but to education generally. To present the ability to play sports or to make music or to appreciate adult humor or to have a well-ordered personality or any of the other abilities covered by MI as *important* and *essential* to the goals of education is a valuable theoretical advance, and Gardner should be applauded for his eloquence in humanizing abilities that are all too often given the short end of the educational stick. In fact, I have made use of the concept of multiple intelligences as a helpful schematic for organizing the effects of several innovations in gifted education (Breen & White, 1996a, 1996b). But, to embrace MI uncritically, without examining with care its implications for the complexities involved when applying this concept to gifted children, is unwise and perhaps even dangerous.

Consider one possible avenue of excess. Gardner (1991) asserts that, until now, "most schools in most cultures have stressed a certain combination of linguistic and logical intelligences," and although he admits that this "combination is important for mastering the agenda of school," he nonetheless insists that "we have gone too far in ignoring the other intelligences," thereby failing to "take advantage of the ways in which multiple intelligences can be exploited to further the goals of schools and the broader culture" (p. 81).

As already noted, Gardner's appeal to develop the possibilities inherent in intelligences other than that which embodies linguistic and logical abilities is laudatory in perfecting the abilities of the gifted child as an integrated human whole. But, the potential danger resides in failing to preserve the fact that what Gardner calls the "linguistic and logical" intelligence is also the locus of an undeniably *directive* function in relation to these other abilities. And this directive function must surely be preserved.

Unfortunately, the concept of MI—at least insofar as it has entered the popular mind—generates for some on the educational scene a kind of pedagogical democracy that has dangerous implications. For if an educator believed that all intelligences are equal in value, there would be no reason against selecting any one of them and then inviting children—gifted or otherwise—to enjoy themselves by making music, dancing, playing sports, socializing, all in the name of "educating" that intelligence and thereby, it is hoped, educating the person as a whole.

Consider two examples, both real-life pedagogical experiences of Maureen Breen (retired French teacher in the International Baccalaureate Program at Lincoln Park High School in Chicago), both justified by their advocates as proper applications of "multiple intelligences."

1. A professional sports franchise is contemplating a move from its home in a large urban area to a neighboring suburb. The idea is evolved of having students respond to this situation by addressing it according to the seven intelligences (e.g., determining how much money would be saved by the move [logico-mathematical], writing letters to local politicians supporting or criticizing the move [linguistic], etc.). The justification for this application of MI is that the students *liked* the sports team and therefore they would enjoy employing the seven intelligences in their educational interaction with this situation.

2. Keeping a journal is a popular pedagogical device. To broaden her students' experience of colonial life, a social studies teacher has each child select an occupation and then write an "imaginative" account of that life. The seven intelligences would be addressed collectively as each student described how his or her occupation—carpenter, judge, surveyor, homemaker, seamstress, merchant—is practiced and how it contributes to the social well-being of the community.

These two examples illustrate a pair of excesses to which MI is subject. First, MI can be applied to a phenomenon or event that may possess a certain local celebrity, but which has little or no lasting educational value. Thus, the sheer exercise of multiple intelligences will not, by itself, be useful educationally if the *content* of this exercise lacks substance. The point is not to denigrate sports franchises and the individuals who follow their results, only to suggest that some subjects are intrinsically more important than others and that the application of MI cannot make something relatively unimportant into something important.

Second, the content toward which MI is directed may be perfectly appropriate, but the *approach* to that content must respect basic intellectual norms. Children can incisively write imaginative accounts of occupations in colonial times, but only if their prior understanding has been fully equipped with appropriate facts about those occupations. To exercise the seven intelligences only or even primarily through the imagination helps only the imagination, not students' comprehension of the reality toward which their imagination is directed. In this case, academically important issues are touched only in a tangential way because of the newly found "appropriateness" of addressing the seven intelligences.

Edutainment is a hybrid name for these styles of education—ungrounded appeals to fun or entertainment as a suitable basis for innovation in the name of educating a specific type of neglected intelligence. But, playing to such an isolated specification is an indulgence and surely a mistake. Before a musical or dramatic evocation or enhancement or even a "fun" extension of a particular concept or lesson can be secured, the nature of that concept or lesson must be at least provisionally understood by the child. To attempt to instill understanding of a given subject by having gifted children perform purely imaginative representations derived from that subject in isolation from what might old-fashionedly be termed "intellectual knowledge" presumes that the musical or spatial intelligences required for these enhancement activities are somehow sufficiently verbal and cognitive enough in and of themselves to inform that one intelligence that is naturally suited for displaying the student's knowledge of the subject matter.

This assumption is, at best, dubious. Unless these activities are *directed* by knowledge of the subject matter grounding these activities, their educational purpose will not be properly understood. Thus, it is essential to place priority, again, on that intelligence—or intersection of intelligences—that provides the gifted child with the understanding of what other intelligences may well be capable of reinforcing and vivifying. It may be suggested that the intelligences involved in dance or theater or music or any of the other forms of nonlinguistic or logical intelligence must follow the lead of that intelligence that governs knowledge about a given subject matter.

Although doubtlessly well intentioned, these "edutainments" will result in little more than quick fixes and poor substitutions for the lack of grounding in foundational skills required by even the most gifted children. If, in thoughtless subservience to the democratic character of the concept of multiple intelligence, a generation of teachers were to forgo teaching what they know (e.g., rudimentary linguistic skills such as diagramming sentences), then this kind of knowledge would be lost and, once lost, would become very difficult for the succeeding generation to restore.

The point is not a reactionary cry for the curricular rigidity of the pedagogical past—when, in fact, gifted education was effectively nonexistent. The point is only to remind educators of the gifted that, although they bear the heavy responsibility of maximizing *all* the intelligences—or abilities—of *all* their students, these abilities are not all equal in all respects. An oversimplified and overly zealous development of the useful and important concept of multiple intelligences should not obscure this fundamental truth.

References

Breen, M., & White, D. (1996a). The oldest cave art: An essay on giftedness and excellence. *Gifted Child Today, 19*(2), 28–31, 46. [Reprinted, with minor modifications, as Chapter 12]

Breen, M., & White, D. (1996b). The philosophy of French Funetics: An essay in applied gifted intelligence. *Roeper Review, 19*(1), 44–50. [Reprinted, with minor modifications, as Chapter 13]

Delisle, J. (1996). Multiple intelligences: Convenient, simple, wrong. *Gifted Child Today, 19*(6), 12–13.

Gardner, H. (1983). *Frames of mind: The theory of multiple intelligences.* New York: BasicBooks.

Gardner, H. (1991). *The unschooled mind: How children think and how schools should teach.* New York: BasicBooks.

CHAPTER 17

Philosophy and Theory in the Study of Gifted Children

What was Plato like as a child and, later, as an adolescent? Was he precociously brilliant and voluble, amazing everyone in Athens with his gifts for language and reasoned insight, or was he quiet, reserved, and only average in his studies, effectively concealing the greatness that was to come? There is no way to answer this question now, but it brings to mind the obvious point that even the most profound philosophers were once children, perhaps manifestly gifted, perhaps not. And this truism is set in opposition by another: Children, all children, have been virtually ignored by philosophers, at least as a subject for systematic study.

The key word here is *systematic*, for children have certainly appeared in the work of many philosophers. Plato himself spends significant time and energy in the *Republic* laying down what he believes to be the appropriate educational system for those children, younger and through adolescence, who will eventually function in their maturity as the guardians of the just state. In the course of this discussion, the nature of children is either described or implicit. And a number of other philosophers have discussed or referred to children in one context or another, although typically without making them the focal point of their concern. Yet, on the whole, it is a fair generalization that philosophers in the West have tended to assume that the most compelling aspects of the human condition originate sometime after adolescence cools off and at the point when we have lurched, more or less prepared, into adulthood.

Nonetheless, substantive material is available for reflective inquiry, assuming the interested student of philosophical perspectives on childhood knows where to look. In fact, this quest has been markedly facilitated by a book of essays edited by Susan M. Turner and Gareth B. Matthews: *The Philosopher's Child: Critical Essays in the*

Western Tradition (1998). This work provides a review of positions on the nature of children as developed by some of the pivotal figures in Western philosophy—among them Plato, Aristotle, the Stoics, Hobbes, Locke, Kant, Rousseau, Mill, and Wittgenstein.

Of course, none of the accounts of philosophers' stances on the nature of children is specifically limited to gifted children. The reflections of these philosophers were intended to cover all children, regardless of any divisions or distinctions that may subsequently be applied to children understood collectively as a single class. The fact that this fundamental priority underlies classical and modern philosophical accounts of children is indirectly beneficial in several respects to reasoned inquiry concerning the gifted. First, if the accounts studied are even approximately correct in their claims about the nature of all children, then any derivation from these accounts for purposes of defining or clarifying traits distinctive to the gifted will reflect the universal base providing the foundational notions and principles in the formulation of these traits. Thus, any subsequent claim made about an aspect of the gifted will always be viewed against the backdrop of a theoretical position produced on the basis of deliberations about all children, not just a preselected group. Second, when sharply delimited classifications of what exactly constitutes "giftedness" (and subdivisions of this category) are in dispute—which seems to be inevitable, both as a matter of theory and in applied educational and social policy—then the fact that any such division has been derived from a theoretical position that has included all children will, or at least should, strengthen the reliability of such classifications. Finally, the more that is known about gifted children as derived from this theoretical base, the more it will be possible to apply that knowledge to such children, especially with respect to the broad diversity of their capacities and individual characteristics.

Preliminary Philosophical Survey

The following summaries recapitulate portions of two essays in *The Philosopher's Child* devoted to figures who reside at both ends of the historical spectrum: the Stoic philosophers in the Hellenistic and Roman eras and the contemporary political philosopher John Rawls (1921–2002). It will become evident that the intersection of these two approaches to children produces theoretical differences that, in turn, generate concepts and hypotheses with a timely relevance to important issues in understanding giftedness.

John Rawls' theory of justice was one of the most discussed positions in ethics and political philosophy in the latter half of the 20th century, and it continues to interest contemporary philosophers. One of the pivotal concepts in that theory is the notion of *stability*. As the authors of the essay on Rawls, Samantha Brennan and Robert Noggle (1998), state, "[t]o be stable, a conception of justice must be capable of gaining our allegiance, of providing us with motivation to support the institutions which it endorses" (p. 214). Thus, for Rawls, it is not sufficient simply to develop a coherent and compelling theory of justice; he must also show why that theory would be chosen as worthy against competing theories, thus ensuring stability in the polity governed by this theoretical—and, if chosen, applied—approach to justice.

In the course of explaining and justifying his notion of stability, Rawls applies the well-known account of moral development advanced by Jean Piaget and Lawrence Kohlberg. According to this theory, moral development occurs in three stages. The authors outline Rawls' version of the theory as follows.

The first stage is the "morality of authority" (the authors assert that the counterpart Piaget stage is called the "morality of heteronomy"), when the child is "utterly helpless and completely dependent on the parent" (p. 214).

Rawls refers to the second stage as the "morality of association," which Piaget calls the "morality of cooperation" (p. 216). Here associations and cooperative activities participated in by children "spark the development of the child's sense of justice; the skills the child learns as she cooperates are the building blocks of the morality of association" (p. 216). The playing of games is one of the principal means emphasized by Piaget for instilling a sense of justice; the authors summarize: "as children see that the rules of games make cooperation possible, and as they develop the desire to cooperate with others, they come to respect the rules that make cooperation possible" (p. 217).

The third and final stage for Rawls is produced when the child desires to comply with the principles of justice purely out of respect for them "as principles" (here the authors quote Rawls directly), rather than because of "ties of friendship and fellow feeling for others, and . . . concern for the approbation of the wider society" (p. 217). But, it is crucial to see the reason why, according to Rawls, we embrace this third stage of justice from the standpoint of principle (Brennan and Noggle again quote Rawls): "We develop a desire to apply and to act upon the principles of justice once we realize how social arrangements answering to them have promoted our good and that of those with whom we are affiliated" (p. 217). In other words, according to Rawls, the second stage of moral development fosters the sense of cooperation through the acceptance of rules and the third stage broadens this acceptance to the rules of justice as soon as we realize that these rules have satisfied our self-interest and the self-interests of those close to us in some way. Thus, the principle of justice is accorded respect precisely because of its benefits to ourselves and to others around us.

Compare this account of moral development with that described by Lawrence C. Becker in his essay on "Stoic Children" (1998). Stoic philosophers (e.g., Epictetus, Seneca, Marcus Aurelius) exercised a leading influence in Hellenistic and Roman intellectual life during the period from about 300 B.C. until 200 A.D. As an essential component in their analysis of human nature, these philosophers presented a theory of moral development that reacted against the Epicurean belief that what motivated infants was the desire to seek pleasure and avoid pain. According to the Stoics, infants in the cradle are motivated by their attachment to and affection for themselves. This affection results in the attempt to satisfy all their primal impulses. Thus, it was clear to the Stoics, says Becker, "that infants often subordinated pleasure-seeking to other pursuits such as efforts to move, to explore their environment, to observe, respond, mimic and learn" (p. 49). As a result, "the initial, conditional affection for the things as means to ends is converted . . . into an affection that is quite independent of perceptions of a thing's instrumental worth" (p. 49). Becker illustrates the point as follows: "it does not matter that the breast is dry, the brightly colored object is dulled, the blanket is no longer warm, the cradle is no longer big enough." As long as these phenomena have been appropriated into our range of active interests, "we have affection for them in themselves, for their own sakes." In short, they have "intrinsic value for us" (p. 50).

In general, then, true belief, correct conduct, and rule following for its own sake are recognized as important whether or not any of these activities are useful for our immediate interests. "Children come to value, for its own sake, doing things in the right way for the right reasons" (Becker, 1998, p. 51). Furthermore, on the Stoic account, "the infant's natural, initial focus on self-preservation and self-interest for its own sake is very quickly supplemented by an equally natural focus on the needs and interests of others, as ends in themselves" (p. 53). One essential way in which this focus on the needs and interests of others is informed revolves around the virtue of justice. Thus, justice becomes a value to the child primarily not because it is a virtue that will contribute directly to his or her own personal well-being, but because it is a virtue that, if properly implemented, will contribute to *everyone's* well-being.

The difference between these two accounts of moral development may appear initially to be slight, more a matter of emphasis than of substance. But, upon closer examination, certain developmental differences become stark and dramatic. For Rawls, justice emerges from the interaction of groups, principally (as Piaget emphasizes) when the members of these groups are at play in games; for the Stoics, a sense of justice develops as the result of the recognition that processes and people have an intrinsic value, quite apart from the immediate usefulness of those processes and people to the individual child.

If the Stoic account is correct, then the child has an inherent receptivity for disinterested value. But, since the value is disinterested, the nature of the value must be defined and described in terms detailing how it is possible for the child to be receptive toward this kind of apprehension. Here is one possible account based on Stoic principles: The end valued is somehow attractive, an attraction that emerges apart from the gratification of interest in a directly physical or emotional sense. The child recognizes not only that acting for an end will produce a good or beneficial result in this particular case and these particular circumstances, but also that the relation of controlling an action in order to achieve an end is good and beneficial.

This recognition has two phases that are distinguishable developmentally. First comes the realization that this relation exists, abstractly, in the sense that its implementation can be effected in a wide variety of ways and for a wide variety of human agents. Thus, the child senses that it is not only good that justice is done to him or her—it is also good, indeed it is even better, that justice is done to everyone. As a result, the comprehensive relation between justice as such and all individuals affected by justice comprises part of the truly valuable aspect of justice—a virtue that, when duly applied, has an obvious importance for an individual's self-interest. Second, the Stoic account suggests that the child then senses and appreciates this fundamental relation by focusing on the fact that justice itself grounds that relation through its own unique value. To understand and appreciate an end as intrinsically valuable (as valuable in itself apart from its immediate benefit to the observer) is to recognize a kind of reality that is abstract, divorced from the realm of the observer's immediate self-interest. And the attraction, the lure that beckons even the young child, is the fulfillment the mind experiences when it comes into contact with something characterized with a certain specified abstract content that the mind explicitly recognizes as abstract. Exactly how this transition is accomplished in the mind of the child is, of course, a process that must be described more fully and with appropriate psychological experimentation and data. The relevant point for present purposes is only that the Stoic position offers this transition as a possibility worthy of consideration in the formation of a child's sense of value.

It has been mentioned above that the Stoic account is intended for all children, not just for those children who are gifted. However, what on the Stoic account defines the developmental process of acquiring receptivity to and appreciation of values such as justice at an early age can, with appropriate expansion, also contribute toward an explanation of two characteristics of the gifted once they have developed this kind of recognition: (a) the tendency toward increased sensitivity to justice and its opposite, injustice; and (b) the drive to attain perfection.

Justice as Fairness

It has often been observed that the gifted tend to be acutely sensitive to justice as fairness, a trait manifested primarily toward instances of injustice since these instances flagrantly violate the respect that the virtue of justice itself so rightly deserves. Note that this phenomenon is not readily explainable on the Rawls/Piaget model of moral development. For if all children learn their sense of justice primarily by participating in cooperative ventures such as games and if it is assumed that equal numbers of gifted and nongifted children participate in playing games, then there would be no reason for the gifted to be more developmentally sensitive to injustice than the nongifted.

By contrast, the Stoic model of moral development affords suitable grounds for an explanation. The Stoic account allows for the possibility that gifted children are more sensitive to infringements against justice because they can more clearly recognize justice *as a principle,* rather than merely as a practical, immediately sensed guideline defining or characterizing events in which people interact in certain mutually beneficial ways. Thus, when the gifted child observes what is perceived to be an injustice perpetrated against other individuals, he or she acutely feels the wrongness of such actions, not because these actions damage his or her own self-interest as such, but because the unjust action is experienced as a violation against the *principle* of justice. As we have seen, although the Rawls/Piaget account of moral development would also have justice recognized as a principle, this recognition is characterized more in terms of the benefits conferred by justice, rather than on the apprehension of the principle of justice by itself, with its own inherent value.

Since, however, the gifted are capable of perceiving and understanding the importance of this principle as being equal to, if not greater than, particular concrete instances of actions or behavior considered just or unjust, it will follow that violations of the principle are reacted to with the same, perhaps even greater, intensity and fervor than if a particular person—either themselves or a friend—had been treated unjustly. The Stoic account suggests that the gifted have internalized the principle of justice as fairness to a degree that exceeds the counterpart sensitivity of their nongifted peers, and they reflect this greater apprehension by their broader, more sensitive, and intense response to violations of justice experienced in their environment, whether that environment is contoured by immediate or remote personal boundaries.

The Pursuit of Excellence

The recognition that a given end is valuable for its own sake apart from any dimension of immediate self-interest, whether subtle or crass, locates the affective and intellectual nature of the gifted child on a level of reality that allows a ready transfer to other objectives that share characteristics with this kind of reality. The inherently valuable end described above is justice understood as a principle. But, when their child grows and develops, this apprehension radiates in similar ways into diverse realms of experience. Thus, one of the most common—and, for teachers of the gifted, often exasperating—characteristics of gifted children is their intense desire for perfection. Dissatisfaction with their work because it is deemed to be less than perfect is frequently recognized as a characteristic of this age group. These individuals seem to be striving to attain a degree of excellence in their endeavors that always remains a measure beyond the limits of realistic actualization.

The student appraises his or her own work. It is good, thinks the student, indeed it is perhaps deemed to be very good. But, it could be better. There may or may not be time and opportunity for additional labor on the project. But, even if time and opportunity are available and the project is improved, it remains less than perfect, less worthy than it might have been—with the student fully, perhaps even painfully, aware of this gap between the reality at hand, however good it may be, and the possibility of a level of achievement that is in some sense visible, but remains distant from the realm of practical realization.

This cycle of unrequited labor has no end, to the painful distress of the individual attempting to circumnavigate it. In practice, the cycle will conclude either when the project must be submitted in order to fulfill a stated deadline or, if the project is self-initiated, when the student simply and perhaps grudgingly decides that life and time must be allowed to march on. It becomes evident that this student is seeking a level of perfection that exists only in the mind's eye, that is, it is perfection as an abstraction, as a sort of ideal goal that is not and, importantly, may never be achievable.

The desire to pursue excellence is, according to this hypothesis, a recognition of the abstract nature of excellence as a value existing for its own sake. The gifted child does not aspire to excellence to appease or impress others, whether friend, student, or teacher, since only one so gifted is aware, as a dimension of self-knowledge, of this ideal level of achievement. Thus, the often all-too-real motive of self-aggrandizement is lacking. The gifted child is not actually in competition with others; he or she is competing with a standard that exists in a realm of reality that is accessible only to the mind of the individual beset by this kind of competition. In a very real sense, the child is striving to be excellent just for the sake of being as good as possible. The child has won an awareness of excellence *as a principle* existing in its own right, apart from the public validation of awards or the articulated compliments of others, whether peers, teachers, or judges. This awareness is of a principle commanding respect and beckoning to the gifted child to be approached and, if possible, appropriated. But, even if excellence cannot be appropriated fully, the drive to approximate it as closely as possible remains no less intense and demanding to the individual caught in the subtle apprehension of this state of ideal perfection.

Conclusion

The two examples of giftedness illuminated by the Stoic account of moral development should not be logically linked. The point is not to claim, or even to intimate, that a gifted child who is sensitive to injustice will also, and inevitably, be driven by perfectionism (or vice versa). The suggestion is only that the recognition of the possible relevance of a theory of moral development observed and described by Stoic philosophers can provide a basis for explaining these two different characteristics of the gifted.

It is essential to emphasize that these explanations, as presented here, are viable only at the theoretical level. If they are judged worthy of consideration by educators and professional students of the gifted, then empirical instruments will determine whether or not, or the extent to which, these explanations cohere with observable data and thus become eligible to serve as guiding principles for additional research and educational policy.

In a more fundamental sense, however, the value of the lines of thought pursued above is independent of empirical validation or disconfirmation in these particular cases. It was, after all, the observation of the differences in approach toward explaining moral development taken by Stoic philosophers and John Rawls that provided the impetus for the explorations in aspects of the theory of giftedness illustrated above. And it was the close juxtaposition of these two positions in *The Philosopher's Child* that established a narrative setting greatly facilitating the generation of these ideas. The primary, point, then is not to insist on the truth, or even necessarily the relevance, of the hypotheses offered here in explaining increased sensitivity to justice and the seeking of perfection. The point is that these philosophers have afforded us sufficient breadth of thought to present a wide horizon of theoretical possibilities for study and reflection and for practical application to the areas of giftedness and gifted education.

In conclusion, it is worth keeping in mind that the fact that major figures in Western philosophy have not directly reflected on and analyzed children in general, much less gifted children, should not deter the contemporary student of giftedness from investigating what philosophy may have to offer in this area. The history of philosophy, especially those moments when philosophers have thought about children, provides a storehouse of concepts and reasoned positions that, with appropriate development, can offer theoretical insight into the many diverse phenomena that constitute giftedness at all age levels.

References

Becker, L. C. (1998). Stoic children. In S. M. Turner & G. Matthews (Eds.), *The philosopher's child: Critical essays in the Western tradition* (pp. 45–61). Rochester, NY: University of Rochester Press.

Brennan, S., & Noggle, R. (1998). Rawls' neglected childhood: Reflections on the original position, stability, and the child's sense of justice. In S. M. Turner & G. Matthews (Eds.), *The philosopher's child: Critical essays in the Western tradition* (pp. 203–232). Rochester, NY: University of Rochester Press.

Turner, S. M., & Matthews, G. (Eds.). (1998). *The philosopher's child: Critical essays in the Western tradition*. Rochester, NY: University of Rochester Press.

EPILOGUE

Philosophical Visions and the Challenge of Education

The reader who has traversed some or all of this book has examined life, or at least a few strands of it, with the help of philosophical thought. The primary-source readings of Part I presented an opportunity to think about friendship, time, knowledge, the existence of God, perception, freedom and society, choice, social justice, feminism, and the meaning of technology. The abstract principles underlying such inquiry then withdrew from direct consideration, but were applied in Part II to a series of dramatic ways for improving critical thinking, the pursuit of excellence through drawing, learning a foreign language, and instilling love for the music of the opera. Finally, the philosophical dimension proper returned in Part III, a set of reflections on the general importance of theory in gifted education, the potential pitfalls involved in employing a current view of the complexities of intelligence, and a glimpse at examples of what can be learned about gifted students by paying attention to philosophical reflection on children in general.

The search for wisdom and self-esteem by gifted children, indeed all children, seen as a continually growing self-awareness of their abilities in thinking and understanding is one of the dominant themes—both in theory and in practice—pervading *The Examined Life*. Furthermore, those who have followed the sequence of topics consecutively, from the concept of friendship analyzed in Chapter 1 through to the suggestions about appreciating the nature of gifted children in Chapter 17, may appreciate more fully the relevance of the kind of theoretical reflection proper to philosophy for securing a more balanced and perceptive understanding of the gifted.

Teachers and administrators in gifted education, as well as parents of the gifted, are invited to consider whether some or all of the topics addressed above are relevant to their concerns as educators. Determining the extent of this relevance is, of course, up to the individual reader. However, *The Examined Life* will have served its primary purpose if any questions, definitions, or problems pertaining to gifted education are examined by those who have a practical stake in these matters with a fundamental respect for the kind of thinking exemplified by the discussions advanced in this book. A serious and sustained pursuit of philosophy is, to state the obvious, not an automatic solution for any of the concerns facing gifted education or any type of education. But, the forces of philosophy are considerable, its legacy is long, and the insight its principles provide can only assist in rendering these concerns as open to solution as possible.

Additional Readings in Philosophy

The following is a miniature bibliography in philosophy. It is divided into three sections and arranged according to three types of works recommended to give young people (as well as the interested adult) additional experience with philosophy:

General

Gaarder, J. (1996). *Sophie's world: A novel about the history of philosophy*. New York: Berkley Books.

A worldwide best-selling work—a remarkable blend of philosophy and an imaginative story involving a young girl and her adventures with a gentle, but somewhat mysterious philosophy teacher. The accounts of philosophers begin with the Greeks, cover the entire history of philosophy, and are noteworthy for their accuracy and fairness. Also interspersed into the development of the plot are more general discussions of cultural, social, and religious factors relevant to the progression of philosophy. Highly recommended as a source for young people who would like to know more about philosophy.

Jacobs, J. A. (2001). *A philosopher's compass*. New York: Harcourt College Publishers.

A remarkably clear introduction to the major questions and problems of philosophy. The discussion also includes a number of helpful hints and strategies for improving a student's critical thinking skills, as well as the ability to write with force and conviction about philosophical matters. The work is primarily intended for an undergraduate audience, but the clarity of the writing is such that younger readers would profit greatly from reading it and taking its lessons to heart.

Durant, W. J. (1991). *The story of philosophy: The lives and opinions of the great philosophers* (Rev. ed.). New York: Pocket.

This is an extremely readable and accurate account of the history of philosophy, with additional biographical features relevant to the philosophers themselves. A good source to provide a more challenging and concentrated review of philosophy than the more generalized accounts given in *Sophie's World*.

Russell, B. (1959). *The problems of philosophy*. London: Oxford University Press.

This famous little book, by one of the great mathematician-philosophers of the 20th century, is a lucid description of the major problems that have occupied philosophers since the Greeks (e.g., appearance and reality, truth and falsehood, knowledge and opinion). There is also a splendid concluding chapter on the value of philosophy. Russell was mordantly witty when he wanted to be, but here he restricts himself to laying out philosophical problems in clear and carefully modulated prose. Recommended for slightly older (or more advanced younger) students.

Barrett, W. (1962). *Irrational man: A study in existential philosophy.* New York: Doubleday.

Existentialism is one of the most important movements in 20th-century philosophy, and Barrett's work is generally acknowledged as one of the clearest and most accessible treatment of the major figures in Existentialism: Kierkegaard, Nietzsche, Sartre, and Heidegger. The work also includes considerable analysis of the background conditions from which Existentialism arose. Barrett's prose is clear, and he is sympathetic to the way the Existentialists approached and analyzed the problems that drew them to philosophy. Younger students who read, or even merely read in, this book will secure a solid background in philosophical issues and in the Existentialist perspective on these issues.

Smullyan, R. M. (1986). *What is the name of this book? The riddle of Dracula and other logical puzzles.* New York: Simon & Schuster.

This is a "fun book" that subtly introduces a host of philosophical problems through several hundred logical puzzles and paradoxes. Smullyan writes clearly with an irrepressible sense of humor. Students who like logic and critical thinking will enjoy this book—and they will also learn a great deal about logic and language. The complexity of some puzzles and paradoxes may be more appropriate for older students, but the bulk of the book could be read and savored by younger students (and curious adults).

Philosophy and Popular Culture

Irwin, W. (Ed.). (2002). *The Matrix and philosophy.* Chicago: Open Court.

A series of essays by contemporary philosophers on themes derived from the remarkable universe of the first of the three *Matrix* films. Anyone even vaguely familiar with this film or with any of the three in the trilogy will doubtless have some interest in the issues raised by the authors. The essays offer a varied approach to classical philosophical issues and introduce the reader to a number of important philosophical positions from past thinkers. Films of this caliber are decidedly philosophical and afford an excellent opportunity for the kind of reflective inquiry common to philosophy.

Irwin, W. (Ed). (1999). *Seinfeld and philosophy: A book about everything and nothing.* Chicago: Open Court.

The comedy of *Seinfeld* is not to everyone's taste, but for those viewers who admired—if not craved—this show and who possess a reflective bent, the essays in this volume present a worthy introduction to philosophical inquiry. Questions pertaining to the nature of reality, how we know what we know, and what sorts of behavior should or should not be permitted are all considered by the authors. "Not that there's anything wrong with that . . ."

Irwin, W., Conard, M. T., & Skoble, A. J. (Eds). (2001). *The Simpsons and philosophy: The d'oh! of Homer.* Chicago: Open Court.

Can cartoons be philosophical? *The Simpsons* works on many levels, and the essays in this volume indicate that the answer is an unequivocal "yes." Viewers of the long-running series will be invited to elevate their responses to the often biting humor to a more theoretical and abstract level. It may be observed that taking these issues seriously and continuing to be a resolute fan of Homer, Bart, Marge, Lisa, Maggie, and the rest of the Springfield gang are not logically incompatible!

Philosophy as Literature

De Saint-Exupéry, A. (1968). *The little prince* (K. Woods, Trans.). New York: HarBrace.

This timeless work beguiles and educates the reader on a number of levels, one of which is decidedly philosophical. The prince, the fox, the snake, the rose, and the aviator all interact to present a number of thoughtful positions on friendship, love, and dealing with "the other." Highly recommended for students who like to think deeply about important issues that originate from a literary—and, in this case, fanciful—narrative.

Camus, A. (1946). *The stranger.* New York: Random House.

A 20th-century classic animating a completely different world from *The Little Prince* and *Harry Potter.* Meursault, the hero (or, perhaps, antihero), drifts through his world with no apparent deep feelings for anything. However, he is trapped in a complex set of life-and-death circumstances during which he discovers a number of important facts—many philosophical in scope. Recommended for older students (and mature younger ones) as an important vision of reality depicted by a prominent French existentialist.

Bradbury, R. (1953). *Fahrenheit 451.* New York: Ballantine.

Science fiction affords a rich field for philosophical thought, and this well-known classic is an especially fertile source. Questions about the effects of technology, the nature of happiness, the importance of emotions, the status of the outsider (the "book people"), and the crucial relevance of simply being in a position to know about and question ideas—these are just some of the issues that arise from this book in a stark and dramatic way.

Silverstein, S. (1974). *Where the sidewalk ends.* New York: HarperCollins.

These quirky and occasionally somber poems go directly to that region in the spirit of young people where they do their most private—and profound—thinking. *Saturday Review* said that the poems are "tender, funny, sentimental, philosophical, and ridiculous in turn, and they're for all ages." Recommended for evoking aspects of young people's experience that intersect with philosophical concerns: values, friendship, and what is real beyond the point "where the sidewalk ends."

Rowling, J. K. (1997). *Harry Potter and the sorcerer's stone.* New York: Scholastic.

On the surface of things, young Harry Potter is a future wizard, not a philosopher. But, the world he inhabits is fully inflected with philosophical concepts, puzzles, and paradoxes. All it takes is a short step back from the vivid characterizations and intricately wrought plot to appreciate the mystery and wonder that surround Harry and his youthful cohorts as they learn the fine art of becoming wizards and witches at Hogwarts School. Questions in ethics (Is power more important than good?), epistemology (How can we know ghosts and trolls?), metaphysics (How do spells work?), and many more quandaries of this sort are natural responses to this excellent work of fiction. Pursuing these questions in a philosophical way will not interfere in the least with participating in Harry's wizardly and wondrous world. The subsequent volumes in the series maintain levels of thought that are well worth taking seriously from a philosophical perspective.

Index

About the Author

David A. White has a doctorate in philosophy from the University of Toronto and has taught philosophy in colleges and universities since 1967. He has written seven books and more than 50 articles in philosophy, literary criticism, and educational theory. In 1985, he received a Fellowship from the American Council of Learned Societies to study the function of myth in Plato's philosophy. Since 1993, he has taught programs in philosophy for the gifted centers and various magnet schools of the Chicago Public School system, the International Baccalaureate program at Lincoln Park High School in Chicago, and Northwestern University's Center for Talent Development, grades 4–9. Dr. White is an adjunct associate professor in the Philosophy Department of DePaul University and also teaches for DePaul's American Studies program. David is married to a philosopher, Mary Jeanne Larrabee, and has two sons, Daniel (the mathematician) and Colin (the explorer in the world of computers). He may be reached to comment on *The Examined Life*—or for general philosophical discussion—at dwhite6886@aol.com.

About the Cover

The cover of *The Examined Life* is a reproduction of "The Death of Socrates," painted in 1787 by the French master Jacques-Louis David (1748–1825). According to Plato's dialogues, Socrates devoted himself to examining life, his own and those of his fellow Athenians. As a result of this sustained inquiry, Socrates faced perhaps life's greatest and most challenging mystery—the arrival of death—with courageous calmness, born from his thoughtful attention to matters that make a wise approach to living so important. Socrates, 70 years old when he died, appears in the painting as an individual flowing with vibrant energy, pointing upward toward the region of higher and nobler realities, which, he believed, should command our attention. In contrast, many of the painting's other figures are bent with grief at the impending event, suggesting that they had yet to master the self-control displayed by Socrates as he is about to consume the cup of poison, the instrument of his death.

Readers of *The Examined Life*, whether younger or more practiced in life, may be inspired by the example of Socrates to embark on the type of reflection he so well exemplified and to persevere in the pursuit of philosophy as a guide to the future, both when life becomes difficult, as it inevitably will, and even when lighter moments carry the day. Socrates' example of applied philosophical wisdom is, at its pinnacle, dramatic and thankfully rare, but philosophical examination has valuable consequences for all our decisions and courses of action, whether small or large—if only the opportunity to engage in such reflection is embraced. It may be hoped that *The Examined Life* will introduce readers to these adventures in thought, both for the present and on into the future.